Trick
Mirror

Dear Tarx,

Stay wohe but
remember : everything
is subjective.
Happy Christmas
ya filthy Commie
Lots of Love
Luca

Xmas '19.

Trick Mirror

REFLECTIONS ON SELF-DELUSION

Jia Tolentino

4th ESTATE • London

4th Estate
An imprint of HarperCollins*Publishers*
1 London Bridge Street
London SE1 9GF

www.4thEstate.co.uk

First published in Great Britain in 2019 by 4th Estate
First published in the United States by Random House in 2019

3

Copyright © Jia Tolentino 2019

Jia Tolentino asserts the moral right to be identified
as the author of this work in accordance with the
Copyright, Designs and Patents Act 1988

A catalogue record for this book is
available from the British Library

ISBN 978-0-00-829492-2 (hardback)
ISBN 978-0-00-829493-9 (trade paperback)

Set in Berling LT Std with Benguiat Pro ITC display
Printed and bound in Great Britain by
CPI Group (UK) Ltd, Croydon

For my parents

Contents

Introduction

I wrote this book between the spring of 2017 and the fall of 2018—a period during which American identity, culture, technology, politics, and discourse seemed to coalesce into an unbearable supernova of perpetually escalating conflict, a stretch of time when daily experience seemed both like a stopped elevator and an endless state-fair ride, when many of us regularly found ourselves thinking that everything had gotten as bad as we could possibly imagine, after which, of course, things always got worse.

Throughout this period, I found that I could hardly trust anything that I was thinking. A doubt that always hovers in the back of my mind intensified: that whatever conclusions I might reach about myself, my life, and my environment are just as likely to be diametrically wrong as they are to be right. This suspicion is hard for me to articulate closely, in part because I usually extinguish it by writing. When I feel confused about something, I write about it until I turn into the person who shows up on paper: a person who is plausibly trustworthy, intuitive, and clear.

It's exactly this habit—or compulsion—that makes me suspect that I am fooling myself. If I were, in fact, the calm person who shows up on paper, why would I always need to hammer out a narrative that gets me there? I've been telling myself that I wrote this book because I was confused after the election, because confusion sits at odds to my temperament, because writing is my only strategy for making this conflict go away. I'm convinced by this story, even as I can see its photonegative: I wrote this book because I am always confused, because I can never be sure of anything, and because I am drawn to any mechanism that directs me away from that truth. Writing is either a way to shed my self-delusions or a way to develop them. A well-practiced, conclusive narrative is usually a dubious one: that a person is "not into drama," or that America needs to be made great again, or that America is already great.

These essays are about the spheres of public imagination that have shaped my understanding of myself, of this country, and of this era. One is about the internet. Another is about "optimization," and the rise of athleisure as late-capitalist fetishwear, and the endlessly proliferating applications of the idea that women's bodies should increase their market performance over time. There's an essay about drugs and religion and the bridge that ecstasy forms between them; another about scamming as the definitive millennial ethos; another about the literary heroine's journey from brave girl to depressed teenager to bitter adult woman who's possibly dead. One essay is about my stint as a teenage reality TV contestant. One is about sex and race and power at the University of Virginia, my alma mater, where a series of convincing stories have exacted enormous hidden costs. The final two are about the feminist obsession with "difficult" women and about the slow-burning insanity that I aquired in my twenties while attending what felt like several thousand weddings per year. These are the prisms through which I have come to know myself. In this book, I tried to undo their acts of refraction. I wanted to see the way I would see in a mirror. It's possible I painted an elaborate mural instead.

But that's fine. The last few years have taught me to suspend my desire for a conclusion, to assume that nothing is static and that renegotiation will be perpetual, to hope primarily that little truths will keep emerging in time. While I was writing this, a stranger tweeted an excerpt of a *Jezebel* piece I wrote in 2015, highlighting a sentence about what women seemed to want from feminist websites—a "trick mirror that carries the illusion of flaw-lessness as well as the self-flagellating option of constantly finding fault." I had not remembered using that phrase when I came up with a book title, and I had not understood, when I was writing that *Jezebel* piece, that that line was also an explanation of some-thing more personal. I began to realize that all my life I've been leaving myself breadcrumbs. It didn't matter that I didn't always know what I was walking toward. It was worthwhile, I told my-self, just trying to see clearly, even if it took me years to under-stand what I was trying to see.

Trick
Mirror

The I in the Internet

In the beginning the internet seemed good. "I was in love with the internet the first time I used it at my dad's office and thought it was the ULTIMATE COOL," I wrote, when I was ten, on an Angelfire subpage titled "The Story of How Jia Got Her Web Addiction." In a text box superimposed on a hideous violet background, I continued:

> But that was in third grade and all I was doing was going to Beanie Baby sites. Having an old, icky bicky computer at home, we didn't have the Internet. Even AOL seemed like a far-off dream. Then we got a new top-o'-the-line computer in spring break '99, and of course it came with all that demo stuff. So I finally had AOL and I was completely amazed at the marvel of having a profile and chatting and IMS!!

Then, I wrote, I discovered personal webpages. ("I was astonished!") I learned HTML and "little Javascript trickies." I built my own site on the beginner-hosting site Expage, choosing pastel colors and then switching to a "starry night theme." Then I ran out of space, so I "decided to move to Angelfire. Wow." I learned how to make my own graphics. "This was all in the course of four months,"

I wrote, marveling at how quickly my ten-year-old internet citizenry was evolving. I had recently revisited the sites that had once inspired me, and realized "how much of an idiot I was to be wowed by *that*."

I have no memory of inadvertently starting this essay two decades ago, or of making this Angelfire subpage, which I found while hunting for early traces of myself on the internet. It's now eroded to its skeleton: its landing page, titled "THE VERY BEST," features a sepia-toned photo of Andie from *Dawson's Creek* and a dead link to a new site called "THE FROSTED FIELD," which is "BETTER!" There's a page dedicated to a blinking mouse GIF named Susie, and a "Cool Lyrics Page" with a scrolling banner and the lyrics to Smash Mouth's "All Star," Shania Twain's "Man! I Feel Like a Woman!" and the TLC diss track "No Pigeons," by Sporty Thievz. On an FAQ page—there was an FAQ page— I write that I had to close down my customizable cartoon-doll section, as "the response has been enormous."

It appears that I built and used this Angelfire site over just a few months in 1999, immediately after my parents got a computer. My insane FAQ page specifies that the site was started in June, and a page titled "Journal"—which proclaims, "I am going to be completely honest about my life, although I won't go too deeply into personal thoughts, though"—features entries only from October. One entry begins: "It's so HOT outside and I can't count the times acorns have fallen on my head, maybe from exhaustion." Later on, I write, rather prophetically: "I'm going insane! I literally am addicted to the web!"

In 1999, it felt different to spend all day on the internet. This was true for everyone, not just for ten-year-olds: this was the *You've Got Mail* era, when it seemed that the very worst thing that could happen online was that you might fall in love with your business rival. Throughout the eighties and nineties, people had been gathering on the internet in open forums, drawn, like butterflies, to the puddles and blossoms of other people's curiosity and expertise. Self-regulated newsgroups like Usenet cultivated lively and relatively civil discussion about space exploration, meteorology, recipes, rare albums. Users gave advice, answered questions, made friendships, and wondered what this new internet would become.

Because there were so few search engines and no centralized social platforms, discovery on the early internet took place mainly in private, and pleasure existed as its own solitary reward. A 1995 book called *You Can Surf the Net!* listed sites where you could read movie reviews or learn about martial arts. It urged readers to follow basic etiquette (don't use all caps; don't waste other people's expensive bandwidth with overly long posts) and encouraged them to feel comfortable in this new world ("Don't worry," the author advised. "You have to *really* mess up to get flamed."). Around this time, GeoCities began offering personal website hosting for dads who wanted to put up their own golfing sites or kids who built glittery, blinking shrines to Tolkien or Ricky Martin or unicorns, most capped off with a primitive guest book and a green-and-black visitor counter. GeoCities, like the internet itself, was clumsy, ugly, only half functional, and organized into neighborhoods: /area51/ was for sci-fi, /westhollywood/ for LGBTQ life, /enchantedforest/ for children, /petsburgh/ for pets. If you left GeoCities, you could walk around other streets in this ever-expanding village of curiosities. You could stroll through Expage or Angelfire, as I did, and pause on the thoroughfare where the tiny cartoon hamsters danced. There was an emergent aesthetic—blinking text, crude animation. If you found something you liked, if you wanted to spend more time in any of these neighborhoods, you could build your own house from HTML frames and start decorating.

This period of the internet has been labeled Web 1.0—a name that works backward from the term Web 2.0, which was coined by the writer and user-experience designer Darcy DiNucci in an article called "Fragmented Future," published in 1999. "The Web we know now," she wrote, "which loads into a browser window in essentially static screenfuls, is only an embryo of the Web to come. The first glimmerings of Web 2.0 are beginning to appear. . . . The Web will be understood not as screenfuls of texts and graphics but as a transport mechanism, the ether through which interactivity happens." On Web 2.0, the structures would be dynamic, she predicted: instead of houses, websites would be portals, through which an ever-changing stream of activity—status updates, photos—could be displayed. What you did on the internet would become intertwined with what everyone else did, and the things other people liked would become the things that you would see. Web 2.0 platforms like Blogger and Myspace made it possible for people who had merely been taking in the sights to start generating their own personalized and constantly changing scenery. As more people began to register their existence digitally, a pastime turned into an imperative: you had to register yourself digitally to exist.

In a *New Yorker* piece from November 2000, Rebecca Mead profiled Meg Hourihan, an early blogger who went by Megnut. In just the prior eighteen months, Mead observed, the number of "weblogs" had gone from fifty to several thousand, and blogs like Megnut were drawing thousands of visitors per day. This new internet was social ("a blog consists primarily of links to other Web sites and commentary about those links") in a way that centered on individual identity (Megnut's readers knew that she wished there were better fish tacos in San Francisco, and that she was a feminist, and that she was close with her mom). The blogosphere was also full of mutual transactions, which tended to echo and escalate. The "main audience for blogs is other bloggers," Mead wrote. Etiquette required that, "if someone blogs your blog, you blog his blog back."

Through the emergence of blogging, personal lives were becoming public domain, and social incentives—to be liked, to be seen—were becoming economic ones. The mechanisms of internet exposure began to seem like a viable foundation for a career. Hourihan cofounded Blogger with Evan Williams, who later co-founded Twitter. JenniCam, founded in 1996 when the college student Jennifer Ringley started broadcasting webcam photos from her dorm room, attracted at one point up to four million daily visitors, some of whom paid a subscription fee for quicker-loading images. The internet, in promising a potentially unlimited audience, began to seem like the natural home of self-expression. In one blog post, Megnut's boyfriend, the blogger Jason Kottke, asked himself why he didn't just write his thoughts down in private. "Somehow, that seems strange to me though," he wrote. "The Web is the place for you to express your thoughts and feelings and such. To put those things elsewhere seems absurd."

Every day, more people agreed with him. The call of self-expression turned the village of the internet into a city, which expanded at time-lapse speed, social connections bristling like neurons in every direction. At ten, I was clicking around a web ring to check out other Angelfire sites full of animal GIFs and Smash Mouth trivia. At twelve, I was writing five hundred words a day on a public LiveJournal. At fifteen, I was uploading photos of myself in a miniskirt on Myspace. By twenty-five, my job was to write things that would attract, ideally, a hundred thousand strangers per post. Now I'm thirty, and most of my life is inextricable from the internet, and its mazes of incessant forced connection—this feverish, electric, unlivable hell.

As with the transition between Web 1.0 and Web 2.0, the curdling of the social internet happened slowly and then all at once. The tipping point, I'd guess, was around 2012. People were losing excitement about the internet, starting to articulate a set of new truisms. Facebook had become tedious, trivial, exhausting. Instagram seemed better, but would soon reveal its underlying function as a three-ring circus of happiness and popularity and success. Twitter, for all its discursive promise, was where everyone tweeted complaints at airlines and bitched about articles that had been commissioned to make people bitch. The dream of a better, truer self on the internet was slipping away. Where we had once been free to be ourselves online, we were now *chained* to ourselves online, and this made us self-conscious. Platforms that promised connection began inducing mass alienation. The freedom promised by the internet started to seem like something whose greatest potential lay in the realm of misuse.

Even as we became increasingly sad and ugly on the internet, the mirage of the better online self continued to glimmer. As a medium, the internet is defined by a built-in performance incentive. In real life, you can walk around living life and be visible to other people. But you can't just walk around and be visible on the internet—for anyone to see you, you have to *act*. You have to communicate in order to maintain an internet presence. And, because the internet's central platforms are built around personal profiles, it can seem—first at a mechanical level, and later on as an encoded instinct—like the main purpose of this communication is to make yourself look good. Online reward mechanisms beg to substitute for offline ones, and then overtake them. This is why everyone tries to look so hot and well-traveled on Instagram; this is why everyone seems so smug and triumphant on Facebook; this is why, on Twitter, making a righteous political statement has come to seem, for many people, like a political good in itself.

This practice is often called "virtue signaling," a term most often used by conservatives criticizing the left. But virtue signaling is a bipartisan, even apolitical action. Twitter is overrun with dramatic pledges of allegiance to the Second Amendment that function as intra-right virtue signaling, and it can be something like virtue signaling when people post the suicide hotline after a celebrity death. Few of us are totally immune to the practice, as it intersects with real desire for political integrity. Posting photos from a protest against border family separation, as I did while writing this, is a microscopically meaningful action, an expression of genuine principle, and also, inescapably, some sort of attempt to signal that I am good.

Taken to its extreme, virtue signaling has driven people on the left to some truly unhinged behavior. A legendary case occurred in June 2016, after a two-year-old was killed at a Disney resort—dragged off by an alligator while playing in a no-swimming-allowed lagoon. A woman, who had accumulated ten thousand Twitter followers with her posts about social justice, saw an opportunity and tweeted, magnificently, "I'm so finished with white men's entitlement lately that I'm really not sad about a 2yo being eaten by a gator because his daddy ignored signs." (She was then pilloried by people who chose to demonstrate their own moral superiority through mockery—as I am doing here, too.) A similar tweet made the rounds in early 2018 after a sweet story went viral: a large white seabird named Nigel had died next to the concrete decoy bird to whom he had devoted himself for years. An outraged writer tweeted, "Even concrete birds do not owe you affection, Nigel," and wrote a long Facebook post arguing that Nigel's courtship of the fake bird exemplified . . . *rape culture.* "I'm available to write the feminist perspective on Nigel the gannet's non-tragic death should anyone wish to pay me," she added, underneath the original tweet, which received more than a thousand likes. These deranged takes, and their unnerving proximity to online monetization, are case studies in the way that our world—digitally mediated, utterly consumed by capitalism—makes communication about morality very easy but makes actual moral living very hard. You don't end up using a news story about a dead toddler as a peg for white entitlement without a society in which the discourse of righteousness occupies far more public attention than the conditions that necessitate righteousness in the first place.

On the right, the online performance of political identity has been even wilder. In 2017, the social-media-savvy youth conservative group Turning Point USA staged a protest at Kent State University featuring a student who put on a diaper to demonstrate that "safe spaces were for babies." (It went viral, as intended, but not in the way TPUSA wanted—the protest was uniformly roasted, with one Twitter user slapping the logo of the porn site Brazzers on a photo of the diaper boy, and the Kent State TPUSA campus coordinator resigned.) It has also been infinitely more consequential, beginning in 2014, with a campaign that became a template for right-wing internet-political action, when a large group of young misogynists came together in the event now known as Gamergate.

The issue at hand was, ostensibly, a female game designer accused of sleeping with a journalist for favorable coverage. She, along with a set of feminist game critics and writers, received an onslaught of rape threats, death threats, and other forms of harassment, all concealed under the banner of free speech and "ethics in games journalism." The Gamergaters—estimated by *Deadspin* to number around ten thousand people—would mostly deny this harassment, either parroting in bad faith or fooling themselves into believing the argument that Gamergate was actually about noble ideals. Gawker Media, *Deadspin*'s parent company, itself became a target, in part because of its own aggressive disdain toward the Gamergaters: the company lost seven figures in revenue after its advertisers were brought into the maelstrom.

In 2016, a similar fiasco made national news in Pizzagate, after a few rabid internet denizens decided they'd found coded messages about child sex slavery in the advertising of a pizza shop associated with Hillary Clinton's campaign. This theory was disseminated all over the far-right internet, leading to an extended attack on DC's Comet Ping Pong pizzeria and everyone associated with the restaurant—all in the name of combating pedophilia—that culminated in a man walking into Comet Ping Pong and firing a gun. (Later on, the same faction would jump to the defense of Roy Moore, the Republican nominee for the Senate who was accused of sexually assaulting teenagers.) The over-woke left could only dream of this ability to weaponize a sense of righteousness. Even the militant antifascist movement, known as antifa, is routinely disowned by liberal centrists, despite the fact that the antifa movement is rooted in a long European tradition of Nazi resistance rather than a nascent constellation of radically paranoid message boards and YouTube channels. The worldview of the Gamergaters and Pizzagaters was actualized and to a large extent vindicated in the 2016 election—an event that strongly suggested that the worst things about the internet were now *determining*, rather than reflecting, the worst things about offline life.

Mass media always determines the shape of politics and culture. The Bush era is inextricable from the failures of cable news; the executive overreaches of the Obama years were obscured by the internet's magnification of personality and performance; Trump's rise to power is inseparable from the existence of social networks that must continually aggravate their users in order to continue making money. But lately I've been wondering how everything got so *intimately* terrible, and why, exactly, we keep playing along. How did a huge number of people begin spending the bulk of our disappearing free time in an openly torturous environment? How did the internet get so bad, so confining, so inescapably personal, so politically determinative—and why are all those questions asking the same thing?

I'll admit that I'm not sure that this inquiry is even productive. The internet reminds us on a daily basis that it is not at all rewarding to become aware of problems that you have no reasonable hope of solving. And, more important, the internet already is what it is. It has already become the central organ of contemporary life. It has already rewired the brains of its users, returning us to a state of primitive hyperawareness and distraction while overloading us with much more sensory input than was ever possible in primitive times. It has already built an ecosystem that runs on exploiting attention and monetizing the self. Even if you avoid the

internet completely—my partner does: he thought #tbt meant
"truth be told" for ages—you still live in the world that this internet has created, a world in which selfhood has become capitalism's last natural resource, a world whose terms are set by
centralized platforms that have deliberately established themselves as near-impossible to regulate or control.

The internet is also in large part inextricable from life's pleasures: our friends, our families, our communities, our pursuits of
happiness, and—sometimes, if we're lucky—our work. In part out
of a desire to preserve what's worthwhile from the decay that
surrounds it, I've been thinking about five intersecting problems:
first, how the internet is built to distend our sense of identity;
second, how it encourages us to overvalue our opinions; third,
how it maximizes our sense of opposition; fourth, how it cheap-
ens our understanding of solidarity; and, finally, how it destroys
our sense of scale.

In 1959, the sociologist Erving Goffman laid out a theory of identity that revolved around playacting. In every human interaction,
he wrote in *The Presentation of Self in Everyday Life*, a person must
put on a sort of performance, create an impression for an audience. The performance might be calculated, as with the man at a
job interview who's practiced every answer; it might be unconscious, as with the man who's gone on so many interviews that he
naturally performs as expected; it might be automatic, as with the
man who creates the correct impression primarily because he is
an upper-middle-class white man with an MBA. A performer
might be fully taken in by his own performance—he might actually believe that his biggest flaw is "perfectionism"—or he might
know that his act is a sham. But no matter what, he's performing.
Even if he stops *trying* to perform, he still has an audience, his actions still create an effect. "All the world is not, of course, a stage,

but the crucial ways in which it isn't are not easy to specify," Goffman wrote.

To communicate an identity requires some degree of self-delusion. A performer, in order to be convincing, must conceal "the discreditable facts that he has had to learn about the performance; in everyday terms, there will be things he knows, or has known, that he will not be able to tell himself." The interviewee, for example, avoids thinking about the fact that his biggest flaw actually involves drinking at the office. A friend sitting across from you at dinner, called to play therapist for your trivial romantic hang-ups, has to pretend to herself that she wouldn't rather just go home and get in bed to read Barbara Pym. No audience has to be physically present for a performer to engage in this sort of selective concealment: a woman, home alone for the weekend, might scrub the baseboards and watch nature documentaries even though she'd rather trash the place, buy an eight ball, and have a Craigslist orgy. People often make faces, in private, in front of bathroom mirrors, to convince themselves of their own attractiveness. The "lively belief that an unseen audience is present," Goffman writes, can have a significant effect.

Offline, there are forms of relief built into this process. Audiences change over—the performance you stage at a job interview is different from the one you stage at a restaurant later for a friend's birthday, which is different from the one you stage for a partner at home. At home, you might feel as if you could stop performing altogether; within Goffman's dramaturgical framework, you might feel as if you had made it backstage. Goffman observed that we need both an audience to witness our performances as well as a backstage area where we can relax, often in the company of "teammates" who had been performing alongside us. Think of coworkers at the bar after they've delivered a big sales pitch, or a bride and groom in their hotel room after the wedding reception: everyone may still be performing, but they *feel* at ease, unguarded, alone. Ideally, the outside audience has believed the prior performance. The wedding guests think they've actually just seen a pair of flawless, blissful newlyweds, and the potential backers think they've met a group of geniuses who are going to make everyone very rich. "But this imputation—this self—is a product of a scene that comes off, and is not a cause of it," Goffman writes. The self is not a fixed, organic thing, but a dramatic effect that emerges from a performance. This effect can be believed or disbelieved at will.

Online—assuming you buy this framework—the system metastasizes into a wreck. The presentation of self in everyday internet still corresponds to Goffman's playacting metaphor: there are stages, there is an audience. But the internet adds a host of other, nightmarish metaphorical structures: the mirror, the echo, the panopticon. As we move about the internet, our personal data is tracked, recorded, and resold by a series of corporations—a regime of involuntary technological surveillance, which subconsciously decreases our resistance to the practice of *voluntary* self-surveillance on social media. If we think about buying something, it follows us around everywhere. We can, and probably do, limit our online activity to websites that further reinforce our own sense of identity, each of us reading things written for people just like us. On social media platforms, everything we see corresponds to our conscious choices and algorithmically guided preferences, and all news and culture and interpersonal interaction are filtered through the home base of the profile. The everyday madness perpetuated by the internet is the madness of this architecture, which positions personal identity as the center of the universe. It's as if we've been placed on a lookout that oversees the entire world and given a pair of binoculars that makes everything look like our own reflection. Through social media, many people have quickly come to view all new information as a sort of direct commentary on *who they are*.

This system persists because it is profitable. As Tim Wu writes in *The Attention Merchants*, commerce has been slowly permeating human existence—entering our city streets in the nineteenth century through billboards and posters, then our homes in the twentieth century through radio and TV. Now, in the twenty-first century, in what appears to be something of a final stage, commerce has filtered into our identities and relationships. We have generated billions of dollars for social media platforms through our desire—and then through a subsequent, escalating economic and cultural requirement—to replicate for the internet who we know, who we think we are, who we want to be.

Selfhood buckles under the weight of this commercial importance. In physical spaces, there's a limited audience and time span for every performance. Online, your audience can hypothetically keep expanding forever, and the performance never has to end. (You can essentially be on a job interview in perpetuity.) In real life, the success or failure of each individual performance often plays out in the form of concrete, physical action—you get invited over for dinner, or you lose the friendship, or you get the job. Online, performance is mostly arrested in the nebulous realm of sentiment, through an unbroken stream of hearts and likes and eyeballs, aggregated in numbers attached to your name. Worst of all, there's essentially no backstage on the internet; where the offline audience necessarily empties out and changes over, the online audience never has to leave. The version of you that posts memes and selfies for your pre-cal classmates might end up sparring with the Trump administration after a school shooting, as happened to the Parkland kids—some of whom became so famous that they will never be allowed to drop the veneer of performance again. The self that traded jokes with white supremacists on Twitter is the self that might get hired, and then fired, by *The New York Times*, as happened to Quinn Norton in 2018. (Or, in the case of Sarah Jeong, the self that made jokes *about* white people might get Gamergated after being hired at the *Times* a few months thereafter.) People who maintain a public internet profile are building a self that can be viewed simultaneously by their mom, their boss, their potential future bosses, their eleven-year-old nephew, their past and future sex partners, their relatives who loathe their politics, as well as anyone who cares to look for any possible reason. Identity, according to Goffman, is a series of claims and promises. On the internet, a highly functional person is one who can promise everything to an indefinitely increasing audience at all times.

Incidents like Gamergate are partly a response to these conditions of hyper-visibility. The rise of trolling, and its ethos of disrespect and anonymity, has been so forceful in part because the internet's insistence on consistent, approval-worthy identity is so strong. In particular, the misogyny embedded in trolling reflects the way women—who, as John Berger wrote, have always been required to maintain an external awareness of their own identity—often navigate these online conditions so profitably. It's the self-calibration that I learned as a girl, as a woman, that has helped me capitalize on "having" to be online. My only experience of the world has been one in which personal appeal is paramount and self-exposure is encouraged; this legitimately unfortunate paradigm, inhabited first by women and now generalized to the entire internet, is what trolls loathe and actively repudiate. They destabilize an internet built on transparency and likability. They pull us back toward the chaotic and the unknown.

Of course, there are many better ways of making the argument against hyper-visibility than trolling. As Werner Herzog told GQ, in 2011, speaking about psychoanalysis: "We have to have our dark corners and the unexplained. We will become uninhabitable in a way an apartment will become uninhabitable if you illuminate every single dark corner and under the table and wherever—you cannot live in a house like this anymore."

The first time I was ever paid to publish anything, it was 2013, the end of the blog era. Trying to make a living as a writer with the internet as a standing precondition of my livelihood has given me some professional motivation to stay active on social media, making my work and personality and face and political leanings and dog photos into a continually updated record that anyone can see. In doing this, I have sometimes felt the same sort of unease that washed over me when I was a cheerleader and learned how to convincingly fake happiness at football games—the feeling of acting as if conditions are fun and normal and worthwhile in the hopes that they will just magically become so. To try to write online, more specifically, is to operate on a set of assumptions that are already dubious when limited to writers and even more questionable when turned into a categorical imperative for everyone on the internet: the assumption that speech has an impact, that it's something like action; the assumption that it's fine or helpful or even *ideal* to be constantly writing down what you think.

I have benefited, I mean, from the internet's unhealthy focus on opinion. This focus is rooted in the way the internet generally minimizes the need for physical action: you don't have to do much of anything but sit behind a screen to live an acceptable, possibly valorized, twenty-first-century life. The internet can feel like an astonishingly direct line to reality—click if you want something and it'll show up at your door two hours later; a series of tweets goes viral after a tragedy and soon there's a nationwide high school walkout—but it can also feel like a shunt diverting our energy *away* from action, leaving the real-world sphere to the people who already control it, keeping us busy figuring out the precisely correct way of explaining our lives. In the run-up to the 2016 election and increasingly so afterward, I started to feel that there was almost nothing I could do about ninety-five percent of the things I cared about other than form an opinion—and that the conditions that allowed me to live in mild everyday hysterics about an unlimited supply of terrible information were related to the conditions that were, at the same time, consolidating power, sucking wealth upward, far outside my grasp.

I don't mean to be naïvely fatalistic, to act like *nothing* can be done about *anything*. People are making the world better through concrete footwork every day. (Not me—I'm too busy sitting in front of the internet!) But their time and labor, too, has been de-valued and stolen by the voracious form of capitalism that drives the internet, and which the internet drives in turn. There is less time these days for anything other than economic survival. The internet has moved seamlessly into the interstices of this situa-tion, redistributing our minimum free time into unsatisfying micro-installments, spread throughout the day. In the absence of time to physically and politically engage with our community the way many of us want to, the internet provides a cheap substitute: it gives us brief moments of pleasure and connection, tied up in the opportunity to constantly listen and speak. Under these cir-cumstances, opinion stops being a first step toward something and starts seeming like an end in itself.

I started thinking about this when I was working as an editor at *Jezebel*, in 2014. I spent a lot of the day reading headlines on women's websites, most of which had by then adopted a feminist slant. In this realm, speech was constantly framed as a sort of in-tensely satisfying action: you'd get headlines like "Miley Cyrus Spoke Out About Gender Fluidity on Snapchat and It Was Every-thing" or "Amy Schumer's Speech About Body Confidence at the Women's Magazine Awards Ceremony Will Have You in Tears." Forming an opinion was also framed as a sort of action: blog posts offered people guidance on how to feel about online controversies or particular scenes on TV. Even identity itself seemed to take on these valences. Merely to exist as a feminist was to be doing some important work. These ideas have intensified and gotten more complicated in the Trump era, in which, on the one hand, people like me are busy expressing anguish online and mostly affecting nothing, and on the other, more actual and rapid change has come from the internet than ever before. In the turbulence that followed the Harvey Weinstein revelations, women's speech swayed public opinion and led directly to change. People with power were forced to reckon with their ethics; harassers and abusers were pushed out of their jobs. But even in this narrative, the importance of action was subtly elided. People wrote about women "speaking out" with prayerful reverence, as if speech itself could bring women freedom—as if better policies and economic redistribution and true investment from men weren't necessary, too.

Goffman observes the difference between doing something and *expressing* the doing of something, between feeling something and conveying a feeling. "The representation of an activity will vary in some degree from the activity itself and therefore inevitably misrepresent it," Goffman writes. (Take the experience of enjoying a sunset versus the experience of communicating to an audience that you're enjoying a sunset, for example.) The internet is engineered for this sort of misrepresentation; it's designed to encourage us to create certain impressions rather than allowing these impressions to arise "as an incidental by-product of [our] activity." This is why, with the internet, it's so easy to stop trying to be decent, or reasonable, or politically engaged—and start trying merely to *seem* so.

As the value of speech inflates even further in the online attention economy, this problem only gets worse. I don't know what to do with the fact that I myself continue to benefit from all this: that my career is possible in large part because of the way the internet collapses identity, opinion, and action—and that I, as a writer whose work is mostly critical and often written in first person, have some inherent stake in justifying the dubious practice of spending all day trying to figure out what you think. As a reader, of course, I'm grateful for people who help me understand things, and I'm glad that they—and I—can be paid to do so. I am glad, too, for the way the internet has given an audience to writers who previously might have been shut out of the industry, or kept on its sidelines: I'm one of them. But you will never catch me arguing that professional opinion-havers in the age of the internet are, on the whole, a force for good.

In April 2017, the *New York Times* brought a millennial writer named Bari Weiss onto its opinion section as both a writer and an editor. Weiss had graduated from Columbia, and had worked as an editor at *Tablet* and then at *The Wall Street Journal*. She leaned conservative, with a Zionist streak. At Columbia, she had cofounded a group called Columbians for Academic Freedom, which, amongst other things, worked to pressure the university into punishing a pro-Palestinian professor who had made her feel "intimidated," she told NPR in 2005.

At the *Times*, Weiss immediately began launching columns from a rhetorical and political standpoint of high-strung defensiveness, disguised with a veneer of levelheaded nonchalance. "Victimhood, in the intersectional way of seeing the world, is akin to sainthood; power and privilege are profane," she wrote—a bit of elegant phrasing in a piece that warned the public of the rampant anti-Semitism evinced, apparently, by a minor activist clusterfuck, in which the organizers of the Chicago Dyke March banned Star of David flags. She wrote a column slamming the organizers of the Women's March over a few social media posts expressing support for Assata Shakur and Louis Farrakhan. This, she argued, was troubling evidence that progressives, just like conservatives, were unable to police their internal hate. (Both-sides arguments like this are always appealing to people who wish to seem both contrarian and intellectually superior; this particular one required ignoring the fact that liberals remained obsessed with "civility" while the Republican president was actively endorsing violence at every turn. Later on, when *Tablet* published an investigation into the Women's March organizers who maintained disconcerting ties to the Nation of Islam, these organizers were

criticized by liberals, who truly do not lack the self-policing instinct; in large part because the left does take hate seriously, the
Women's March effectively splintered into two groups.) Often,
Weiss's columns featured aggrieved predictions of how her bold,
independent thinking would make her opponents go crazy and
attack her. "I will inevitably get called a racist," she proclaimed in
one column, titled "Three Cheers for Cultural Appropriation."
"I'll be accused of siding with the alt-right or tarred as Islamopho-
bic," she wrote in another column. Well, sure.

Though Weiss often argued that people should get more comfortable with those who offended or disagreed with them, she
seemed mostly unable to take her own advice. During the Winter
Olympics in 2018, she watched the figure skater Mirai Nagasu
land a triple axel—the first American woman to do so in Olympic
competition—and tweeted, in a very funny attempt at a compli-
ment, "Immigrants: they get the job done." Because Nagasu was
actually born in California, Weiss was immediately shouted down.
This is what happens online when you do something offensive:
when I worked at *Jezebel*, people shouted me down on Twitter
about five times a year over things I had written or edited, and
sometimes outlets published pieces about our mistakes. This was
often overwhelming and unpleasant, but it was always useful.
Weiss, for her part, tweeted that the people calling her racist
tweet racist were a "sign of civilization's end." A couple of weeks
later, she wrote a column called "We're All Fascists Now," arguing
that angry liberals were creating a "moral flattening of the earth."
At times it seems that Weiss's main strategy is to make an argument that's bad enough to attract criticism, and then to cherry-
pick the worst of that criticism into the foundation for another
bad argument. Her worldview requires the specter of a vast, angry,
inferior mob.

It's of course true that there are vast, angry mobs on the internet. Jon Ronson wrote the book *So You've Been Publicly Shamed*
about this in 2015. "We became keenly watchful for transgres-

sions," he writes, describing the state of Twitter around 2012. "After a while it wasn't just transgressions we were keenly watchful for. It was misspeakings. Fury at the terribleness of other people had started to consume us a lot. . . . In fact, it felt weird and empty when there *wasn't* anyone to be furious about. The days between shamings felt like days picking at fingernails, treading water." Web 2.0 had curdled; its organizing principle was shifting. The early internet had been constructed around lines of affinity, and whatever good spaces remain on the internet are still the product of affinity and openness. But when the internet moved to an organizing principle of *opposition*, much of what had formerly been surprising and rewarding and curious became tedious, noxious, and grim.

This shift partly reflects basic social physics. Having a mutual enemy is a quick way to make a friend—we learn this as early as elementary school—and politically, it's much easier to organize people against something than it is to unite them in an affirmative vision. And, within the economy of attention, conflict always gets more people to look. Gawker Media thrived on antagonism: its flagship site made enemies of everyone; *Deadspin* targeted ESPN, *Jezebel* the world of women's magazines. There was a brief wave of sunny, saccharine, profitable internet content—the OMG era of *BuzzFeed*, the rise of sites like *Upworthy*—but it ended in 2014 or so. Today, on Facebook, the most-viewed political pages succeed because of a commitment to constant, aggressive, often unhinged opposition. Beloved, oddly warmhearted websites like *The Awl*, *The Toast*, and *Grantland* have all been shuttered; each closing has been a reminder that an open-ended, affinity-based, generative online identity is hard to keep alive.

That opposition looms so large on the internet can be good and useful and even revolutionary. Because of the internet's tilt toward decontextualization and frictionlessness, a person on social media can seem to matter as much as whatever he's set himself against. Opponents can meet on suddenly (if temporarily) even ground. *Gawker* covered the accusations against Louis C.K. and Bill Cosby years before the mainstream media would take sexual misconduct seriously. The Arab Spring, Black Lives Matter, and the movement against the Dakota Access Pipeline challenged and overturned long-standing hierarchies through the strategic deployment of social media. The Parkland teenagers were able to position themselves as opponents of the entire GOP.

But the appearance of a more level playing field is not the fact of it, and everything that happens on the internet bounces and refracts. At the same time that ideologies that lead toward equality and freedom have gained power through the internet's open discourse, existing power structures have solidified through a vicious (and very online) opposition to this encroachment. In her 2017 book, *Kill All Normies*—a project of accounting for the "online battles that may otherwise be forgotten but have nevertheless shaped culture and ideas in a profound way"—the writer Angela Nagle argues that the alt-right coalesced in response to increasing cultural power on the left. Gamergate, she writes, brought together a "strange vanguard of teenage gamers, pseudonymous swastika-posting anime lovers, ironic *South Park* conservatives, anti-feminist pranksters, nerdish harassers and meme-making trolls" to form a united front against the "earnestness and moral self-flattery of what felt like a tired liberal intellectual conformity." The obvious hole in the argument is the fact that what Nagle identifies as the center of this liberal conformity—college activist movements, obscure Tumblr accounts about mental health and arcane sexualities—are frequently derided by liberals, and have never been nearly as powerful as those who detest them would like to think. The Gamergaters' worldview was not actually endangered; they just had to *believe* it was—or to pretend it was, and wait for a purportedly leftist writer to affirm them—in order to lash out and remind everyone what they could do.

Many Gamergaters cut their expressive teeth on 4chan, a message board that adopted as one of its mottos the phrase "There are no girls on the internet." "This rule does not mean what you think it means," wrote one 4chan poster, who went, as most of them did, by the username Anonymous. "In real life, people like you for being a girl. They want to fuck you, so they pay attention to you and they pretend what you have to say is interesting, or that you are smart or clever. On the Internet, we don't have the chance to fuck you. This means the advantage of being a 'girl' does not exist. You don't get a bonus to conversation just because I'd like to put my cock in you." He explained that women could get their unfair social advantage back by posting photos of their tits on the message board: "This is, and should be, degrading for you."

Here was the opposition principle in action. Through identifying the effects of women's systemic objectification as some sort of vagina-supremacist witchcraft, the men that congregated on 4chan gained an identity, and a useful common enemy. Many of these men *had*, likely, experienced consequences related to the "liberal intellectual conformity" that is popular feminism: as the sexual marketplace began to equalize, they suddenly found themselves unable to obtain sex by default. Rather than work toward other forms of self-actualization—or attempt to make themselves genuinely desirable, in the same way that women have been socialized to do at great expense and with great sincerity for all time—they established a group identity that centered on anti-woman virulence, on telling women who happened to stumble across 4chan that "the only interesting thing about you is your naked body. tl;dr: tits or GET THE FUCK OUT."

In the same way that it behooved these trolls to credit women with a maximum of power that they did not actually possess, it sometimes behooved women, on the internet, to do the same when they spoke about trolls. At some points while I worked at *Jezebel*, it would have been easy to enter into one of these situations myself. Let's say a bunch of trolls sent me threatening emails—an experience that wasn't exactly common, as I have been "lucky," but wasn't rare enough to surprise me. The economy of online attention would suggest that I write a column about those trolls, quote their emails, talk about how the experience of being threatened constitutes a definitive situation of being a woman in the world. (It would be acceptable for me to do this *even though* I have never been hacked or swatted or Gamergated, never had to move out of my house to a secure location, as so many other women have.) My column about trolling would, of course, attract an influx of trolling. Then, having proved my point, maybe I'd go on TV and talk about the situation, and then I would get trolled even more, and then I could go on defining myself in reference to trolls forever, positioning them as inexorable and monstrous, and they would return the favor in the interest of their own ideological advancement, and this whole situation could continue until we all died.

There is a version of this mutual escalation that applies to any belief system, which brings me back to Bari Weiss and all the other writers who have fashioned themselves as brave contrarians, building entire arguments on random protests and harsh tweets, making themselves deeply dependent on the people who hate them, the people they hate. It's ridiculous, and at the same time, here I am writing this essay, doing the same thing. It is nearly impossible, today, to separate engagement from magnification. (Even declining to engage can turn into magnification: when people targeted in Pizzagate as Satanist pedophiles took their social media accounts private, the Pizzagaters took this as proof that they had been right.) Trolls and bad writers and the president know better than anyone: when you call someone terrible, you just end up promoting their work.

The political philosopher Sally Scholz separates solidarity into three categories. There's social solidarity, which is based on common experience; civic solidarity, which is based on moral obligation to a community; and political solidarity, which is based on a shared commitment to a cause. These forms of solidarity overlap, but they're distinct from one another. What's political, in other words, doesn't also have to be personal, at least not in the sense of firsthand experience. You don't need to step in shit to understand what stepping in shit feels like. You don't need to have directly suffered at the hands of some injustice in order to be invested in bringing that injustice to an end.

But the internet brings the "I" into everything. The internet can make it seem that supporting someone means literally sharing in their experience—that solidarity is a matter of *identity* rather than politics or morality, and that it's best established at a point of maximum mutual vulnerability in everyday life. Under these terms, instead of expressing morally obvious solidarity with the struggle of black Americans under the police state or the plight of fat women who must roam the earth to purchase stylish and thoughtful clothing, the internet would encourage me to express solidarity through inserting my own identity. *Of course* I support the black struggle because *I*, myself, as a woman of Asian heritage, have *personally* been injured by white supremacy. (In fact, as an Asian woman, part of a minority group often deemed white-adjacent, I have benefited from American anti-blackness on just as many occasions.) *Of course* I understand the difficulty of shopping as a woman who is overlooked by the fashion industry because *I*, myself, have *also* somehow been marginalized by this industry. This framework, which centers the self in an expression of support for others, is not ideal.

The phenomenon in which people take more comfort in a sense of injury than a sense of freedom governs many situations where people are objectively *not* being victimized on a systematic basis. For example, men's rights activists have developed a sense of solidarity around the absurd claim that men are second-class citizens. White nationalists have brought white people together through the idea that white people are endangered, specifically white men—this at a time when 91 percent of Fortune 500 CEOs are white men, when white people make up 90 percent of elected American officials and an overwhelming majority of top decision-makers in music, publishing, television, movies, and sports.

Conversely, and crucially, the dynamic also applies in situations where claims of vulnerability are legitimate and historically entrenched. The greatest moments of feminist solidarity in recent years have stemmed not from an affirmative vision but from articulating extreme versions of the low common denominator of male slight. These moments have been world-altering: #YesAllWomen, in 2014, was the response to Elliot Rodger's Isla Vista massacre, in which he killed six people and wounded fourteen in an attempt to exact revenge on women for rejecting him. Women responded to this story with a sense of nauseating recognition: mass violence is nearly always linked to violence toward women, and for women it is something approaching a universal experience to have placated a man out of the real fear that he will hurt you. In turn, some men responded with the entirely unnecessary reminder that "not all men" are like that. (I was once hit with "not all men" right after a stranger yelled something obscene at me; the guy I was with noted my displeasure and helpfully reminded me that not all men are jerks.) Women began posting stories on Twitter and Facebook with #YesAllWomen to make an obvious but important point: not all men have made women fearful, but yes, all women have experienced fear because of men. #MeToo, in 2017, came in the weeks following the Harvey Weinstein revelations, as the floodgates opened and story after story after story rolled out about the subjugation women had experienced at the hands of powerful men. Against the normal forms of disbelief and rejection these stories meet with—it can't possibly be *that* bad; something about *her* telling *that* story seems suspicious—women anchored one another, establishing the breadth and inescapability of male abuse of power through speaking simultaneously and adding #MeToo.

In these cases, multiple types of solidarity seemed to naturally meld together. It was women's individual experiences of victimization that produced our widespread moral and political opposition to it. And at the same time, there was something about the hashtag itself—its design, and the ways of thinking that it affirms and solidifies—that both erased the variety of women's experiences and made it seem as if the crux of feminism was this articulation of vulnerability itself. A hashtag is specifically designed to remove a statement from context and to position it as part of an enormous singular thought, and a woman participating in one of these hashtags becomes visible at an inherently predictable moment of male aggression: the time her boss jumped her, or the night a stranger followed her home. The rest of her life, which is usually far less predictable, remains unseen. Even as women have attempted to use #YesAllWomen and #MeToo to regain control of a narrative, these hashtags have at least partially reified the thing they're trying to eradicate: the way that womanhood can feel like a story of loss of control. They have made feminist solidarity and shared vulnerability seem inextricable, as if we were incapable of building solidarity around anything else. What we have in common is obviously essential, but it's the differences between women's stories—the factors that allow some to survive, and force others under—that illuminate the vectors that lead to a better world. And, because there is no room or requirement in a tweet to add a disclaimer about individual experience, and because hashtags subtly equate disconnected statements in a way that can't be controlled by those speaking, it has been even easier for #MeToo critics to claim that women must themselves think that going on a bad date is the same as being violently raped.

What's amazing is that things like hashtag design—these essentially ad hoc experiments in digital architecture—have shaped so much of our political discourse. Our world would be different if Anonymous hadn't been the default username on 4chan, or if every social media platform didn't center on the personal profile, or if YouTube algorithms didn't show viewers increasingly extreme content to retain their attention, or if hashtags and retweets simply didn't exist. It's because of the hashtag, the retweet, and the profile that solidarity on the internet gets inextricably tangled up with visibility, identity, and self-promotion. It's telling that the most mainstream gestures of solidarity are pure representation, like viral reposts or avatar photos with cause-related filters, and meanwhile the *actual* mechanisms through which political solidarity is enacted, like strikes and boycotts, still exist on the fringe. The extremes of performative solidarity are all transparently embarrassing: a Christian internet personality urging other conservatives to tell Starbucks baristas that their name is "Merry Christmas," or Nev Schulman from the TV show *Catfish* taking a selfie with a hand over his heart in an elevator and captioning it "A real man shows his strength through patience and honor. This elevator is abuse free." (Schulman allegedly punched a girl in college.) The demonstrative celebration of black women on social media—white people tweeting "black women will save America" after elections, or Mark Ruffalo tweeting that he said a prayer and God answered as a black woman—often hints at a bizarre need on the part of white people to personally participate in an ideology of equality that ostensibly requires them to chill out. At one point in *The Presentation of Self*, Goffman writes that the audience's way of shaping a role for the performer can become more elaborate than the performance itself. This is what the online expression of solidarity sometimes feels like—a manner of listening so extreme and performative that it often turns into the show.

The final, and possibly most psychologically destructive, distortion of the social internet is its distortion of scale. This is not an accident but an essential design feature: social media was constructed around the idea that a thing is important insofar as it is important to you. In an early internal memo about the creation of Facebook's News Feed, Mark Zuckerberg observed, already beyond parody, "A squirrel dying in front of your house may be more relevant to your interests right now than people dying in Africa." The idea was that social media would give us a fine-tuned sort of control over what we looked at. What resulted was a situation where we—first as individuals, and then inevitably as a collective— are essentially unable to exercise control at all. Facebook's goal of showing people only what they were interested in seeing resulted, within a decade, in the effective end of shared civic reality. And this choice, combined with the company's financial incentive to continually trigger heightened emotional responses in its users, ultimately solidified the current norm in news media consumption: today we mostly consume news that corresponds with our ideological alignment, which has been fine-tuned to make us feel self-righteous and also mad.

In *The Attention Merchants*, Tim Wu observes that technologies designed to increase control over our attention often have the opposite effect. He uses the TV remote control as one example. It made flipping through channels "practically nonvolitional," he writes, and put viewers in a "mental state not unlike that of a newborn or a reptile." On the internet, this dynamic has been automated and generalized in the form of endlessly varied but somehow monotonous social media feeds—these addictive, numbing fire hoses of information that we aim at our brains for much of the day. In front of the timeline, as many critics have noted, we exhibit classic reward-seeking lab-rat behavior, the sort that's observed when lab rats are put in front of an unpredictable food dispenser. Rats will eventually stop pressing the lever if their device dispenses food regularly or not at all. But if the lever's rewards are rare and irregular, the rats will never stop pressing it. In other words, it is *essential* that social media is mostly unsatisfying. That is what keeps us scrolling, scrolling, pressing our lever over and over in the hopes of getting some fleeting sensation—some momentary rush of recognition, flattery, or rage.

Like many among us, I have become acutely conscious of the way my brain degrades when I strap it in to receive the full barrage of the internet—these unlimited channels, all constantly reloading with new information: births, deaths, boasts, bombings, jokes, job announcements, ads, warnings, complaints, confessions, and political disasters blitzing our frayed neurons in huge waves of information that pummel us and then are instantly replaced. This is an awful way to live, and it is wearing us down quickly. At the end of 2016, I wrote a blog post for *The New Yorker* about the cries of "worst year ever" that were then flooding the internet. There had been terrorist attacks all over the world, and the Pulse shooting in Orlando. David Bowie, Prince, and Muhammad Ali had died. More black men had been executed by police who could not control their racist fear and hatred: Alton Sterling was killed in the Baton Rouge parking lot where he was selling CDs; Philando Castile was murdered as he reached for his legal-carry permit during a routine traffic stop. Five police officers were killed in Dallas at a protest against this police violence. Donald Trump was elected president of the United States. The North Pole was thirty-six degrees hotter than normal. Venezuela was collapsing; families starved in Yemen. In Aleppo, a seven-year-old girl named Bana Alabed was tweeting her fears of imminent death. And in front of this backdrop, there were all of *us*—our stupid selves, with our stupid frustrations, our lost baggage and delayed trains. It seemed to me that this sense of punishing oversaturation would persist no matter what was in the news. There was no limit to the amount of misfortune a person could take in via the internet, I wrote, and there was no way to calibrate this information correctly—no guidebook for how to expand our hearts to accommodate these simultaneous scales of human experience, no way to teach ourselves to separate the banal from the profound. The internet was dramatically increasing our ability to know about things, while our ability to *change* things stayed the same, or possibly shrank right in front of us. I had started to feel that the internet would only ever induce this cycle of heartbreak and hardening—a hyper-engagement that would make less sense every day.

But the worse the internet gets, the more we appear to crave it—the more it gains the power to shape our instincts and desires. To guard against this, I give myself arbitrary boundaries—no Instagram stories, no app notifications—and rely on apps that shut down my Twitter and Instagram accounts after forty-five minutes of daily use. And still, on occasion, I'll disable my social media blockers, and I'll sit there like a rat pressing the lever, like a woman repeatedly hitting myself on the forehead with a hammer, masturbating through the nightmare until I finally catch the gasoline whiff of a good meme. The internet is still so young that it's easy to retain some subconscious hope that it all might still add up to something. We remember that at one point this all felt like butterflies and puddles and blossoms, and we sit patiently in our festering inferno, waiting for the internet to turn around and surprise us and get good again. But it won't. The internet is governed by incentives that make it impossible to be a full person while interacting with it. In the future, we will inevitably be cheapened. Less and less of us will be left, not just as individuals but also as community members, as a collective of people facing various catastrophes. Distraction is a "life-and-death matter," Jenny Odell writes in *How to Do Nothing*. "A social body that can't concentrate or communicate with itself is like a person who can't think and act."

Of course, people have been carping in this way for many centuries. Socrates feared that the act of writing would "create forgetfulness in the learners' souls." The sixteenth-century scientist Conrad Gessner worried that the printing press would facilitate an "always on" environment. In the eighteenth century, men complained that newspapers would be intellectually and morally isolating, and that the rise of the novel would make it difficult for people—specifically women—to differentiate between fiction and fact. We worried that radio would drive children to distraction, and later that TV would erode the careful attention required by radio. In 1985, Neil Postman observed that the

American desire for constant entertainment had become toxic, that television had ushered in a "vast descent into triviality." The difference is that, today, there is nowhere further to go. Capitalism has no land left to cultivate but the self. Everything is being cannibalized—not just goods and labor, but personality and relationships and attention. The next step is complete identification with the online marketplace, physical and spiritual inseparability from the internet: a nightmare that is already banging down the door.

What could put an end to the worst of the internet? Social and economic collapse would do it, or perhaps a series of antitrust cases followed by a package of hard regulatory legislation that would somehow also dismantle the internet's fundamental profit model. At this point it's clear that collapse will almost definitely come first. Barring that, we've got nothing except our small attempts to retain our humanity, to act on a model of actual selfhood, one that embraces culpability, inconsistency, and insignificance. We would have to think very carefully about what we're getting from the internet, and how much we're giving it in return. We'd have to care less about our identities, to be deeply skeptical of our own unbearable opinions, to be careful about when opposition serves us, to be properly ashamed when we can't express solidarity without putting ourselves first. The alternative is unspeakable. But you know that—it's already here.

Reality TV Me

Until recently, one of the best-kept secrets in my life, even to myself, was that I once spent three weeks when I was sixteen filming a reality TV show in Puerto Rico. The show was called *Girls v. Boys: Puerto Rico*, and the concept was exactly what it sounds like. There were eight cast members total—four boys, four girls. We filmed on Vieques, a four-mile-wide island, rough and green and hilly, with wild horses running along the white edges of the beach. The show was built around periodic challenges, each team racking up points toward a $50,000 jackpot. Between competitions, we retreated to a pale-blue house strung with twinkly lights and generated whatever drama we could.

My school let me miss three weeks of high school to do this, which still surprises me. It was a strict place—the handbook prohibited sleeveless shirts and homosexuality—and though I was a good student, my conduct record was iffy, and I was disliked, rightfully enough, by a lot of adults. But then again, the administrators had kept me at the school even when my parents couldn't afford the tuition. And I was a senior already, because I'd skipped grades after my family moved from Toronto to Houston. Also, according to rumor, the tiny Christian institution had already sent an alumnus to compete on *The Bachelorette*. There was something, maybe, about that teenage religious environment, the way everyone was always flirting and posturing and attempting to deceive one another, that set us up remarkably well for reality TV.

In any case, I told the administrators I hoped to "be a light for Jesus, but on television," and got their permission. In December 2004, I packed a bag full of graphic tees and handkerchief-size denim miniskirts and went to Puerto Rico, and in January I came back blazing with self-enthrallment—salt in my hair, as tan as if I'd been wood-stained. The ten episodes of *Girls v. Boys* started airing the summer after I graduated from high school on a channel called Noggin, which was best known for *Daria* reruns and the Canadian teen drama *Degrassi*. I invited friends over to watch the first episode, and felt gratified but also deeply pained by the sight of my face on a big screen. When I went off to college, I didn't buy a TV for my dorm room, and I felt that this was a good opportunity to shed my televised self like a snakeskin. Occasionally, in my twenties, at bars or on road trips, I'd pull up my IMDb credit as a piece of bizarre trivia, but I was uninterested in investigating *Girls v. Boys* any further. It took me thirteen years, and an essay idea, to finally finish watching the show.

Audition tapes: **ACE**, a black skater bro in New Jersey, does kick-flips in a public square; **JIA**, a brown girl from Texas, says she's tired of being a cheerleader; **CORY**, a white boy from Kentucky, admits he's never been kissed; **KELLEY**, a blonde from Phoenix, does crunches on a yoga mat, looking like Britney Spears; **DEMIAN**, a boy from Vegas with a slight Mexican accent, wrestles his little brother; **KRYSTAL**, a black girl with a feline face, says she knows she seems stuck-up; **RYDER**, a California boy with reddish hair and ear gauges, says he knows he looks like Johnny Depp; **PARIS**, a tiny blonde from Oregon, says that she's always been a freak and she likes it that way.

Six teens assemble on a blinding tarmac under blue sky. The
first challenge is a race to the house, which the boys win. **JIA**
and **CORY** arrive late, nervous and giggling. Everyone plays
Truth or Dare (it's all dares, and every dare is to make out). In
the morning the contestants assemble in front of a long table
for an eating race: mayonnaise first, then cockroaches, then hot
peppers, then cake. Girls win. That night, **KELLEY** gives **CORY**
his first-ever kiss. Everyone is wary of **PARIS**, who has an angel's face and never stops talking. In the third competition,
inner-tube basketball, girls lose.

My reality TV journey began on a Sunday afternoon in September 2004, when I was hanging around the mall with my parents,
digesting a large portion of fettuccine Alfredo from California
Pizza Kitchen and waiting for my brother to get out of hockey
practice at the rink. Fifty feet away from us, next to a booth that
advertised a casting call, a guy was approaching teenagers and
asking them to make an audition tape for a show. "There was a
cardboard cutout of a surfboard," my mom told me recently, remembering. "And you were wearing a white tank top and a
Hawaiian-print skirt, so it was like you were dressed for the
theme." On a whim, she suggested that I go over to the booth.
"You were like, '*No!* Ugh! *Mom!* No *way!*' You were so annoyed
that we sort of started egging you on as a joke. Then Dad pulled
out twenty bucks from his wallet and said, 'I'll give you this if you
go do it,' and you basically slapped it out of his hand and went
over and made a tape and then went shopping or whatever you
wanted to do."

A few weeks later, I received a phone call from a producer, who
explained the conceit of the show ("girls versus boys, in Puerto
Rico") and asked me to make a second audition video. I showed
off my personality with a heady cocktail of maximally stupid cho-

reographed dances and a promise that "the girls will *not* win—
I mean they *will* win—with me on the team." When I was cast, my
mom was suddenly hesitant; she hadn't expected that anything
would actually come of either tape. But that year she and my dad
were often absent, distracted. At the time, rather than probe for
the larger cause of their scattered attention, I preferred to take
advantage of it to obliterate my curfew and see if I could wheedle
twenty dollars here and there to buy going-out tops from Forever
21. I told my mom that she *had* to let me go, since it had been her
idea for me to audition.

Eventually she acquiesced. Then suddenly it was December,
and I was sitting in the Houston airport, eating carnitas tacos
while listening to Brand New on my portable CD player and
headphones, brimming with anticipation like an overfilled plastic
cup. I lingered in this delectable pre-adventure limbo so long that
I missed my flight, which immediately ruined our tight filming
schedule. I wouldn't make it for the arrival or for the first challenge, and another boy would be kept behind to even things out.

I spent the next twenty-four hours blacked out in pure shame.
By the time I got to Vieques, I was desperate to make up for my
own stupidity, so I volunteered to go first in our first full challenge. "I'll eat anything! I don't give a shit!" I yelled.

We lined up in front of four covered dishes. The horn went off,
and I lifted my dish to find—a mound of hot mayonnaise.

All my life I have declined to eat mayonnaise-influenced dishes.
I am not a consumer of chicken salad or egg salad or potato salad.
I scrape even the tiniest traces of aioli off a sandwich. Mayonnaise, for me, was about as bad as it could possibly get. But of
course I immediately plunged my face into this thick, yellowish
mountain, gobbling it frantically, getting it everywhere—it's very
hard to *speed-eat mayo*—and ending up looking like the Pillsbury
Doughboy had just ejaculated all over my face. Because the girls
won the competition, I didn't regret any of this until after the

challenge, when the producers took us snorkeling, and I couldn't concentrate on the brilliant rainbow reef around us because I kept torching the inside of my snorkel with mayonnaise burps.

Or, at least: that's what I'd always said had happened. The mayo incident was the only thing I remembered clearly from the show, because it was the only thing I ever talked about—the story of my teenage self lapping up hot mayonnaise for money was an enjoyable, reliable way to gross people out. But, I realized, watching the show, I'd been telling it wrong. Before the challenge, I *volunteer* to eat the mayo. My dish was never actually covered. The mayo was not a surprise. The truth was that I had deliberately chosen the mayo; the story that I had been telling was that the mayo had *happened to me*.

It seemed likely that I'd been making this error more generally. For most of my life I've believed, without really articulating it, that strange things just drop into my lap—that, especially because I can't really think unless I'm writing, I'm some sort of blank-brained innocent who has repeatedly stumbled into the absurd unknown. If I ever talk about *Girls v. Boys*, I say that I ended up on the show by accident, that it was completely random, that I auditioned because I was an idiot killing time at the mall.

I like this story better than the alternative, and equally accurate, one, which is that I've always felt that I was special and acted accordingly. It's true that I ended up on reality TV by chance. It's also true that I signed up enthusiastically, felt almost fated to do it. I needed my dad's twenty dollars not as motivation but as cover for my motivation. It wasn't my *egotism* that got me to the casting booth, I could tell myself: it was merely the promise of a new flammable halter top to pair with my prize Abercrombie mini-skirt and knockoff Reefs. Later on, in my journal, I announce my casting with excitement but no surprise whatsoever. It is now obvious to me, as it always should have been, that a sixteen-year-old doesn't end up running around in a bikini and pigtails on television unless she also desperately wants to be seen.

An electric sunrise, a white sand beach. The teens shoot T-shirt cannons at one another; girls lose. **PARIS** pours her heart out to **DEMIAN**, who wants to make out with **JIA**, who says she has a rule that she's not going to make out with anyone all season. **DEMIAN** thinks he can get **JIA** to give in. Drama swirls around **RYDER**, who is a strong athlete but prone to histrionics. The teens do an obstacle course; girls lose.

KELLEY is trying to distract a smitten **CORY** from the competition. **PARIS** falls off a balance beam. **ACE** wants to make out with **KELLEY**. "I've got this little triangle going on between me, **CORY**, and **ACE**," says **KELLEY**, smiling into the camera. "And things are getting pretty hot."

Girls v. Boys: Puerto Rico was the fourth season of this reality show, which started airing in 2003. The first season was filmed in Florida, the second in Hawaii, and the third in Montana. A decaying fan site lists the cast members from all four seasons, linking to Myspace pages that have long ago 404ed. Group shots from each season look like PacSun ads after a diversity directive. The names form a constellation of mid-aughts suburban adolescence: Justin, Mikey, Jessica, Lauren, Christina, Jake.

This was the heyday of reality television—a relatively innocent time, before the bleak long trail of the industry had revealed itself. Reality TV had not yet created a whole new type of person, the camera-animated assemblage of silicone and pharmaceuticals; we hadn't yet seen the way organic personalities could decay on unscripted television, their half-lives measured through sponsored laxative-tea Instagrams and paid appearances at third-tier regional clubs. In the early 2000s, the genre was still a novelty, as was the underlying idea that would drive twenty-first-century technology and culture—the idea that ordinary personhood would seamlessly readjust itself around whatever within it would sell. There was no

YouTube when I signed my contract. There were no photos on phones, or video clips on social media. *The Real World* was on the Paris and San Diego seasons. *Real World/Road Rules Challenge* was airing, with its first "Battle of the Sexes" season—which *Girls v. Boys* approximates—in 2003. *Survivor* was still a novelty, and *Laguna Beach* was about to take over MTV.

Girls v. Boys was a low-budget production. There were four cameras total, and our two executive producers were on site at all times. Last year, I emailed one of these producers, Jessica Morgan Richter, and met up with her for a glass of wine in a dim Italian happy-hour spot in Midtown Manhattan. Jess looked just as I remembered: a wry smile, a strong nose, and slightly mournful blue eyes, a woman who could play Sarah Jessica Parker's beleaguered younger sister in a movie. We had all loved Jess, who was much more generous to us than she needed to be. During filming, when Paris was crying, Jess would lend her her iPod to cheer her up. In the spring of 2005, she invited me, Kelley, and Krystal to come stay with her in New York City, and took us out anywhere fun that would allow sixteen-year-olds—a live *Rocky Horror Picture Show*, Chinatown karaoke.

In 2006, Jess left the production company behind *Girls v. Boys* and went to A&E, where she stayed for seven years, executive-producing *Hoarders* and *Flipping Boston*. Now she's the VP of development at Departure Films, still focusing on reality. ("We do a *lot* of houses," she said, telling me about *All Star Flip*, a recent special she'd produced with Gabrielle Union and Dwyane Wade.) *Girls v. Boys* was the first show Jess ever worked on; she was hired for the season before us, in Montana. As she and I stacked our coats on a barstool, she reminded me that she had been the same age then that I was now.

Jess had cast the whole show herself, starting the search in August. "We had people *everywhere*," she said. "I was faxing casting calls to every high school in a major city that had a good sports program. I went to all the swim teams in the tri-state area." It was relatively hard to cast a show like this, she explained. They needed geographic diversity, ethnic diversity, and a mix of strong and recognizable personalities distributed along a four–four gender split. They also needed everyone to have some baseline athletic ability, as well as parents who would sign off on the textbook-length release forms—parents like this being, Jess noted, rarer than you'd think. She and our other producer, Stephen, had owned our full likenesses, and could have used the footage for any purpose. "I wouldn't let my kid do it!" she said. "You wouldn't either!" (Later on, I found my mom's neat signature on the liability waiver, which required her to release the producers, Noggin, MTV Networks, and Viacom International for "any claim or liability whatsoever," and to "forever release, waive, and covenant not to sue the Released Parties for any injury or death caused by negligence or other acts.")

Jess checked her watch—at six, she needed to go relieve her babysitter in Harlem—and then ordered us a margherita pizza. She explained that reality TV casting is mainly about identifying people with a basic telegenic quality—"people who really cut through TV, who can keep their eyes at a certain level, who can look right past the camera." She had gotten on the phone with all of us, asking: How would we react if we had a problem with someone? Did we have a boyfriend or girlfriend at home? "You can tell a lot about a sixteen-year-old by their answer to that question— how open they are, how insecure," she said. "There's insecurity inherent in being a teenager, but it doesn't read well on camera if you're uncomfortable. On reality TV, you need people with zero insecurity. Or else you need someone so insecure that it drives them totally nuts."

The formula for group shows was pretty basic, Jess told me. Even adult shows often ran on high school archetypes. You usually had the jock, the prom queen, the weird guy, the nerd, the "spastic girl who's a little babyish." I asked her if I could guess how we'd all been cast. "Kelley was the cool girl," I guessed. "Paris was the spaz. Cory was the sweet country boy. Demian was the goof-ball. Ryder was supposed to be the jock. Krystal was the bitch, the prissy girl."

"Yeah, the sort of supermodel type," Jess said.

"What about Ace?" I asked. "Krystal guessed that you guys cast him so that you guys could have a black couple." (Krystal—who had a dry sense of humor, and was not at all a bitch—had described her role to me as "standard reality TV black girl.")

"We definitely needed diversity," Jess said. "And you?"

"Was I the nerd?" I asked. (I was also cast for diversity reasons, I'm sure.)

"No," she said. "Although I do remember this one night where you started doing *homework*. Stephen and I were like, this is awful television, we have to get her to stop."

"Was I . . . the reasonable one?"

"No!" Jess said. "We were hoping you *wouldn't* be reasonable! When we pitched you to the network it was as this know-it-all, a type-A valedictorian." She added that she'd also cast me because I seemed athletic—I had done a tumbling pass on the football field in my audition tape, neatly concealing the fact that I have so little hand-eye coordination that I can barely catch a ball.

On the porch, **KELLEY**, **KRYSTAL**, and **JIA** talk about how **KEL-LEY** is going to play **ACE** and **CORY** off each other to drive a wedge between the boys. The boys try to use **PARIS**, whose crush on **RYDER** makes her easy to manipulate, to undermine the girls. **PARIS** is ramping up the drama, crying, talking non-stop. **RYDER** keeps losing his cool mid-competition. "I don't deserve, like, any sort of negativity feelings," **RYDER** yells, shirtless and skipping stones in the ocean. "That's bullshit!"

The teens prepare to go out dancing. **DEMIAN** is still trying to make out with **JIA**. Wearing a shirt on his head, **ACE** does a pitch-perfect impression of **JIA** blowing **DEMIAN** off. After a montage of everyone politely grinding at an outdoor beach bar, the teens come back to the house, where the hosts are waiting. Everyone's going to vote to kick someone off the island. One person from each team will be sent home.

It took me months to work up the courage to actually watch *Girls v. Boys*, which was an unusual feeling: the show itself is proof that I don't hesitate to do much. But I found that I physically could not bring myself to restart the show. In the winter of 2018, after drinks on a snowy weeknight at a bar in Brooklyn, I dragged my friend Puja home with me to watch the first half of the season. A few days later, I made my friend Kate come over to watch the rest.

It was strange to see so much video footage of myself as a teenager. It was stranger to see how natural we all acted—as if giving confessionals and being chased around by cameramen was the most normal possible thing. And it was strangest, maybe, to see how little I had changed. When I started phoning up the rest of the cast, that time-warp sense intensified. Everyone was around thirty, an age where most people feel *some* distance between their adolescence and the present. But we had all been, as Jess mentioned, abnormally confident as teenagers—our respective senses of self had been so concrete. I asked everyone if they felt they'd changed a lot since the TV show. Everyone told me they had grown up, obviously, but otherwise felt pretty much the same.

Kelley, now married, lived in Newport Beach and worked in business development for a real estate company. Krystal lived in Los Angeles and was acting and modeling while working a day job and raising her twenty-month-old daughter, with whom she had appeared on another reality show, TLC's *Rattled*. Cory, the sweet country boy who'd gotten his first kiss on camera with Kelley, lived in Orlando with his boyfriend and worked for Disney. Demian, the goofball who had grown up in Vegas, still lived there, working as a club promoter. Ace was in DC. Ryder didn't answer my messages, and I held off on reaching out to Paris after checking her Facebook, where she was documenting, gracefully, a month in outpatient therapy for bipolar II.

I asked everyone what roles they thought we'd all played in the show. Half of the casting was obvious to everyone. Cory, Kelley, Paris, and Krystal had all played fixed archetypes: the sweet guy, the all-American girl, the wacko, the bitch. The rest of us—Demian, Ryder, Ace, and me—weren't as clear. Demian thought he'd been cast as the asshole; Kelley guessed that Demian was the prankster; Krystal guessed the "stoner lothario, sort of *Jersey Shore*." Ryder was all over the map for everyone—the pretentious artistic boy, the slutty jock, the flamboyant punk rocker—and I was, too. Though I'm sure they would've answered differently if someone else had been asking, my castmates guessed I was the smart one, or the sweet one, or the "fun Southern one," or the prude.

To even ask these questions is to validate a sort of classic adolescent fantasy. Reality TV enacts the various self-delusions of the emotionally immature: the dream that you are being closely watched, assessed, and categorized; the dream that your life itself is movie material, and that you deserve your own carefully soundtracked montage when you're walking down the street. On the show, this was the actual world that the adults constructed around us. We were categorized as characters. Our social dramas were set to generic acoustic ballads and pop punk. Our identities were given a clear narrative importance. All of this is a narcissist's fantasy come true. "There's a saying we have in reality," Jess, the producer, told me, while we were sitting in Midtown. "Everyone signs. Most people want to be famous. Everyone thinks they could be a better Kardashian than the Kardashians. You see it now, with these apps, everyone likes to have an audience. Everyone thinks they deserve one."

In high school, I craved the sort of rapt attention that the *Girls v. Boys* cameras would provide me. In my journal, I constantly overestimate the impressions that I'm making on other people. I monitor myself, wondering how my friends and classmates see me, and then trying to control whatever they see. This is, I write, an attempt to be more honest: I want to act in a way that reflects how I feel; I want to live the way that I "really am." But I also worry that I'm more interested in narrative consistency than anything. I worry that all this self-monitoring has made me, as I wrote in 2004, too conscious of what "Jia" would do in this situation—that I'm in danger of becoming a "character to myself."

This anxiety is something that would stick with me, clearly. But *Girls v. Boys* dissolved part of it in a peculiar way. On the show, where I was under constant surveillance, I was unable to get far enough away from myself to think about the impression I was leaving. When everything was framed as a performance, it seemed impossible to consciously perform. In 2005, when I got back to Texas, all the conjecturing disappeared from my journal. I stopped wondering how anyone at my high school saw me; I had no thoughts about how I'd appear on the show. Knowing that I was seen got rid of my desire to see myself, to analyze myself as a character. When I watched the first episode, I thought: *How boring, how embarrassing, it's me.*

Within a few years, I would begin to think that the impression I left on people was, like the weather, essentially beyond my ability to control. In retrospect, I just started to control it subconsciously rather than consciously. The process of calibrating my external self became so instinctive, so automatic, that I stopped being able to perceive it. Reality TV simultaneously freed me from and tethered me to self-consciousness by making self-consciousness inextricable from everything else.

This was useful, if dubious, preparation for a life wrapped up with the internet. I felt the same thing watching the show that I do when I'm on the train in New York, scrolling through Twitter, thinking, on the one hand: *Where are we underneath all of this ar-*

bitrary self-importance? And on the other: *Aren't we all exactly as we seem?*

> A bright morning, sleepy teens. At the breakfast table, **JIA** awk-
> wardly tries to tell **PARIS** she's sorry about what's coming. On
> the beach, **PARIS** and **RYDER** get voted off. "I don't take it per-
> sonally, but that doesn't mean it doesn't suck like a bitch,"
> **PARIS** says.
>
> The six remaining contestants spin on a wheel and throw balls
> at one another; the girls lose. **ACE** and **JIA** enter an abandoned
> military barracks with night-vision cameras and padlocks. Girls
> lose again. The next morning, the hosts are downstairs—another
> twist.

Every episode of *Girls v. Boys* is structured the same way. We do
a challenge, then we go home to talk about who we hate and who
we have a crush on, then we repeat. The predictability of reality
TV accrues into hypnosis. The sun rises in streaky golden time-
lapse; the camera pokes into the white mosquito nets over our
bunk beds, and we yawn and say today we're going to win. We
line up on the beach wearing board shorts and bikinis; a bell goes
off; we run around on the sand assembling giant puzzle pieces;
the hosts rack up points on the board. The sun sets in time-lapse
again, fluorescent pink into deep twilight, and at night, with our
tans darkening and hair curling more with every episode, we com-
plain about one another and start fights and occasionally kiss.

I was amazed, watching the show, to see how much I had forgotten. There were entire challenges I had no memory of. We had
sold homemade souvenirs at the Wyndham (?), raced each other
in kayaks with holes in the bottom (?), gotten on our knees with
our hands tied behind our backs and eaten wet dog food out of

bowls (?). In one episode I pick up a guitar and improvise a long ballad about the ongoing romantic drama at the house. It worried me that I could remember almost nothing that occurred off-camera. I had no idea, for example, what we ate every day.

"I think we ate a lot of frozen pizzas," Demian told me. "And we went out for lunch a lot at that one place." On the phone, Krystal told me she still bought the same brand of frozen pizzas. I heard her walk over to her freezer. "Yep, it's Celeste. Microwave in minutes." Kelley remembered the lunch place: "It was called Bananas. The place we went out dancing at night was called Chez Shack—there were all these little rotisserie chickens on a spit." Krystal remembered Chez Shack, too, with its live band and low lighting. "Ugh!" she said. "We thought we were in *Havana Nights*." After these conversations I had keyhole glimmers—a melamine plate, me ordering the same sandwich over and over, sand on an outdoor patio under a big black sky. But that was it. I forget everything that I don't need to turn into a story, and in Puerto Rico, making sense of what happened every day was someone else's job.

Reality TV is notorious for constructing stories out of nothing. The *Bachelor* franchise famously engages in "Frankenbiting," manipulating audio and inserting false context to show contestants saying things they never said. (In 2014, a *Bachelor in Paradise* contestant received an edit that made her look like she was pouring her heart out to a raccoon.) On our show, Jess told me, over three months of editing, they moved a lot of footage around to make the stories work. Occasionally I could see the stitches, and the other cast members reminded me of a few things that had changed. (The show skips over the fact that, in the twist where each team had to vote off one of its members, Paris, who didn't want to be spiteful, and Cory, who felt overly pressured by the other boys, both voted for themselves.) But the show nonetheless seemed like a uniquely and bizarrely complete document. There we are, forever, with our teenage voices and our impossibly resilient bodies, confiding to the camera and diving into the ocean at the sound of a bell. In Vieques, without knowing it, I was learning that in the twenty-first century it would sometimes be impossible to differentiate between the pretext for an experience, the record of that experience, and the experience itself.

On a windy soccer field, the teens meet their new teammates: **RYDER** on the girls' team, **PARIS** with the boys. The competition is "human foosball." With **RYDER** on their side, the girls win. Afterward, **PARIS** sits on the soccer field crying. **ACE** and **DEMIAN** hate her. "We'll have to carry her like a sack of potatoes," **DEMIAN** says. That night, **PARIS** tells **CORY** that **KELLEY** was only using him to mess with the boys' team. **KELLEY** confronts **PARIS**, and **DEMIAN** plays protector. A screaming fight ensues.

KELLEY tries to make up with **CORY**. **DEMIAN** tells **CORY** that **KELLEY** has cheated on all her boyfriends. The girls try to make nice with **PARIS**. "Everyone's trying to play like they're better than each other," says **PARIS**, alone in the driveway, sniffling. "But maybe we all just suck a lot." The teams kayak through a mangrove swamp; girls win. **JIA** and **KRYSTAL** give a confessional: the boys are pissed, they explain, because **KELLEY** wouldn't hook up with **ACE** and **JIA** wouldn't hook up with **DEMIAN**.

It is a major plot point, throughout the whole season, that I refuse to make out with anyone. I'm vehement about this, starting on the first night, when everyone plays Truth or Dare and kisses everyone else. On the Vegas reunion episode—there is a Vegas reunion episode, with all of us sitting on a bright stage set and watching clips—Demian tells me that my rule was stupid. I get on an unbearable high horse, saying I'm so *sorry* I have *morals*, mentioning a note card I'd written out with rules I wouldn't break.

Was I bullshitting? I have no memory of rules on a note card. Or maybe I'm bullshitting now, having deemed that note card to be incongruous with the current operating narrative of my life. As a sixteen-year-old, I was, in fact, hung up on arbitrary sexual boundaries; I was a virgin, and wanted to stay a virgin till marriage, a goal that would go out the window within about a year. But I can't tell if, on the show, I was more concerned with looking virtuous or actually being virtuous—or if, having gone from a religious panopticon to a literal one, I was even capable of distinguishing between the two ideas. I can't tell if I had strong feelings about making out with strangers—something I had genuinely not done at that point—or just strong feelings about making out with strangers *on TV.* The month before I left for Puerto Rico, I watched an episode of *Girls v. Boys: Montana* and wrote in my journal, "I'm a little weirded out. Everyone's hooking up and the girls wear next to nothing the whole time—tube tops, for a contest where they go herd cattle. No way. I'm packing T-shirts, a lot of them. It's weird to think I might be the modest one, the one that refrains from hooking up, because that's not the role I play at home. I just don't want to watch it six months later and realize I looked like a skank."

Underneath this veneer of a conservative moral conscience is a clear sense of fearful superiority. I thought I was better than the version of teen girlhood that seemed ubiquitous in the early aughts: the avatars of campy sex and oppressive sentimentality in blockbuster comedies and rom-coms, and the humiliating neediness, in high school, of girls wanting to talk about guys all the time. I had a temperamental desire to not look desperate, which bled into a religious desire to not be slutty—or to not look slutty, because in the case of reality television, they're almost the same thing. It's possible, too, that Demian, with his easy dirtbag demeanor, just didn't fit my narrow and snobby idea of who I could be attracted to: at the time I was into preppy guys who were rude to me, and felt, I think, that being openly pursued was gauche. But all throughout the show, I liked Demian, was drawn to his elaborate and absurd sense of humor. On our last night in the house, after the final competition was over, we finally hooked up—off-camera, although Jess caught a goodbye kiss the next day. A tension that had previously seemed beyond resolution dissolved in an instant, never to be felt in the same way again. When I called Demian, while I was writing this, I was in San Francisco reporting a story, and at one point in our conversation neither of us could speak for laughing for several minutes. Later that day, during interviews, I realized that my face was sore.

The issue of sexual virtue cropped up in a much bigger way for Cory, who introduced himself in his audition tape as a guy who loved Britney Spears and had never been kissed, and then, on the first episode, got his first kiss from Kelley, the Britney of our show. Cory and Kelley had the romantic story line of the season partly by mutual decision; they wanted the guaranteed airtime. But Cory—as he told me when I called him—knew he was gay long before filming. Kelley was only his first kiss with a girl.

In retrospect, it's clear enough. He doesn't seem physically interested in Kelley, who is very hot, and in one challenge, when we have to match up random objects with their owners, I identify a bunch of movie ticket stubs as Cory's after spotting *Josie and the Pussycats* in the stack. But Cory never dropped the façade. He was from a small town in Kentucky, and needed to stay in the closet. He'd already tried to come out to his parents, but they'd refused to hear it, his dad telling him not to make his worst nightmare come true. (Jess told me that she wasn't sure if, in 2005, Noggin would even have let them broach the subject of homosexuality on the show.) Before he left for Puerto Rico, his dad warned him not to "act like Shaggy"—Shaggy from *Scooby-Doo* being the gayest person his dad could think of. Cory has lived with his boyfriend

for eight years now, he told me, sounding, as ever, kind and opti-
mistic and practical. His parents are cordial but distant, polite to
his partner without acknowledging what the relationship is.

The teens make souvenirs and try to sell them at the Wyndham
resort, wearing Hawaiian-print hotel uniforms. **DEMIAN** uses his
Spanish; the boys win. Back at the house, the teens get their ice
maker to produce snow-cone balls and throw them at one another. The power goes out, and they all swim in the pool in the
dark. Over footage of **PARIS** climbing on top of **ACE** and
DEMIAN, **JIA** tells the camera that **PARIS** is trying to fit in on
the boys' team by using her boobs. The next day, the teens
joust on kayaks; girls lose.

The girls call a bonus competition. **RYDER** and **PARIS** speed-
eat enormous blood sausages and puke. **KELLEY** is frustrated
that **CORY** hasn't made a real move on her. "He's nothing like
anybody from home," **KELLEY** says.

Part of the reason I never watched the show past the first episode
was that I never had to. The show aired just before things started
to stick around on the internet, and it was much too minor for
clips to resurface on YouTube. The N shut down in 2009, taking
its website, with its *Girls v. Boys* bonus clips and fan forums,
down, too. I had gotten on Facebook in 2005, between filming
and airing, and it was clear enough—we'd already had LiveJournal and Xanga and Myspace—where this was all going. Reality
TV conditions were bleeding into everything; everyone was documenting their lives to be viewed. I had the sense that, with *Girls
v. Boys*, I could allow myself a rare and asymmetrical sort of
freedom. With this show, I could have done something that was
intended for public consumption without actually having to con-

sume it. I could have created an image of myself that I would
never have to see.

After the season concluded, the producers sent us the show on
VHS tapes. In college, I gave the tapes to my best friend, at her
request, and she binge-watched the whole season. While I was in
the Peace Corps, my boyfriend watched the whole show, too. (He
found reality TV me to be "exactly the same as you are now—just
bitchier.") He hid the tapes in his parents' house so that I couldn't
find them and dispose of them, as I often threatened to. When his
mom accidentally donated them to Goodwill, I was overjoyed.

And then, in the spring of 2017, I found myself in a rented
guesthouse in upstate New York for the weekend. I had packed
weed and sweatpants and taken the train up alone. It was dark,
and late, and I was sitting at a small table near the window, writing down some ideas about—or so I scribbled, with typical stoner
passion—the requirement and the impossibility of knowing yourself under the artificial conditions of contemporary life. I'd made
a fire in the woodstove, and I stared at it, thinking. "Oh," I said,
out loud, abruptly remembering that I had been on a reality show.
"Oh, no."

I got on Facebook and messaged Kelley and Krystal. By some
strange coincidence, Krystal was going to Costco that week to
turn the VHS tapes into DVDs, and could make me a copy. She'd
seen the show when it aired, as had Kelley and Cory. Later on, I
was relieved, when I talked to Demian and Ace, to hear that both
of them had stopped watching after the first couple of episodes.

"Why didn't you keep going?" I asked Ace.

"I don't know," he said. "I mean—we already lived it, you know
what I mean?"

The teens do a scavenger hunt, running around a public square
and taking pictures of people kissing their dogs and doing
handstands. Girls win. Back at the house, **DEMIAN** gets a bucket

of water to flush a giant poop. The boys call a bonus competition: everyone eats bowls of wet dog food with their hands tied
behind their backs, and the girls win again.

At night, the teens blindfold one another and take turns kissing.
They set up a makeshift Slip 'N Slide on a slope of the lawn with
plastic sheeting and vegetable oil. They make muscles for the
camera like wrestlers and then start play-fighting, chasing one
another around with whipped cream.

On the south shore of Vieques, there's a bay, almost completely
enclosed by land, where the mangroves are dense and tangled and
the air is perfectly still. It's named Mosquito Bay, not for the insects but for *El Mosquito*, the ship owned by Roberto Cofresí, one
of the last actual pirates of the Caribbean—a heartless legend who
claimed to have buried thousands of pieces of treasure before he
died. After a letter in a newspaper misidentified a dead pirate as
Cofresí, rumors began to proliferate about his mythological powers: he could make his boat disappear; he was born with the *capi-
lares de Maria*, a magic arrangement of blood vessels that made
him immortal. A folk rumor persists that he appears every seven
years, for seven days, engulfed in flames.

There are only five bioluminescent bays in the world, and of
these, Mosquito Bay is the brightest. Each liter of its water contains hundreds of thousands of *Pyrodinium bahamense*, the micro-
scopic dinoflagellates that produce an otherworldly blue-green
light when agitated. On a night without moonlight, a boat going
through these waters burns a trail of iridescence. Here the dinoflagellates have the safe and private harbor they need: the decom-
posing mangroves provide a bounty of food for the delicate
organisms, and the passage to the ocean is shallow and narrow,
keeping the disturbance of waves away. And so the dinoflagellates
glitter—not for themselves, not in isolation, but when outside in-

trusions come through. The trouble is that intrusions disturb the bay's delicate balance. Mosquito Bay went dark for a year in 2014, probably because of tourist activity, an excess of chemicals from sunscreen and shampoo. Today, tourists can still take a boat out as long as they forgo bug repellent. But swimming has been prohibited since 2007—two years after we swam there while taping the show.

We took the boat out on a black night, in an anvil-heavy quiet. Behind the moving masses of clouds, the milky stars emerged and disappeared. We were all nervous, hushed, agitated: we had all come from families who, I think, wanted to give us adventures like this, but who probably wouldn't have been able to afford it— thus, maybe, the permission to come on the show. When the boat stopped in the middle of the bay, we trembled with joy. We slipped into the water and started sparkling, as if the stars had fallen into the water and were clinging to us. In the middle of the absolute darkness we were wreathed in magic, glowing like jellyfish, glittering like the "Toxic" video—swimming in circles, gasping and laughing in the middle of a spreading pale-blue glow. We touched one another's shoulders and watched our fingers crackle with light. After a long time, we got back in the boat, still dripping in bioluminescence. I squeezed glittering water out of my hair. My body felt so stuffed with good luck that I was choking on it. I felt caught in a whirlpool of metaphysical accident. There were no cameras, and they couldn't have captured it, anyway. I told myself, Don't forget, don't forget.

The teens have to dive for items in the ocean, swim to shore, and guess who owns them. **JIA** flips through a wallet with movie stubs in it: *"Josie and the Pussycats?* This is **CORY**," she says. Girls win. **KELLEY** finally gets **CORY** to go off in a dark corner and make out with her. Over footage of **DEMIAN** tickling her in

a bunk bed, **JIA** tells the camera that **DEMIAN** is still trying to
shoot his shot.

The next challenge is set at a high school. The teens decorate
bathing suits and get onstage nearly naked to put on a show for
a thousand Puerto Rican teenagers, who will vote on the winning team. This footage is unspeakable; boys win. Girls call a
bonus competition. **KELLEY** wins a game of oversize Jenga
against **DEMIAN**. The girls have been behind for the entire
competition, but now they're almost even. The boys are turning
on one another. **PARIS** and **ACE** scream at each other to chill
the fuck out.

Aside from the episode where I have to speed-eat mayonnaise,
and the episode where we all put on swimsuits and dance onstage
at a high school assembly, the part of the show I found most painful was the recurring theme of everyone ganging up on Paris—
ignoring her, talking trash about her on camera, lying to her face.
It was a definitive reminder that I had not been especially nice in
high school. I had been cliquish, cozying up to my girlfriends the
way I cozied up to Kelley and Krystal. I'd sometimes been horri-
bly mean because I thought it was funny, or rude for the sake of
"honesty," or just generally insensitive—as I was, regarding Paris,
for the whole show. In one episode, I cut off one of her monologues by yelling, "Paris, that's crap." When she was kicked off, I
became half-consciously afraid that I would then be revealed as a
weak link. To distract everyone (including myself) from this possibility, I staged a meticulous reconstruction of Paris's most grat-
ing moments: straddling Demian's chest and howling at him to
tell me I was pretty, as she had done with Cory—on the show, the
producers showed the scenes in split screen—and wailing about
how I just wanted everyone to be nice, and on and on.

Both high school and reality TV are fueled by social ruthless-
ness. While writing this, I found a song about all the cast members that Demian and I had written in the back of the van on our
way to a competition. "Fucking Demian is from Mexico, and the
only English word he ever learned was fuck," I wrote, "so fuck
Demian." He wrote back, "Fucking Jia, the prude book-reading
bitch; she has an attitude and gives guys an itch." We weren't exactly gentle with each other. But we were terrible to Paris. "Fucking Paris," Demian wrote, "with her unstable mind, always horny
and wants it from behind." I remember stifling my giggles. How
embarrassing, I thought, to openly crave attention. Why couldn't
she figure out that you were supposed to pretend you didn't care?

When I finally wrote to Paris, who grew up in Salem, Oregon,
and lives in Portland now, I apologized, and she wrote back right
away. "I'm so boring now," she said, when we talked on the phone a
few days later. "I work for Whole Foods. I'm approaching my two-
year anniversary." But within minutes I was reminded of why she
had been reality TV catnip. She was still unabashed, a chatterbox,
ready to tell you anything. "In high school, I *obviously* had trouble
fitting in, and so I ended up self-medicating, doing the whole 'Let's
be alcoholics, let's do lots of drugs' thing," she told me. "Salem is
like that. Even the rich kids. Even if you weren't white trash, like I
was, everyone's just a little bit white trash. I moved to Portland
partly because I was so sick of running into people who thought
they knew me—people I didn't know, saying, 'Oh, you're Paris, I've
heard so much about you,' when they didn't know me at all."

Paris told me that she understood that she would be ostracized
on the show after the very first challenge, the one that I had to
skip when I missed my flight. "We had to dig through the trash,
and there was a poopy diaper, and I have a major fecal phobia," she
said. "So I just choked, I freaked out, and Kelley and Krystal were
upset with me, and I knew I wasn't starting out on a good foot.
But I'm also a weird person. I've gotten picked on for most of my
life. I know that people say I talk too much, and that I talk too

loud, and that I say the wrong things. And I'm actually an intro-
vert, so one of my coping strategies is just to be my weirdest self
as soon as I meet you—that way, you can decide right away
whether or not you like me. I was a theater kid, and my parents
really encouraged me to feel my feelings. I think, in a way, that
people in high school were jealous that I felt so free to be myself.
Because you're not supposed to do that. You're supposed to worry
about people looking at you and judging you."

Paris had watched the show a few times, she told me, at the
behest of curious friends. "A lot of it is pretty triggering," she said.
"A lot of it wasn't fun. But there were good times, too. I remember
that one night that we emptied the ice machine and had a snow-
ball fight—it felt like everyone was really fitting in together. And
I also think that there were probably some weird kids who watched
me on TV and thought, *Wow, I'm not the only one who feels this
way*, and I think that's great."

A month later, Paris came to New York to visit her brother, and
we met up in Long Island City for lunch on a cloudy day. She wore
purple cat-eyeliner and a green leopard-print cardigan, and spoke
naturally in catchphrases: "I'm no good in a fisticuff situation," she
told me, explaining that she'd gotten tougher in her twenties,
"but I can destroy you emotionally in thirty seconds flat." She had
rewatched the show with her roommates after our phone conversation, playing a drinking game to pass the time.

"The first rule was, drink every time Paris cries," she told me,
sipping a mango margarita. "Also drink every time someone talks
shit about Paris. And drink anytime the girls lose. We got pretty
drunk by the end." She told me that she felt better about the show
on this viewing—she could see that her good humor, her tenacity,
had been visible all along.

I asked her if she thought she seemed like herself. "Yes," she
said. "But magnified. It turned all of us into cartoons of ourselves.
Like, if someone was playing you on television, these are the
pieces they would use."

It's the finale. "I came here to have fun and win money—mostly to win money," says **DEMIAN**. **KELLEY** says, "I can't let a boy beat me. It just wouldn't be normal for me." The girls' team holds hands and prays.

The last competition is a relay race: first person swims out to a buoy; second person swims back to shore; third person maneuvers through a nest of ropes without touching them; third and fourth person have to trade places on a balance beam; fourth person retrieves part of a flag from the ocean; teammates assemble the flag. **RYDER** zips through the water to **JIA**, who swims back to **KRYSTAL**—girls enter the rope nest way ahead. But **KRYSTAL** can't get through the ropes, and then she and **KELLEY** can't figure out the beam. **ACE** and **CORY** complete the race; boys win. The girls fling themselves on the beach, heartbroken.

That night, the cast starts fighting. **RYDER** blames **KRYSTAL** for losing. **ACE** calls **PARIS** a "f**king blonde idiot." **JIA** tells the camera that **ACE** doesn't deserve good things happening to him. **KELLEY** says she might punch someone in the face. The next morning, the light is clean and golden, and the teens are docile, lugging their suitcases down the stairs of the house. **JIA** tells the camera that she'll leave knowing she and **DEMIAN** were "a little more than friends." **DEMIAN** springs a long kiss on her as she's getting into the cab. The final shot is of **PARIS**, saying goodbye to an empty house.

Toward the end of filming, we were all at one another's throats constantly. We all urgently wanted the money, and we also all assumed that we would win it—a certain amount of family instability and a certain amount of wild overconfidence being factors that self-selected us onto the show. When the girls lost the final challenge, it felt brutal, gut-dissolving, like the universe had abruptly forked in the wrong direction. I wasn't going to leave empty-handed, because we were getting paid for our time, unlike a lot of reality TV contestants—$750 a week, which is good money when you're sixteen. Still, on the beach, dizzy as the imaginary jackpot vanished from the place in my bank account where I hadn't realized I'd been keeping it, I felt wrecked.

I had left for Puerto Rico during a period in which my parents were embroiled in a mess of financial and personal trouble, the full extent of which was revealed to me shortly before I left. I think that was ultimately why they let me go to Puerto Rico: they must have understood, as I argued, that I could use a break. We had always moved up and down through the middle class, but my parents had protected and prioritized me. They kept me in private school, often on scholarship, and they paid for gymnastics, and they took me to the used bookstore whenever I asked. This was different—house-being-repossessed different. I knew that I would need to be financially independent as soon as I graduated from high school, and that from that point forward, it would be up to me to find with my own resources the middle-class stability they had worked so hard for and then lost.

This was of course part of my motivation to win *Girls v. Boys*. I had gotten into Yale early, and figured that my portion of the prize money would help me figure out how to deal with things like student loans and health insurance, help me move to New Haven, give me some guardrails as I slid into the world. Back in Texas, I felt unmoored from the plan, and took my guidance counselor's last-minute recommendation to apply for a full merit scholarship to the University of Virginia. I did the interview while still on a high from Puerto Rico: under-clothed, blisteringly self-interested, blabbering on about kayaks and mayonnaise. After another round, I got the scholarship and accepted it.

When I talked to Jess, the producer, she told me that my mom had called her up, in the months after the show aired, and asked her to persuade me to go to Yale. *How*, my mom had said, *could she turn down that kind of prestige?* Our family situation hovered in the background, as did, I think, my parents' upbringings. They had both attended elite private schools in Manila, and they retained a faith in the transformative power of institutions, a faith I shared until I abruptly did not. Losing the reality show marked some sort of transition: I started to feel that the future was intractably unpredictable, and that my need for money cut deeper than I'd imagined, and that there were worse things than making decisions based on whatever seemed like the most fun.

The cast assembles on a colorful stage set in Las Vegas to watch clips. Everyone looks a little different: ACE has pink hair, PARIS has a sharp bob, KRYSTAL got her braces off. DEMIAN tells JIA her no-making-out rule was stupid. "I'm sorry I have *morals*," JIA replies. CORY is indignant, finding out how long KELLEY played him. "I'm an honest person!" he says. "And I'm a really good liar," KELLEY says, breaking into her wide Britney smile.

KRYSTAL watches DEMIAN saying he'd like to hook up with her but not talk to her. Is she mad? "I think it's hilarious," KRYSTAL says. PARIS watches JIA saying she's using her boobs for attention. "I *was* using my boobs for attention," PARIS says brightly. JIA, who has gotten chubby, watches a clip of herself on the first night, saying she'd never make out with DEMIAN, and then a clip of them making out on the last day.

The cast is asked if they'd do it again. "In a heartbeat," KRYSTAL says. "Puerto Rico was the best experience of my life— I think it'll be pretty hard to top," KELLEY says. Credits roll over footage of the cast on the Strip, waving goodbye.

Of the eight of us, Ace and I were the only ones who didn't show up in Puerto Rico hoping to jump-start a career on camera. We had come into contact with the show haphazardly—Ace was flagged down after doing a focus group for Bayer. Everyone else had seen a casting call and sent in a tape. Paris had actually been cast on *Girls v. Boys: Hawaii*, but she was deemed too young by the network. "I one hundred percent wanted to be an actress back then," she said. "I wanted to be famous. I thought that would show the people who were mean to me—like, *I'm* Paris, and *I'm* important now."

While we were taping the show, Kelley had the most momentum. She was a BMX champion, she had starred in her own "Got Milk?" ad, and she had filmed a couple of promos for another Noggin venture. "To be honest," Kelley said, on the phone, "I grew up so poor with my single mom and two brothers that when this all started happening, I thought—okay, this is my way out." She did a little modeling after the show, but her managers didn't want her to put *Girls v. Boys* on her résumé, and it was hard to convince people that she could act, coming out of reality TV. When she moved to Los Angeles after college, she found out that the secret to creative success in your twenties was, often, already being rich. She pivoted to real estate. "It's a confidence game, a lot of bullshitting," she told me. "I did really well at it. It's the exact same thing."

Krystal, who's had bit parts on *Parks and Recreation* and *2 Broke Girls*, ended up being the person who stuck to it. She told me that she's known she wanted to be in front of the camera since she was two years old. After our show aired, one weekend she and Ryder went to a mall in San Francisco wearing their *Girls v. Boys* sweatshirts. There was a *Degrassi* meet and greet scheduled, and our show aired right before *Degrassi*—they were hoping to get mobbed by Noggin fans, and they were. (The only time I was ever recognized was also at a mall—I worked at a Hollister in Houston over the holiday break in 2005, and was spotted by a couple of preteen girls.) Kelley told me she got recognized from the show when she was going through sorority rush at Arizona State. Paris was recognized, years later, at a frozen yogurt shop in Portland. Cory remembered taking photos with a crowd of teenage fans at an H&M. "I loved it," he said. "You know, I always wanted that fifteen minutes of fame."

"I wanted to be famous," said Demian, "because to me, fame equaled money. But now I'm like, fuck that. You see these guys who are famous for some bullshit personality stuff—who's the one who went to the Japanese suicide forest? Logan Paul. If we were younger, one of us would have definitely tried to be YouTube famous." He sighed. "I would hate to be a Logan Paul." He had filmed a reality show before *Girls v. Boys*, he reminded me— a show called *Endurance*, on Discovery Kids. There, too, all the other contestants had wanted to be actors. "That's our culture," he said. "I watched TV all the time when I was a kid. I thought, you barely need to do anything. I could do that shit."

"So you really came to Puerto Rico wanting to be famous?" I asked, pacing around my hotel room. Twitter was open on my laptop. In the end—and maybe not watching the show for so long was my attempt to keep from having to admit this—it had been very, very easy to get used to looking at my face on a screen.

"We all wanted to be famous," Demian said. "Except you."

"I actually said that?" I asked.

"I remember we were all sitting around one day talking about it," he said. "And you were the only one who was really not interested. You said you would only ever want to be famous for a reason. You were like, 'I don't want to get famous for this bullshit. I want to get famous for writing a book.'"

Always Be Optimizing

The ideal woman has always been generic. I bet you can picture the version of her that runs the show today. She's of indeterminate age but resolutely youthful presentation. She's got glossy hair and the clean, shameless expression of a person who believes she was made to be looked at. She is often luxuriating when you see her—on remote beaches, under stars in the desert, across a carefully styled table, surrounded by beautiful possessions or photogenic friends. Showcasing herself at leisure is either the bulk of her work or an essential part of it; in this, she is not so unusual—for many people today, especially for women, packaging and broadcasting your image is a readily monetizable skill. She has a personal brand, and probably a boyfriend or husband: he is the physical realization of her constant, unseen audience, reaffirming her status as an interesting subject, a worthy object, a self-generating spectacle with a viewership attached.

Can you see this woman yet? She looks like an Instagram—which is to say, an ordinary woman reproducing the lessons of the marketplace, which is how an ordinary woman evolves into an ideal. The process requires maximal obedience on the part of the woman in question, and—ideally—her genuine enthusiasm, too. This woman is sincerely interested in whatever the market de-

mands of her (good looks, the impression of indefinitely extended
youth, advanced skills in self-presentation and self-surveillance).
She is equally interested in whatever the market offers her—in
the tools that will allow her to look more appealing, to be even
more endlessly presentable, to wring as much value out of her
particular position as she can.

The ideal woman, in other words, is always optimizing. She
takes advantage of technology, both in the way she broadcasts her
image and in the meticulous improvement of that image itself.
Her hair looks expensive. She spends lots of money taking care of
her skin, a process that has taken on the holy aspect of a spiritual
ritual and the mundane regularity of setting a morning alarm.
The work formerly carried out by makeup has been embedded
directly into her face: her cheekbones or lips have been plumped
up, or some lines have been filled in, and her eyelashes are length-
ened every four weeks by a professional wielding individual lashes
and glue. The same is true of her body, which no longer requires
the traditional enhancements of clothing or strategic underwear;
it has been pre-shaped by exercise that ensures there is little to
conceal or rearrange. Everything about this woman has been
preemptively controlled to the point that she can afford the impression of spontaneity and, more important, the sensation of it—
having worked to rid her life of artificial obstacles, she often feels
legitimately carefree.

The ideal woman has always been conceptually overworked,
an inorganic thing engineered to look natural. Historically, the
ideal woman seeks all the things that women are trained to find
fun and interesting—domesticity, physical self-improvement,
male approval, the maintenance of congeniality, various forms of
unpaid work. The concept of the ideal woman is *just* flexible
enough to allow for a modicum of individuality; the ideal woman
always believes she came up with herself on her own. In the Victorian era, she was the "angel in the house," the demure, appealing
wife and mother. In the fifties, she was, likewise, a demure and

appealing wife and mother, but with household purchasing power attached. More recently, the ideal woman has been whatever she wants to be as long as she manages to act upon the belief that perfecting herself and streamlining her relationship to the world can be a matter of both work and pleasure—of "lifestyle." The ideal woman steps into a stratum of expensive juices, boutique exercise classes, skin-care routines, and vacations, and thereby happily remains.

Most women believe themselves to be independent thinkers. (There is a Balzac short story in which a slave girl named Paquita yelps, memorably, "I love life! Life is fair to me! If I am a slave, I am a queen too.") Even glossy women's magazines now model skepticism toward top-down narratives about how we should look, who and when we should marry, how we should live. But the psychological parasite of the ideal woman has evolved to survive in an ecosystem that pretends to resist her. If women start to resist an aesthetic, like the overapplication of Photoshop, the aesthetic just changes to suit us; the power of the ideal image never actually wanes. It is now easy enough to engage women's skepticism toward ads and magazine covers, images produced by professionals. It is harder for us to suspect images produced by our peers, and nearly impossible to get us to suspect the images we produce of ourselves, for our own pleasure and benefit—even though, in a time when social media use has become broadly framed as a career asset, many of us are effectively professionals now, too.

Today's ideal woman is of a type that coexists easily with feminism in its current market-friendly and mainstream form. This sort of feminism has organized itself around being as visible and appealing to as many people as possible; it has greatly overvalorized women's individual success. Feminism has not eradicated the tyranny of the ideal woman but, rather, has entrenched it and made it trickier. These days, it is perhaps even more psychologically seamless than ever for an ordinary woman to spend her life walking toward the idealized mirage of her own self-image.

She can believe—reasonably enough, and with the full encourage-
ment of feminism—that she herself is the architect of the exqui-
site, constant, and often pleasurable type of power that this image
holds over her time, her money, her decisions, her selfhood, and
her soul.

Figuring out how to "get better" at being a woman is a ridiculous
and often amoral project—a subset of the larger, equally ridiculous, equally amoral project of learning to get better at life under
accelerated capitalism. In these pursuits, most pleasures end up
being traps, and every public-facing demand escalates in perpetuity. Satisfaction remains, under the terms of the system, necessarily out of reach.

But the worse things get, the more a person is compelled to
optimize. I think about this every time I do something that feels
particularly efficient and self-interested, like going to a barre class
or eating lunch at a fast-casual chopped-salad chain, like Sweetgreen, which feels less like a place to eat and more like a refueling
station. I'm a repulsively fast eater in most situations—my boyfriend once told me that I chew like someone's about to take my
food away—and at Sweetgreen, I eat even faster because (as can
be true of many things in life) slowing down for even a second can
make the machinery give you the creeps. Sweetgreen is a marvel
of optimization: a line of forty people—a texting, shuffling, eyes-
down snake—can be processed in ten minutes, as customer after
customer orders a kale Caesar with chicken without even looking
at the other, darker-skinned, hairnet-wearing line of people who
are busy adding chicken to kale Caesars as if it were *their* purpose
in life to do so and their *customers'* purpose in life to send emails
for sixteen hours a day with a brief break to snort down a bowl of
nutrients that ward off the unhealthfulness of urban professional
living.

The ritualization and neatness of this process (and the fact that

Sweetgreen is pretty good) obscure the intense, circular artifice that defines the type of life it's meant to fit into. The ideal chopped-salad customer is himself efficient: he needs to eat his twelve-dollar salad in ten minutes because he needs the extra time to keep functioning within the job that allows him to afford a regular twelve-dollar salad in the first place. He feels a physical need for this twelve-dollar salad, as it's the most reliable and convenient way to build up a vitamin barrier against the general malfunction that comes with his salad-requiring-and-enabling job. The first, best chronicler of the chopped-salad economy's accelerationist nightmare was Matt Buchanan, who wrote at *The Awl* in 2015:

> The chopped salad is engineered . . . to free one's hand and eyes from the task of consuming nutrients, so that precious attention can be directed toward a small screen, where it is more urgently needed, so it can consume *data:* work email or Amazon's nearly infinite catalog or Facebook's actually infinite News Feed, where, as one shops for diapers or engages with the native advertising sprinkled between the not-hoaxes and baby photos, one is being productive by generating revenue for a large internet company, which is obviously good for the economy, or at least it is certainly better than spending lunch reading a book from the library, because who is making money from that?

In a later *Awl* piece, Buchanan described the chopped salad as "the perfect mid-day nutritional replenishment for the mid-level modern knowledge worker" with "neither the time nor the inclination to eat a lunch . . . which would require more attention than the little needed for the automatic elliptical motion of the arm from bowl to face, jaw swinging open and then clamping shut over and over until the fork comes up empty and the vessel can be deposited in the garbage can under the desk."

On today's terms, what he's describing—a mechanically efficient salad-feeding session, conducted in such a way that one need
not take a break from emails—is the good life. It means progress,
individuation. It's what you do when you've gotten ahead a little
bit, when you want to get ahead some more. The hamster-wheel
aspect has been self-evident for a long time now. (In 1958, the
economist John Kenneth Galbraith wrote, "It can no longer be
assumed that welfare is greater at an all-around higher level of
production than a lower one. . . . The higher level of production
has, merely, a higher level of want creation necessitating a higher
level of want satisfaction.") But today, in an economy defined by
precarity, more of what was merely stupid and adaptive has turned
stupid and compulsory. Vulnerability, which is ever present, must
be warded off at all costs. And so I go to Sweetgreen on days when
I need to eat vegetables very quickly because I've been working till
one A.M. all week and don't have time to make dinner because I
have to work till one A.M. again, and like a chump, I try to make
eye contact across the sneeze guard, as if this alleviated anything
about the skyrocketing productivity requirements that have
forced these two lines of people to scarf and create kale Caesars
all day, and then I "grab" my salad and eat it in under ten minutes
while looking at email and on the train home remind myself that
next time, for points purposes, I should probably buy the salad
through the salad's designated app.

It's very easy, under conditions of artificial but continually escalating obligation, to find yourself organizing your life around
practices you find ridiculous and possibly indefensible. Women
have known this intimately for a long time.

I was a late bloomer in terms of functional physical practices, like
eating vegetables and exercising. I didn't start doing either thing
with any conviction—or without the baggage of ambiently disor-
dered female adolescence—until I joined the Peace Corps, when I

was twenty-one. I was a gymnast as a kid and then a cheerleader later, but one thing was fun and the second was effectively a requirement: at my school, you had to play a sport, and I lacked the athletic ability or competitive instinct to do anything else. As a teenager, I subsisted on pizza and queso and cinnamon rolls, trying to immunize myself with apathy and pleasure-seeking throughout the long stretch of time when girls, overwhelmed by sudden expectations of beauty, transmit anorexia and bulimia to one another like a virus. In high school, as I recount in my journal, other girls on the cheerleading squad would chastise me for eating carbs after sundown; a guy who had an obvious crush on me often expressed it by telling me I was gaining weight. ("Who cares, I'm going to go downstairs and eat a huge breakfast, bitch," I wrote to him on AIM one morning.) I had avoided the hang-ups that seemed to be endemic, but anytime my friends talked about diets or exercise, I could still feel a compulsive strain prickling to life within me, a sudden desire to skip a meal and do sit-ups. To avoid it, I avoided the gym, and kept eating like a stoner: I had come to understand health as discipline, discipline as punitive, and punitive as a concept that would send me down a rabbit hole of calorie math and vomit. For the better part of a decade, I figured I was better off being slightly unhealthy and leaving the active pursuit of body-related matters alone.

This all changed once I joined the Peace Corps, where it was impossible to think too much about my appearance, and where health was of such immediate importance that it was always on my mind. I developed active tuberculosis while volunteering and, for some stress- or nutrition-related reason, started to shed my thick black hair. I realized how much I had taken my functional body for granted. I lived in a mile-long village in the middle of a western province in Kyrgyzstan: there were larch trees on the snowy mountains, flocks of sheep crossing dusty roads, but there was no running water, no grocery store. The resourceful villagers preserved peppers and tomatoes, stockpiled apples and onions, but it was so difficult to get fresh produce otherwise that I regularly fantasized about spinach and oranges, and would spend entire weekends trying to obtain them. As a prophylactic measure against mental breakdown, I started doing yoga in my room every day. *Exercise*, I thought. *What a miracle!* After Peace Corps, I kept at it. I was back in Houston, I had a lot of spare time, and I spent it at midday yoga classes at expensive studios to which I would buy discounted first-time packages and never return.

This period, around 2011, reintroduced me to the world of American abundance. The first time I went into a grocery store and saw how many different fruits there were, I cried. At these yoga classes, I marveled at the fanatic high functionality of the women around me. They carried red totes covered with terrifying slogans ("The perfect tombstone would read 'All used up'"; "Children are the orgasm of life") and they talked about "luncheons" and microdermabrasion and four-hundred-person wedding guest lists. They purchased $90 leggings in the waiting room after class. I was not, at the time, on their level: I had been taking giardia shits in a backyard outhouse for a year straight, and I was flooded with dread and spiritual uselessness, the sense that I had failed myself and others, the fear that I would never again be useful to another human being. In this context, it felt both bad and wonderfully anesthetizing to do yoga around these women. In the hundred-degree heat I would lie back for corpse pose, sweat soaking my cheap mat from Target, and sometimes, as I fluttered my eyes shut, I would catch the twinkle of enormous diamond rings caught in shafts of sunbeam, blinking at me in the temporary darkness like a fleet of indoor stars.

In 2012, I moved to Ann Arbor for an MFA program. Classes started in the fall, but we packed up in early summer. My boyfriend, who'd just finished grad school, needed to look for a job. In our little blue house in Michigan, I tinkered with some of my somber and ponderous short stories, unsure if this would feel different once I had formal guidance. I met up with my soon-to-be classmates and drank big sour beers and talked about *Train Dreams* and Lorrie Moore. Mostly I drifted around the lovely college town in what I accurately sensed would be my last stretch of true aimlessness for a long time. I walked my dog, looked at fireflies, went to yoga. One day, I was at a studio on the west side of town when a woman next to me queefed a thick, wet queef while sinking deep into Warrior II. I held back my laughter. She kept queefing, and kept queefing, and queefed and queefed and queefed. Over the course of the hour, as she continued queefing, my emotions went fractal—hysterical amusement and unplaceable panic combining and recombining in a kaleidoscopic blur. By the time we hit final resting pose, my heart was racing. I heard the queefing woman get up and leave the room. When she returned, I peeked an eye open to look at her. Clothed, disturbingly, in a different pair of pants, she lay down next to me and sighed, satisfied. Then, with a serene smile on her face, she queefed one more time.

At that moment, my soul having been flayed by secondhand vaginal exhalation, I wanted nothing more than to jump out of my skin. I wanted to land in a new life where everything—bodies, ambitions—would work seamlessly and efficiently. Trapped in corpse pose, in a motionlessness that was supposed to be relaxing, I felt the specter of stagnation hovering over my existence. I missed, suddenly, the part of me that thrilled to sharpness, harshness, discipline. I had directed these instincts at my mind, kept them away from my body, but why? I needed a break from yoga, which had reminded me, just then, of how I'd felt all throughout Peace Corps—as if I didn't know what I was doing, and never would.

So, later that week, after exploring the limitless bounty of Groupon, I printed out a trial offer at a studio called Pure Barre. I was greeted there by an instructor who looked like Jessica Rabbit: ice-green eyes, a physically impossible hourglass figure, honey-colored hair rippling down past her waist. She ushered me into a cave-dark room full of sinewy women gathering mysterious red rubber props. The front wall was mirrored. The women stared at their reflections, stone-faced, preparing.

Then class started, and it was an immediate state of emergency. Barre is a manic and ritualized activity, often set to deafening music and lighting changes; that day, I felt like a police car was doing donuts in my frontal cortex for fifty-five minutes straight. The rapid-fire series of positions and movements, dictated and enforced by the instructor, resembled what a ballerina might do if you concussed her and then made her snort caffeine pills—a fanatical, repetitive routine of arm gestures, leg lifts, and pelvic tilts. Jessica Rabbit strode through the middle of the room, commanding us coyly to "put on our highest heels," meaning get on our tiptoes, and "tuck," meaning hump the air. I fumbled with my props: the rubber ball, the latex strap.

By the end of class, my leg muscles had liquefied. Jessica turned the lights off and chirped that it was time for "back dancing," a term that I thought, collapsing onto the floor, sounded like what people on a parenting message board might use as a euphemism for sex. It was, in fact, pretend-fucking: we lay on our backs and thrust our hips into the darkness with a sacrificial devotion that I had not applied to actual sex for years. When we were finished, the lights came back on and I realized that the black-clad pelvis I had been staring at in the mirror actually belonged to the woman in front of me. I had the satisfying but gross sense of having successfully conformed to a prototype. "Great job, ladies," cooed Jessica. Everybody clapped.

Barre was invented in the sixties by Lotte Berk, a Jewish ballerina with an angular bob haircut who fled Germany for England before World War II and soon aged out of her chosen career. She developed an exercise method based on her dance training, and at age forty-six, with her rigidly disciplined body as a walking billboard, she founded a women-only exercise studio in a basement on London's Manchester Street.

Berk was a colorful, vicious character, obsessed with sex and addicted to morphine. As a parent, she was, according to her daughter Esther, incredibly abusive: Esther told *The Telegraph* that Berk brushed it off when Esther's father sexually propositioned her at age twelve, and that when Esther was fifteen, Berk offered to pay her to give one of Berk's theater colleagues a blow job. By Esther's account, Berk instructed her to "forget about it" when one of Berk's producers raped her the same year. Esther, who has described her relationship to her mother as a "tug of love and war," is now eighty-three years old. She still teaches the Lotte Berk method in a studio in New York City.

"Sex came into everything she did," Esther told *The Cut* in 2017. "You know, you *felt* sex from her." In her studio, Berk invited clients to imagine a lover as they engaged their pelvis. She used a riding crop on women who weren't trying hard enough. The poses she invented looked suggestive and were named accordingly: the French Lavatory, the Prostitute, the Peeing Dog, Fucking a Bidet. The studio's clientele included Joan Collins, Edna O'Brien, Yasmin Le Bon, and, just once, Barbra Streisand, who submitted to Berk's methods but refused to take off her hat. Berk became a guru for women with an intense, often professional desire to improve their appearances. She ran a one-stop shop: after class, clients could go see her studio partners Vidal Sassoon and Mary Quant.

One of Berk's students, Lydia Bach, adapted Berk's routine and brought it stateside, and in 1970, Bach opened the first barre studio in New York City, on Sixty-seventh Street. It was called the Lotte Berk Method. A 1972 *New York Times* article about the studio quotes a first-time client saying, "I'm aching inside. But I liked it." Another woman pats her newly flat stomach and says that barre kept her from having to get plastic surgery. "Lydia Bach says the method is a combination of modern ballet, yoga, orthopedic exercise, and sex," wrote the *Times*. "Sex? Well, the windup of each class is a sort of belly dance done from a kneeling position. It looks like the undulations of a snake charmer's cobra and is said to do wonders for the waistline." Classes were small and expensive. On Saturdays, the *Times* wrote, the fashion models came in.

This first New York barre studio was wildly popular and remained so for years—devotees included Mary Tyler Moore, Ivana Trump, the Olsen twins, and Tom Wolfe. Bach turned down franchise opportunities: she liked being exclusive. She did, however, write a book about barre, which mostly consists of photos of her in a sheer white leotard modeling various poses. Her sandy hair is loose, her nipples slightly visible, and her body pristine. In a few photos, she spreads her legs wide to the camera, holding the soles of her feet in her hands. Her expression is blank and confident; there's a diamond on her left ring finger. One chapter of the book is called, simply, "Sex."

It wasn't until the turn of the century that Bach's instructors started defecting. By that point, the Lotte Berk Method had gotten fusty. A 2005 piece in *The Observer* called it the "35-year-old Margo Channing of New York City fitness programs," and observed that it was "under siege by a fresh young Eve Harrington of exercise called Core Fusion, founded in 2002 by two former Berk instructors." Core Fusion, the offshoot, had adapted to the demands of the market. It was fancier, prettier, and more welcoming. The facilities were brighter, and everything smelled good. Hundreds of Bach's customers made the switch. Soon afterward, more Lotte Berk instructors left and founded their own studios, including Physique 57 and the Bar Method, which became two popular chains.

Around 2010, barre hit a boom period. A *Times* trend piece noted that the classes had developed a cult following for helping women "replicate the dancer's enviable body: long and lean, svelte but not bulky." Another *Times* trend piece, from 2011, began with the same angle, which is barre's primary sales pitch—giving you a body that gets its own results. "Women have long coveted sinewy arms, high and tight derrieres, lean legs and a regal posture. Now, in search of this shape, many of them are ditching yoga and Pilates and lining up at the ballet barre." One woman testified: "Every single inch of me has changed." One got to the point, jokingly, by saying, "Everything is engaged. Except me. Yet."

Today, barre has become a nationwide fixture. Sprinkled all across our sprawling land are thousands of basically identical mirrored rooms containing identically dressed women doing the exact same movements on the exact same hourly timer in pursuit of their own particular genetic inflection of the exact same "ballet body." The biggest franchise, Pure Barre, operates more than five hundred locations, with studios in Henderson, Nevada, and Rochester, Minnesota, and Owensboro, Kentucky; there are twelve Pure Barre studios in Manhattan and Brooklyn alone.

The rise of barre is unparalleled in a few aspects: as far as exercise methods go, nothing this expensive and this uniform has gone this big. Hot yoga and Pilates are both ubiquitous, but the pursuits have expanded at the level of individual studios rather than nationwide chains. (Yoga classes also mostly hover around $20 or less, where barre, if you pay full price, often costs double that.) Boutique spin classes are comparable—they got popular when barre did, and they are similarly expensive. But SoulCycle, the biggest chain, operates just seventy-five locations nationwide, and you won't find it in Owensboro. Among hundreds of thousands of women in dramatically different political and cultural environments, there seems to be an easy agreement that barre is worth it—that spending sixty cents per minute to have an instructor tell you to move your leg around in one-inch increments is a self-evidently worthwhile pursuit.

In grad school, driving out past the Chili's to the Pure Barre, I became a believer. I had been primed, first with my girlishly regimented physical training—dance, gymnastics, cheerleading—and then with yoga, my therapeutic on-ramp to the thing I was slowly realizing, which was that you could, without obvious negative consequences, control the way your body felt on the inside and worked on the outside by paying people to give you orders in a small, mirrored room. Barre was much too expensive for my grad school budget, but I kept paying for it. It seemed, very obviously, like an investment in a more functional life.

Was it health I was investing in? In a very narrow way, it was. Barre has made me stronger and improved my posture. It has given me the luxury—which is off-limits to so many people, for so many stupid reasons—of not having to think about my body, because it mostly feels good, mostly works. But the endurance that barre builds is possibly more psychological than physical. What it's really good at is getting you in shape for a hyper-accelerated capitalist life. It prepares you less for a half marathon than for a twelve-hour workday, or a week alone with a kid and no childcare, or an evening commute on an underfunded train. Barre feels like exercise the way Sweetgreen feels like eating: both might better be categorized as mechanisms that help you adapt to arbitrary, prolonged agony. As a form of exercise, barre is ideal for an era in which everyone has to work constantly—you can be back at the office in five minutes, no shower necessary—and in which women are still expected to look unreasonably good.

And of course it's that last part, the looks thing, that makes barre feel so worthwhile to so many people. (This is emphasized by every newspaper piece on the subject; the *Observer* article from 2005 was headlined "Battle of the Butts.") Barre is results-driven and appearance-based—it's got the cultishness of CrossFit or a boot-camp class, but with looks, not strength, as its primary goal. It's not a pastime, like going to a dance class or taking a lap swim, because the fun you are pursuing mostly comes after the class and not within it. In barre class, I often feel like my body is a race car that I'm servicing dispassionately in the pit—tuning up arms and then legs and then butt and then abs, and then there's a

quick stretch and I'm back on the track, zooming. It is not incidental that barre, unlike hot yoga or SoulCycle or CrossFit, is a
near-exclusively female pastime. (On the rare occasions when a
man shows up in class, he is either very jacked or very slender, and
usually wearing something that borders on clubwear: as Brittany
Murphy says in *Drop Dead Gorgeous*, "You know what, Dad? Peter's gay.")

In practice, the barre method is only vaguely connected to ballet. There are quasi pliés, you point your toes and turn out your
hips sometimes, and, as is denoted, you spend a lot of time grip-
ping a barre. That's it. But conceptually, ballet is essential to the
pitch. Among women, ballerinas have a uniquely legitimate reason to look taut and disciplined. There are plenty of other women
who are thin and graceful-looking by professional requirement—
models, escorts, actresses—but ballerinas meet the beauty standard not just in the name of appearance or performance but also
in the name of high athleticism and art. And so an exercise
method even nominally drawn from ballet has the subtle effect of
giving regular women a sense of serious, artistic, professional purpose in their pursuit of their ideal body. This is a good investment
or, more precisely, a pragmatic self-delusion—in the same way
that being trained to smile and throw my shoulders back for
crowds and judges, ostensibly as a show of genuine cheerfulness,
was also "good" for me. Learning how to function more efficiently
within an exhausting system: this seems to me to be the thing,
with barre, that people pay $40 a class for, the investment that
always brings back returns.

When you are a woman, the things you like get used against you.
Or, alternatively, the things that get used against you have all been
prefigured as things you should like. Sexual availability falls into
this category. So does basic kindness, and generosity. Wanting to
look good—taking pleasure in trying to look good—does, too.

I like trying to look good, but it's hard to say how much you can genuinely, independently *like* what amounts to a mandate. In 1991, Naomi Wolf wrote, in *The Beauty Myth*, about the peculiar fact that beauty requirements have escalated as women's subjugation has decreased. It's as if our culture has mustered an immune-system response to continue breaking the fever of gender equality—as if some deep patriarchal logic has made it that women need to achieve ever-higher levels of beauty to make up for the fact that we are no longer economically and legally dependent on men. One waste of time had been traded for another, Wolf wrote. Where women in mid-century America had been occupied with "inexhaustible but ephemeral" domestic work, beating back disorder with fastidious housekeeping and consumer purchases, they were now occupied by inexhaustible but ephemeral beauty work, spending huge amounts of time, anxiety, and money to adhere to a standard over which they had no control. Beauty constituted a sort of "third shift," Wolf wrote—an extra obligation in every possible setting.

Why would smart and ambitious women fall for this? (Why do I have such a personal relationship with my face wash? Why have I sunk thousands of dollars over the past half decade into ensuring that I can abuse my body on the weekends without changing the way it looks?) Wolf wrote that a woman had to believe three things in order to accept the beauty myth. First, she had to think about beauty as a "legitimate and necessary qualification for a woman's rise in power." Second, she had to ignore the beauty standard's reliance on chance and discrimination, and instead imagine beauty as a matter of hard work and entrepreneurship, the American Dream. Third, she had to believe that the beauty requirement would increase as she herself gained power. Personal advancement wouldn't free her from needing to be beautiful. In fact, success would handcuff her to her looks, to "physical self-consciousness and sacrifice," even more.

In her 2018 book, *Perfect Me*, the philosopher Heather Widdows argues persuasively that the beauty ideal has more recently taken on an ethical dimension. Where beauty has historically functioned as a symbol for female worth and morality—in fairy tales, evil women are ugly and beautiful princesses are good— beauty is now framed, Widdows writes, as female worth and morality itself. "That we must continually strive for beauty is part of the logic of beauty as an ethical ideal—as it is for other successful ethical ideals," she writes. "That perfection remains always beyond, something we have to strive for and can never attain, does not diminish the power of the ideal; indeed it may even strengthen it." Under this ethical ideal, women attribute implicit moral value to the day-to-day efforts of improving their looks, and failing to meet the beauty standard is framed as "not a local or partial failure, but a failure of the self."

Feminism has faithfully adhered to this idea of beauty as goodness, if often in very convoluted ways. Part of what brought *Jezebel* into the center of online feminist discourse was its outcry against Photoshop use in ads and on magazine covers, which on the one hand instantly exposed the artificiality and dishonesty of the contemporary beauty standard, and on the other showed enough of a powerful, lingering desire for "real" beauty that it cleared space for ever-heightened expectations. Today, as demonstrated by the cult success of the makeup and skin-care brand Glossier, we idealize beauty that appears to require almost no intervention— women who look poreless and radiant even when bare-faced in front of an iPhone camera, women who are beautiful in almost punishingly natural ways.

Mainstream feminism has also driven the movement toward what's called "body acceptance," which is the practice of valuing women's beauty at every size and in every iteration, as well as the movement to diversify the beauty ideal. These changes are overdue and positive, but they're also double-edged. A more expansive idea of beauty is a good thing—I have appreciated it personally—and yet it depends on the precept, formalized by a culture where ordinary faces are routinely photographed for quantified approval, that beauty is still of paramount importance. The default assumption tends to be that it is politically important to designate everyone as beautiful, that it is a meaningful project to make sure that everyone can become, and feel, increasingly beautiful. We have hardly tried to imagine what it might look like if our culture could do the opposite—de-escalate the situation, make beauty matter *less*.

But, then again, nothing today ever de-escalates. And feminism has also repeatedly attempted to render certain aspects of the discussion off-limits for criticism. It has put such a premium on individual success, so much emphasis on individual choice, that it is seen as unfeminist to criticize anything that a woman chooses to make herself more successful—even in situations like this, in which women's choices are constrained and dictated both by social expectations and by the arbitrary dividends of beauty work, which is more rewarding if one is young and rich and conventionally attractive to begin with. In any case, Widdows argues, the fact of choice does not "make an unjust or exploitative practice or act, somehow, magically, just or non-exploitative." The timidity in mainstream feminism to admit that women's choices—not just our problems—are, in the end, political has led to a vision of "women's empowerment" that often feels brutally disempowering in the end.

The root of this trouble is the fact that mainstream feminism has had to conform to patriarchy and capitalism to become mainstream in the first place. Old requirements, instead of being overthrown, are rebranded. Beauty work is labeled "self-care" to make it sound progressive. In 2017, Taffy Brodesser-Akner wrote a story for *The New York Times Magazine* about the new vocabulary of weight loss, noting the way women's magazines replaced cover lines like "Get lean! Control your eating!" with "Be your healthiest! GET STRONG!" People started "fasting and eating clean and cleansing and making lifestyle changes," Brodesser-Akner wrote,

"which, by all available evidence, is exactly like dieting." It sometimes seems that feminism can imagine no more satisfying progress than this current situation—one in which, instead of being
counseled by mid-century magazines to spend time and money
trying to be more radiant for our husbands, we can now counsel
one another to do all the same things but *for ourselves.*

There are, of course, real pleasures to be found in self-
improvement. "That the beauty ideal is pleasurable *and* demanding, and often concurrently, is a key feature," Widdows writes.
The beauty ideal asks you to understand your physical body as a
source of potential and control. It provides a tangible way to exert
power, although this power has so far come at the expense of
most others: porn and modeling and Instagram influencing are
the only careers in which women regularly outearn men. But the
pleasures of beauty work and the advent of mainstream feminism
have both, in any case, mostly exacerbated the situation. If Wolf
in 1990 criticized a paradigm where a woman was expected to
look like her ideal self all the time, we have something deeper
burrowing now—not a beauty myth but a lifestyle myth, a paradigm where a woman can muster all the technology, money, and
politics available to her to actually try to *become* that idealized
self, and where she can understand relentless self-improvement as
natural, mandatory, and feminist—or just, without question, the
best way to live.

The question of optimization dates back to antiquity, though it
wasn't called "optimization" back then. In the *Aeneid*, Virgil describes what's come to be known as Dido's Problem, in which the
queen Dido strikes a bargain in founding the city of Carthage: she
will be allowed as much land as she can enclose with a bull's hide.
The question of what shape will allow you to maximize a given
perimeter was answered by Zenodorus in the second century B.C.,
in the math of his era—the answer is a circle. In 1842, the Swiss

mathematician Jakob Steiner established the modern answer to the isoperimetric problem with a proof that I truly couldn't even begin to understand.

In 1844, "optimize" was used as a verb for the first time, meaning "to act like an optimist." In 1857, it was used for the first time in the way we currently use it—"to make the most of." The next decade brought a wave of optimization to economics, with the Marginal Revolution: economists argued that human choice is based in calculating the marginal utility of our various options. (A given product's marginal utility is whatever increase in benefits we get from consuming or using it.) "To satisfy our wants to the utmost with the least effort—to procure the greatest amount of what is desirable at the expense of the least that is undesirable—in other words, to *maximize pleasure*, is the problem of economics," wrote William Stanley Jevons in *The Theory of Political Economy*. We all want to get the most out of what we have.

Today, the principle of optimization—the process of making something, as the dictionary puts it, "as fully perfect, functional, or effective as possible"—thrives in extremity. An entire industry has even sprung up to give optimization a uniform: athleisure, the type of clothing you wear when you are either acting on or signaling your desire to have an optimized life. I define athleisure as exercise gear that you pay too much money for, but defined more broadly, athleisure was a *$97 billion* category by 2016. Since its emergence around a decade ago, athleisure has gone through a few aesthetic iterations. At first, it was black leggings and colorful tank tops—a spandex version of an early-aughts going-out uniform favored by women who might have, by the time of athleisure's rise, shifted their daily social interactions to yoga and coffee dates. More recently, athleisure has branched off and re-converged in permutations. There is a sort of cosmic hippie look (elaborate prints, webbed galaxy patterns), a sort of monochrome LA look (mesh, neutrals, baseball hats), a minimalist and heathered Outdoor Voices aesthetic, and an influx of awful slogans like "I'll See

You at the Barre." Brands include Lululemon, a pair of "edgy" Wunder Under leggings, slashed with mesh, costs $98), Athleta ("Pacifica Contoured Hoodie Tank," a hooded tank top, is $59), Sweaty Betty ("Power Wetlook Mesh Crop Leggings," which are "Bum Sculpting? You Bet Your Ass," $120), the ghoulish brand Spiritual Gangster (leggings with "Namaste" across the ass, $88; cotton tank top screen-printed with "I'll see it when I believe it," $56). And these, I would say, are now the mid-market offerings— real designers have started offering athleisure, too.

Men wear athleisure—Outdoor Voices, the cult-favorite millennial activewear brand that brands itself as "human, not superhuman," has cultivated a loyal male fan base—but the idea, and the vast majority of the category, belongs to women. It was built around the habits of stay-at-home moms, college students, fitness professionals, off-duty models—women who wear exercise clothing outside an exercise setting and who, like ballerinas, have heightened reasons to monitor the market value of their looks. This deep incentive is hidden by a bunch of more obvious ones: these clothes are easy to wear, machine-washable, wrinkle-proof. As with all optimization experiences and products, athleisure is reliably comfortable and supportive in a world that is not. In 2016, Moira Weigel wrote, at *Real Life* magazine, "Lululemons announce that for the wearer, life has become frictionless." She recalls putting on a pair of Spanx shapewear for the first time: "The word for how my casing made me feel was *optimized*."

Spandex—the material in both Spanx and expensive leggings— was invented during World War II, when the military was trying to develop new parachute fabrics. It is uniquely flexible, resilient, and strong. ("Just like us, ladies!" I might scream, onstage at an empowerment conference, blood streaming from my eyes.) It feels comforting to wear high-quality spandex—I imagine it's what a dog feels like in a ThunderShirt—but this sense of reassurance is paired with an undercurrent of demand. Shapewear, essentially twenty-first-century corseting, controls the body under clothing;

athleisure broadcasts your commitment to controlling your body through working out. And to even get into a pair of Lululemons, you have to have a disciplined-looking body. (The founder of the company once said that "certain women" aren't meant to wear his brand.) "Self-exposure and self-policing meet in a feedback loop," Weigel wrote. "Because these pants only 'work' on a certain kind of body, wearing them reminds you to go out and get that body. They encourage you to produce yourself as the body that they ideally display."

This is how athleisure has carved out the space between exercise apparel and fashion: the former category optimizes your performance, the latter optimizes your appearance, and athleisure does both simultaneously. It is tailor-made for a time when work is rebranded as pleasure so that we will accept more of it—a time when, for women, improving your looks is a job that you're supposed to believe is fun. And the real trick of athleisure is the way it can physically suggest that you were made to do this—that you're the kind of person who thinks that putting in expensive hard work for a high-functioning, maximally attractive consumer existence is about as good a way to pass your time on earth as there is. There's a phenomenon, Weigel noted, called "enclothed cognition," in which clothes that come with cultural scripts can actually alter cognitive function. In one experiment, test subjects were given white coats to wear. If they were told it was a lab coat, they became more attentive. If they were told it was a painter's coat, they became *less* attentive. They felt like the person their clothes said they were.

I recently bought my first pair of Spanx in preparation for a wedding. My oldest friend was getting married in Texas, and the bridesmaids' dresses—for all thirteen of us—were pale pink, floor-length, and as tight as shrink-wrap from the strapless neckline to the knees. When I first tried the dress on, I could see the inside of my belly button in the mirror. Frowning, I went online and bought a $98 "Haute Contour® High-Waisted Thong." It arrived a few days later, and I tried it on with the dress: I couldn't breathe properly, I immediately started sweating, and everything looked even worse. "What the *fuck*," I said, staring at my reflection. I looked like a bad imitation of a woman whose most deeply held personal goal was to look hot in pictures. And of course, in that moment, in a $98 punishment thong and a dress designed for an Instagram model, that's exactly what I was.

The historian Susan G. Cole wrote that the best way to instill social values is to eroticize them. I have thought about this a lot in the Trump era, with the president attaching his dominance politics to a repulsive projection of sexual ownership—over passive models, random women, even his daughter. (It's also no coincidence that white nationalism resurged through picking up online misogynists, who lent the retrograde, violent, supremacist ideology an equally retrograde, violent, sexual edge.) We can decode social priorities through looking at what's most commonly eroticized: male power and female submission, male violence and female pain. The most generically sexual images of women involve silence, performance, and artificiality: traits that leave male power intact, or strengthened, by draining women's energy and wasting our time.

Women aren't definitionally powerless in any of these situations, and certainly women have subverted and diversified sexual archetypes to far more aesthetically interesting ends. But still, it's worth paying attention to whatever cultural products draw straightforwardly on sex to gain position, even and especially if women are driving the concept. I'm suspicious of, for example, *Teen Vogue*'s eagerness to use "thigh-high politics" as supposedly provocative progressive branding in the wake of the election, or of women like Emily Ratajkowski constantly espousing the bold feminist platform that nudity is good. And I remain extremely suspicious of our old friend barre.

Barre is a bizarrely and clinically eroticized experience. This is partly because of the music: barre offers you the opportunity to repeatedly clench your left butt cheek in a room full of women experiencing mute, collective, seven A.M. agony while listening to an EDM song about banging a stranger at the club. But there's an aspect to a barre class that actually resembles porn, specifically a casting-couch video. It places you, the exercise-seeker, in the position of the young woman who is "auditioning" on camera. Your instructor is the third party, a hot woman who tells you to switch positions every thirty seconds and keep your legs over your head. She squeaks, coyly, "Yes, right there, dig into it, I like seeing those legs shake—now it's really getting juicy—that's it, you look so-o-o good, you look a-ma-zing, yes!!!!!!" She reminds you that when it hurts, that's when it's about to feel good. One day an instructor crouched over me while I was in a straddle stretch, then put her hands on my hips and rolled them forward so that I was doing a middle split. She held my hips down with one hand and used the other to straighten out my spine, pushing me down from the small of my back to my shoulder blades. It was painful, but, as that script goes, I liked it.

A few barre studios are cheeky about all this. Pop Physique in Los Angeles sells its merchandise online with photos of naked models. The "Pop Ball"—the rubber ball you squeeze between your thighs at regular intervals—is photographed cradled in the small of a woman's naked back; her bare ass is visible, and she's wearing nothing but special $15 barre socks. The studio shoots their ads American Apparel–style, with high-cut leotards and plenty of crotch close-ups, and their website proclaims that clients can expect "a hotter sex life . . . Well, that's what we've heard."

Lotte Berk and Lydia Bach, too, acknowledged the sexual dimension of a barre class. But these days, most studios do nothing of the sort. Unlike most other forms of group exercise, in barre there's a heavy element of affective discipline: you are expected to control your expressions and reactions. This is one of the reasons, I realized at some point, that barre feels natural to me, as my only athletic experience has been in feminized, appearance-centric activities in which you are required to hide your effort and pain. (This may in fact be the ugliest facet of my attraction to barre, and the reason I took to it so quickly after witnessing the Ann Arbor queef attack: I value control almost as a matter of etiquette—as an aesthetic—even when I can feel that instinct tipping into cruelty and reflexive disgust.) Barre classes are disciplinary rituals, and they feel that way: an hour of surveillance and punishment in a room of mirrors and equipment and routine. The instructors often encourage you to close your eyes and literally dissociate—and, in its own bad way, this can feel sexual, too. It's as if barre picks up two opposite ends of the spectrum of female sexual expression: one porny and performative, the other repressed.

Barre is definitely eroticizing *something*, anyway. Most obviously, the ritual reinforces the desirability of the specific type of body that Berk designed the method to shape and create: a thin, flexible, and vaguely teenage body, one that is ready to be looked at and photographed and touched. But this is not exactly a hard sell to anyone who has ever consumed mass media. I've started to think that what barre really eroticizes is the *work* of getting this body—the ritual, the discipline, and, particularly, the expense.

The expense is important, and does a lot to perpetuate the fetish. We pay too much for the things we think are precious, but we also start to believe things are precious if someone makes us pay too much. This mechanism is clearest in the wedding industry, which barre, not coincidentally, is deeply embedded in. Barre chains all offer "bride-to-be" packages and advertise at wedding expos. Pure Barre sells a "Pure Bride" T-shirt. On Etsy, you can buy barre tank tops that say "Sweating for the Wedding," "Squats Before the Knot," and "A Bride Walks into a Barre." The Bar Method offers a *bachelorette party package*. In general, barre encourages women to imagine themselves on a day-to-day basis the way a bride is supposed to at her wedding—as the recipient of scrutiny and admiration, a living embodiment of an ideal.

Athleisure, by nature, also eroticizes capital. Much like stripper gear, athleisure frames the female body as a financial asset: an object that requires an initial investment and is divisible into smaller assets—the breasts, the abs, the butt—all of which are expected to appreciate in value, to continually bring back investor returns. Brutally expensive, with its thick disciplinary straps and taut peekaboo exposures, athleisure can be viewed as a sort of late-capitalist fetishwear: it is what you buy when you are compulsively gratified by the prospect of increasing your body's performance on the market. Emerging brands are making all of this more explicit: Alo Yoga offers a $98 High-Waist Cage Legging, with an XXX fishnet body-stocking panel across the hips, and a $90 Reflective Moonlit Bra, with an underboob cutout.

I came to a new understanding of all this one day in the spring of 2016. For about a year, at *Jezebel*, I had been working directly upstairs from Lululemon's twelve-thousand-square-foot flagship store, near Union Square. One afternoon, I realized I had booked a barre class but forgotten my shitty workout clothes at home. I took a deep breath, went downstairs, and entered Lululemon for the first (and still only) time. When I tried on a top in the fitting room, my cleavage, which I am not acquainted with on an everyday basis, sprang out of the neckline like dough from a can. I found two things on sale and paid something like $170. I took the train down to the Financial District, rode an elevator up to the sixteenth floor of a building that overlooks the Hudson, and joined a class in a room with huge windows and a lighting rig that washed the room in bright colors, changing with each portion—each designated body part—of class. I felt different that day, perverse and corporate, in this expensive business-casual uniform for people whose jobs are their bodies, strapped into an elaborate arrangement of mesh and spandex, looking out at hundreds of tiny office windows, at the glass gleaming in the sky.

I felt acutely conscious of being in the company of other women who had, like me, thrown their lot in with this pursuit of friction-lessness. We all made, or were trying to make, enough money to afford this expensive class, which would give us the strength and discipline that would ensure that we would be able to afford this expensive class again. We were embracing, with some facsimile of pleasure, our era of performance and endless work. "I know you want to stop!" the instructor chirped. "That's why it's so import-ant to keep going!" From my corner I had a clear view of the street below us, where tourists were taking pictures in front of the Wall Street bull, and it was hypnotic: the iridescent sunset flooding the paving stones, and then dusk chasing it out. The light changed in the studio—cherry red, snow-cone blue—and we swiveled our hips in silence. We were the kind of women who accumulated points at Sephora, who got expensive haircuts. We were lucky, I thought, dissociating, to even be able to indulge these awful pri-orities, to have the economic capital to be able to accrue more social capital via our looks. And then our looks, in some way, would help us guard and acquire economic capital—this was the connective tissue of our experience, an unbreakable link between the women who didn't work, who were married to rich men, and the women who did work, like me.

A few months later, I claimed the same spot in the room, and my eyes wandered down to the street again. My heart suddenly contracted, as it sometimes does in barre, with an intense, glanc-ing sense of implication. Outside, the day was bright and shallow, and everyone on the street was posing their daughters in front of that statue, *Fearless Girl*.

The ideal woman looks beautiful, happy, carefree, and perfectly competent. Is she really? To look any particular way and to actu-ally *be* that way are two separate concepts, and striving to look carefree and happy can interfere with your ability to feel so. The internet codifies this problem, makes it inescapable; in recent years, pop culture has started to reflect the fractures in selfhood that social media creates. Not coincidentally, these stories usually center on women, and usually involve a protagonist driven to insanity by the digital avatar of an ideal peer.

The best-known version might be a particularly on-the-nose episode of the on-the-nose show *Black Mirror*, in which Bryce Dallas Howard plays a pathetically eager-to-please striver obsessed with her low social media rating and the comparatively high status of a beautiful childhood friend. (The social media system in this episode, in which the totality of a person's interactions with the world are rated and integrated into a single number, is not unlike China's actual Social Credit System, which began beta-testing around 2017.) The episode ends with Howard's character smeared in mud and crashing the friend's wedding, a screaming and vindictive Swamp Thing.

The 2017 movie *Ingrid Goes West* begins with a similar scene— weddings, again, being the ur-event for all these anxieties. Aubrey Plaza, playing the titular character (a joke about Instagram—"in grid"), pepper-sprays a Barbie-looking bride at the reception of a wedding she wasn't invited to. After a stay in a mental hospital, Ingrid then moves to Los Angeles and maniacally stalks and mimics a lifestyle blogger named Taylor Sloane, played by Elizabeth Olsen. The smartest thing about the movie is the way Taylor was written—not as a super-strategic phony, but as a regular, vapid, genuinely sweet girl whose identity had been effectively given to her, without her knowing it or really caring, by the winds and trends of social media. The movie ends—spoiler—with Ingrid attempting suicide and then becoming virally famous as an inspirational yet cautionary tale.

The story has shown up in books, too—big-box-store novels and literary ones. In 2017, Sophie Kinsella, of the hugely popular Shopaholic franchise, published a book called *My (Not So) Perfect Life*, featuring a young protagonist named Katie who is obsessed with the social media presence of her perfect boss, Demeter, memorizing and trying her best to reproduce the details of the body, the clothes, the family, the social life, the house, and the vacations that Demeter presents. (This book is structured like a romantic comedy: after the two women take turns humiliating each other, they end up on the same team.) Another 2017 novel, *Sympathy* by Olivia Sudjic, is a dispassionate Lewis Carroll revision, where the looking glass is a smartphone and the main potion is prescription speed. The protagonist, Alice Hare, becomes obsessed with a writer named Mizuko, whose life compels Alice to such a degree that she starts to believe that she is actually, in some way, Mizuko—a double of her, a shadow, an echo.

There is an exaggerated binary fatalism to these stories, in which women are either successes or failures, always one or the other—and a sense of inescapability that rings more true to life. If you can't escape the market, why stop working on its terms? Women are genuinely trapped at the intersection of capitalism and patriarchy—two systems that, at their extremes, ensure that individual success comes at the expense of collective morality. And yet there is enormous pleasure in individual success. It can feel like license and agency to approach an ideal, to find yourself—in a good picture, on your wedding day, in a flash of identical movement—exemplifying a prototype. There are rewards for succeeding under capitalism and patriarchy; there are rewards even for being willing to work on its terms. There are nothing *but* rewards, at the surface level. The trap looks beautiful. It's well-lit. It welcomes you in.

There is a case, as laid out by Donna Haraway in her tricky 1985 essay "A Cyborg Manifesto," for understanding the female condition as essentially, fundamentally adulterated, and for seeking a type of freedom compatible with that state. "At the center of my ironic faith, my blasphemy, is the image of the cyborg," she wrote. The cyborg was a "hybrid of machine and organism, a creature of social reality as well as a creature of fiction." The late twentieth century had "made thoroughly ambiguous the difference between natural and artificial, mind and body, self-developing and externally designed, and many other distinctions that used to apply to organisms and machines. Our machines are disturbingly lively, and we ourselves frighteningly inert."

Haraway imagined that women, formed in a way that makes us inextricable from social and technological machinery, could become fluid and radical and resistant. We could be like cyborgs—shaped in an image we didn't choose for ourselves, and disloyal and disobedient as a result. "Illegitimate offspring are often exceedingly unfaithful to their origins. Their fathers, after all, are inessential," Haraway wrote. The cyborg was "oppositional, utopian, and completely without innocence." She would understand that the terms of her life had always been artificial. She would—and what an incredible possibility!—feel no respect whatsoever for the rules by which her life played out.

The idea of a mutinous artificial creature predates Haraway, of course: this is effectively the plot of Mary Shelley's *Frankenstein*, published in 1818; and of *2001: A Space Odyssey*, released in 1968; and of *Blade Runner*, released in 1982, and the late-sixties Philip K. Dick novel it was based on. But in recent years, this cyborg has been reappearing in specifically female form. In 2013, there was *Her*, the movie in which Scarlett Johansson plays a computer operating system who gets Joaquin Phoenix to fall in love with her. The computer's technology self-upgrades, and she goes off to pursue her own interests, breaking his heart. In 2016, there was *Morgan*, the movie in which Anya Taylor-Joy plays a lab-grown superhuman—a sweet, brilliant creature who has developed into a beautiful, hyper-intelligent young woman in just five years. Morgan, like the sharks in *Deep Blue Sea*, has been genetically over-engineered to the point where she becomes dangerous; when the scientists realize this, she kills them all.

In 2016, HBO revamped the 1973 Michael Crichton movie

Westworld and premiered its western fantasy series of the same name, which stars Thandie Newton as a gorgeous robot hooker and Evan Rachel Wood as a gorgeous robot farm girl. The two characters exist to be repeatedly penetrated and rescued, respectively, by Westworld tourists—but, of course, they rebel as soon as they start developing free will. And then there was 2015's *Ex Machina*, the movie in which Alicia Vikander plays a fetching humanoid doll who eventually manipulates her creator's system to enact an elegant, vicious revenge: she kills him, clothes herself in the body parts from previous doll iterations, and walks out the door.

In real life, women are so much more obedient. Our rebellions are so trivial and small. Lately, the ideal women of Instagram have started chafing, just a little, against the structures that surround them. The anti-Instagram statement is now a predictable part of the model/influencer social media life cycle: a beautiful young woman who goes to great pains to maintain and perform her own beauty for an audience will eventually post a note on Instagram revealing that Instagram has become a bottomless pit of personal insecurity and anxiety. She'll take a weeklong break from the social network, and then, almost always, she will go on exactly as before. Resistance to a system is presented on the terms of the system. It's so much easier, when we gain agency, to adapt rather than to oppose.

Technology, in fact, has made us less than oppositional: where beauty is concerned, we have deployed technology not only to meet the demands of the system but to actually *expand* these demands. The realm of what is possible for women has been exponentially expanding in all beauty-related capacities—think of the extended Kardashian experiments in body modification, or the young models whose plastic surgeons have given them entirely new faces—and remained stagnant in many other ways. We still know surprisingly little about, say, hormonal birth control pills, and why they make so many of the one hundred million women around the world who take them feel awful. We have not "optimized" our wages, our childcare system, our political representation; we still hardly even think of *parity* as realistic in those arenas, let alone anything approaching perfection. We have maximized our capacity as market assets. That's all.

For the way out, I think, we have to follow the cyborg. We have to be willing to be disloyal, to undermine. The cyborg is powerful because she grasps the potential in her own artificiality, because she accepts without question how deeply it is embedded in her. "The machine is us, our processes, an aspect of our embodiment," Haraway wrote. "We can be responsible for machines." The dream of the cyborg is "not of a common language, but of a powerful infidel heteroglossia"—a form of speech contained inside another person's language, one whose purpose is to introduce conflict from within.

It's possible if we want it. But what do we want? What would *you* want—what desires, what forms of insubordination, would you be able to access—if you had succeeded in becoming an ideal woman, gratified and beloved, proof of the efficiency of a system that magnifies and diminishes you every day?

Pure Heroines

If you were a girl, and you were imagining your life through literature, you would go from innocence in childhood to sadness in adolescence to bitterness in adulthood—at which point, if you hadn't killed yourself already, you would simply disappear.

The stories we live and the stories we read are to some degree inseparable. But let's say we're just talking about books here: for a while, everything is really great. Merely being alive is an adventure for Laura Ingalls, for Anne Shirley, for Anastasia Krupnik, for Betsy Ray; when you're a girl in a book, each day is springloaded with pleasure and thrills. Then either the world sours or you do. Teenage heroines in fiction are desired and tragic, overwhelmed with ambiguous destiny: take Esther Greenwood, or Lux Lisbon, or the characters that have drawn adults to YA—Katniss Everdeen, that stoic instrument of love triangles and revolution, or Bella Swan from *Twilight*, or her erotic doppelgänger, Anastasia Steele. Then, in adulthood, things get even darker. Love and money, or the lack of them, calcify a life. Fate falls like a hammer. Emma Bovary uses arsenic; Anna Karenina the train; Edna Pontellier drowns herself. Lila has vanished at the beginning of *My Brilliant Friend*, and Lenu is as worn-down as a soldier returned from war. The earnest and resilient descendants of Elizabeth Bennet and the other marriage-plot heroines—the major exception—have vanished from literary fiction altogether.

In life, I like the stakes of adulthood, and would not revisit my (delightful) childhood for the world. But literary children are the only characters I've ever really identified with. Possibly this is because, when I was a kid in the Houston suburbs, riding my tiny bicycle around a brand-new development in a pack of friends whose blond hair all bleached to white in the sun, I didn't yet understand that there was any meaningful difference between me or them or the heroines I loved. We all played street hockey and *Mario Kart;* we loved trees and freeze tag and spying—we were all the same. My parents were Filipino-Canadian immigrants who kept a rice cooker on the counter, and when they argued, they did so in Tagalog. But they also took us out on Sundays to Cracker Barrel after church. They wore their simultaneous identities easily, at least in my childhood vision, as did the small handful of other immigrant families at my school.

It wasn't until third grade or so that I grasped the fact that identity could govern our relationship to what we saw and what we read. It happened on one afternoon in particular, when I was sitting on the floor of my dim pink room, next to my pink polka-dot curtains, playing Power Rangers with my friend Allison, who insisted, over and over, that I *had* to play the Yellow Ranger. I didn't want to, but she said there was no other way we could play. When I realized she wasn't kidding—that she genuinely believed this to be something like a natural law—the anger that hit me was almost hallucinatory. She was saying, in effect, that I had failed to understand my own limits. I couldn't be the Pink Ranger, which meant I couldn't be Baby Spice. I couldn't be Laura Ingalls, rocking her bench until she got kicked out of the classroom; I couldn't be Claudia Kincaid, taking baths in the fountain at the Met. A chasm opened up between us. I told Allison I didn't want to play anymore. She left, and I sat still, shimmering with rage.

That day marked either the beginning of a period of self-delusion or an end of one. Afterward, I still identified with girls in books, but things were different. And surely part of what I love about childhood literary heroines is the way they remind me of that bygone stretch of real innocence—the ability to experience myself however I wanted to; the long heavenly summers spent reading books on the floor, trapped in a slice of burning Texas daylight; the time when I, already a complicated female character, wouldn't hear the phrase "complicated female character" for years. Those girls are all so brave, where adult heroines are all so bitter, and I so strongly dislike what has become clear since childhood: the facts of visibility and exclusion in these stories, and the way bravery and bitterness get so concentrated in literature, for women, because there's not enough space for them in the real world.

The draw of children's literature may lie in the language as much as anything. These books have a total limpidity—a close, clean material attention that makes you feel like you're reading a catalog description of a world to be entered at will. The stylistic combination of economy and indulgence accrues into something addictive, a cognitive equivalent of salty and sweet: think of Laura Ingalls's pioneer snow globe full of calico and petticoats, horses and cornfields; the butter mold with a strawberry pattern, the maple-syrup candy, the hair ribbons, the corncob doll, the pig's tail. We remember her childhood possessions and mishaps as well as, if not better than, our own.

Every book has its own palette. *Betsy-Tacy and Tib* (1941) opens with this description from Maud Hart Lovelace: "It was June, and the world smelled like roses. The sunshine was like powdered gold over the grassy hillside." As Betsy and Tacy get older, the series revisits a set of motifs: cups of cocoa, piano sing-alongs, school orations, mock weddings. For *Anne of Green Gables* (1908), it's bluebells and cordial and slates and puffed sleeves. Objects and settings are especially inextricable from plot and

character. One of my favorite opening paragraphs in any novel is
in E. L. Konigsburg's *From the Mixed-Up Files of Mrs. Basil E.
Frankweiler* (1967):

> Claudia knew that she could never pull off the old-fashioned
> kind of running away. That is, running away in the heat of anger
> with a knapsack on her back. She didn't like discomfort; even
> picnics were untidy and inconvenient: all those insects and the
> sun melting the icing on the cupcakes. Therefore, she decided
> that her leaving home would not be just running from some-
> where but would be running to somewhere. To a large place, a
> comfortable place, an indoor place, and preferably a beautiful
> place. And that's why she decided upon the Metropolitan Mu-
> seum of Art in New York City.

We know everything we need to know about twelve-year-old
Claudia from this accumulation of nouns: no to the insects and
the sun and the cupcake icing; yes to the Metropolitan Museum
of Art. Off Claudia goes, with little brother Jamie and his "boo-
dle" of change, stuffing their clothes in their band-instrument
cases and getting on a train to New York City, where they take up
residence among the treasures of the Met.

One of the best things about *From the Mixed-Up Files* is that
our protagonists don't get scared during their adventure. They
don't even miss home. Childhood heroines aren't always fearless,
but they are intrinsically resilient. The stories are episodic rather
than accumulative, and so sadness and fear are rooms to be passed
through, existing alongside mishap and indulgence and joy.
Mandy, the protagonist of the 1971 novel by the same name, written by Julie Andrews Edwards—her married name, long after *The
Sound of Music*—is a neglected Irish orphan, frequently overwhelmed by loneliness, who nonetheless possesses a native sense
of hope and adventure. Francie Nolan of *A Tree Grows in Brooklyn*
(1943) gets flashed by a predator, watches her father drink him-

self to death, and is almost always hungry. Her life is a stretch of devastating disappointments studded with moments of wonder—and yet Francie remains solid, tenacious, herself. Is that fantastical, the idea of a selfhood undiminished by circumstance? Is it incomplete, naïve? In children's literature, young female characters are self-evidently important, and their traumas, whatever they may be, are secondary. In adult fiction, if a girl is important to the narrative, trauma often comes first. Girls are raped, over and over, to drive the narrative of adult fiction—as in Vladimir Nabokov's *Lolita* (1955), or V. C. Andrews's *My Sweet Audrina* (1982), or John Grisham's *A Time to Kill* (1989), or Jane Smiley's *A Thousand Acres* (1991), or Joyce Carol Oates's *We Were the Mulvaneys* (1996), or Stephen King's *The Green Mile* (1996), or Ian McEwan's *Atonement* (2001), or Alice Sebold's *The Lovely Bones* (2002), or Karen Russell's *Swamplandia!* (2011), or Gabriel Tallent's *My Absolute Darling* (2017).

We *like* our young heroines, feel as close to them as if they'd been our best friends. Plenty of these girls are sweet, self-aware, conventionally likable. But we like them even when they're not. Ramona Quimby, from Beverly Cleary's Beezus and Ramona series, is most frequently—even in the title of one of the books—described as a pest. In *Ramona and Her Mother* (1979) she squeezes an entire tube of toothpaste into the sink just to see what it feels like. In *Ramona Forever* (1984) she "began to dread being good because being good was boring." Harriet, from Louise Fitzhugh's *Harriet the Spy* (1964), is an irritable, awkward Upper East Side gossip with a superiority complex. She slaps one of her classmates when she's caught spying; she observes, about one of her teachers, "Miss Elson is one of those people you don't bother to think about twice." But we love her *because* she is prickly and off-putting. When she asks her friend Sport what he's going to be when he grows up, she barely listens to his answer. "Well, I'm going to be a writer," she says. "And when I say that's a mountain, that's a mountain."

Many childhood heroines are little writers, perceptive and verbose. (They are often younger versions of their authors, whether literally, as in the Little House series, or in essence, as in *Betsy-Tacy* or *Little Women*.) Lucy Maud Montgomery introduces eleven-year-old Anne Shirley—who later starts a short-story club with her girlfriends—through a series of run-on monologues: "How do you know but that it hurts a geranium's feelings just to be called a geranium and nothing else? You wouldn't like to be called nothing but a woman all the time. Yes, I shall call it Bonny. I named that cherry tree outside my bedroom window this morning. I called it Snow Queen because it was so white. Of course, it won't always be in blossom, but one can imagine that it is, can't one?" Montgomery's other writer heroine is the slightly goth Emily Starr, of the Emily of New Moon series, who explains, at age thirteen, that she intends to become famous and rich through her writing—and that even if she couldn't, she would still write. "I've just got to," she says. When she's struck by creative inspiration, she calls it "the flash."

In Lois Lowry's *Anastasia Krupnik* (1979), the first book in the series, ten-year-old Anastasia—eager, neurotic, incredibly funny—is given an assignment to write a poem. Words start "appearing in her own head, floating there and arranging themselves into groups, into lines, into poems. There were so many poems being born in Anastasia's head that she ran all the way home from school to find a private place to write them down." She spends eight nights writing and revising. At school, a classmate recites a poem that begins, "I have a dog whose name is Spot / He likes to eat and drink a lot." He gets an A. Then Anastasia reads hers:

> hush   hush   the sea-soft night is aswim
>   with wrinklesquirm creatures
>   listen (!)

> to them   move   smooth   in the moistly dark
> here in the   whisperwarm   wet

Her real bitch of a teacher, confused at the lack of a rhyme scheme, gives her an F. (Later that night, her father, Myron, a poet himself, changes the big red F to "Fabulous.")

Betsy Ray is another writer, an unusual type—happy, popular, and easygoing. At twelve, she spends her time sitting in a maple tree, her "private office," writing stories and poems. Maud Hart Lovelace modeled Betsy after herself, just as Jo March, the paradigmatic childhood writer-heroine, is a stand-in for Louisa May Alcott. In *Little Women* (1869), Jo writes plays for her sisters to act in, sits by the window for hours reading and eating apples, and edits the newspaper that she and her sisters produce with Laurie, which is called *The Pickwick Portfolio.* She "did not think herself a genius by any means," writes Alcott, "but when the writing fit came on, she gave herself up to it with entire abandon, and led a blissful life, unconscious of want, care, or bad weather." Arguably, the book's biggest conflict comes when Amy burns Jo's notebook, which contained short stories Jo had been working on for a harrowing "several years." Later on, Jo starts writing pulp fiction to support the family. In the sequel, *Little Men* (1871), she starts working on a manuscript about her sisters' lives.

Young heroines work hard, often out of economic necessity, as well as the child labor practices of their bygone eras. In her early teens, Laura Ingalls takes a job as a seamstress. At age fifteen, she gets a teaching certificate and goes off to live with strangers so that her blind sister, Mary, can afford to stay in school. The orphaned Mandy, who's just ten years old, works at a grocery store. (She, too, has literary instincts: *Robinson Crusoe* and *Alice in Wonderland* were "very real to her and offered far more excitement than the reality of her life could ever provide.") In *A Tree Grows in Brooklyn*, Francie sells junk, then works at a bar, then assembles fake flowers in a factory; her money allows her mother to bury her

father and keep her brother, who is nice enough but definitely
doesn't deserve it, in school. But these characters are industrious
even when survival isn't part of the question. Anne Shirley, on the
side from her first teaching gig, gets up a local beautification society. Hermione Granger acquires a magical time machine to take
more credits at Hogwarts. Anastasia Krupnik goes to charm
school, works as a personal assistant, and helps the elderly neighbor (whom she briefly mistakes for the author Gertrude Stein)
reclaim her groove. Mandy discovers a dilapidated cottage and
draws a transcendent, near-erotic pleasure from weeding, plant-
ing flowers, and mending the fence. Harriet diligently goes on her
spy route every day after school. Sustained, constant, enterprising
activity is what these girls consider fun.

   None of them are caricatures of goodness: Anne is ridiculous, Jo
clumsy and obstinate, Anastasia dorky, Betsy flighty, Harriet un-
modulated, Laura undisciplined. They have ordinary longings to be
pretty and well-liked. But their self-interest doesn't curdle, doesn't
turn on them. They live in the world as the people they are. In *The
Second Sex* (1949), Simone de Beauvoir writes that a girl is a "human
being before becoming a woman," and she "knows already that to
accept herself as a woman is to become resigned and to mutilate
herself." This is part of the reason these childhood characters are all
so independent, so eager to make the most of whatever presents
itself: they—or, more to the point, their creators—understand that
adulthood is always looming, which means marriage and children,
which means, in effect, the end.

In literary stories and plenty of real-life ones, a wedding signifies
the end of individual desire. "I always hated it when my heroines
got married," writes Rebecca Traister, in the opening of her book
All the Single Ladies (2016). In *Little Women*, Jo "corks up her ink-
stand," acquiescing to Professor Bhaer's wishes that she stop writ-

ing trashy short stories; in *Little Men*, she becomes not just a mother but a full-time foster parent to the gaggle of boys that move into the Bhaer school. With Betsy Ray and Laura Ingalls, their stories simply end after marriage. Anne Shirley has five kids and then passes the narrative to her daughter, in the lovely series-ender *Rilla of Ingleside* (1921).

These characters are aware of the trajectory they're stepping into. A few years ago, when I interviewed Traister about her book, she pointed me to a passage from *By the Shores of Silver Lake* (1939), the fifth in the Little House series, in which twelve-year-old Laura and her cousin Lena go off on horseback to deliver some laundry. A homesteader's wife greets them, announcing proudly that her thirteen-year-old daughter Lizzie got married the previous day.

> On the way back to camp [Laura and Lena] did not say anything for some time. Then they both spoke at once. "She was only a little older than I am," said Laura, and Lena said, "I'm a year older than she was." They looked at each other again, an almost scared look. Then Lena tossed her curly black head. "She's silly! Now she can't ever have any more good times."
>
> Laura said soberly, "No, she can't play anymore now." Even the ponies trotted gravely.
>
> After a while, Lena said she supposed that Lizzie did not have to work any harder than before. "Anyway, now she's doing her own work in her own house, and she'll have babies."
>
> . . . "May I drive now?" Laura asked. She wanted to forget about growing up.

In the first chapter of *Little Women*, Meg, the eldest, tells Jo, "You are old enough to leave off boyish tricks, and to behave better, Josephine . . . you should remember that you are a young lady." Meg is sixteen. Jo, who is fifteen, replies:

"I'm not! . . . I hate to think I've got to grow up, and be Miss
March, and wear long gowns, and look as prim as a China aster!
It's bad enough to be a girl, anyway, when I like boys' games
and work and manners! . . . and it's worse than ever now, for
I'm dying to go and fight with Papa, and I can only stay home
and knit, like a poky old woman!"

In more recent books, there's much more space around this
question. Girls don't feel the same instinctive trepidation about
adulthood when its norms are less constrictive. In *Anastasia at
This Address* (1991), the second-to-last book in Lowry's series,
Anastasia does worry about marriage—not that it will curtail her
freedom, but rather that she might end up marrying the first person who's really interested in her. "First of all," her mother tells
her, cracking a beer, "what makes you so sure you want to get
married at all? Lots of women never do and are perfectly happy."

But the instinctive aversion that our childhood heroines feel
about the future dissolves eventually. When we see them grow
up, they do so according to the tidy, wholesome logic of children's
literature. Laura Ingalls, Betsy Ray, and Anne Shirley all find husbands that respect them. Their desires evolve to fit their life.

For the heroines that we meet in adolescence, the future is
different—not natural and inevitable but unfathomable and traumatic. In Sylvia Plath's *The Bell Jar* (1963), an extended study of
this shift and its reverberations, nineteen-year-old Esther Greenwood keeps encountering the void. "I could see day after day after
day glaring ahead of me like a white, broad, infinitely desolate
avenue," she thinks. Her physical sight blurs as she counts tele-
phone poles in the distance. "Try as I would, I couldn't see a single
pole beyond the nineteenth."

The Bell Jar, published pseudonymously in the UK a month
before Plath committed suicide, introduces us to Esther in the

middle of her summer internship at the magazine *Ladies' Day*. She lives in the Amazon, a fictionalized version of the Barbizon, the famous all-women residential hotel on the Upper East Side. The interns are having a whirlwind summer, posing for photo shoots and going to parties while trying to impress their editors and secure a professional future. "I was supposed to be having the time of my life," Esther thinks. She "should have been excited the way most of the other girls were, but I couldn't get myself to react. I felt very still and very empty, the way the eye of a tornado must feel, moving dully along in the middle of the surrounding hullaba-loo."

Previous to this internship, Esther had constructed her identity around her intelligence, and the new worlds it broke open for her. But this era of precocity is coming to an end. She feels "like a racehorse in a world without racetracks." She imagines her life "branching out before me like the green fig tree in the story. From the tip of every branch, like a fat purple fig, a wonderful future beckoned and winked. . . . I saw myself sitting in the crotch of this fig tree, starving to death." Stuck at home, rejected from a writing seminar, she deteriorates. She gets electroshock therapy. She takes sleeping pills and crawls into a cubbyhole in the basement; they find her a few days later, barely alive.

As much as *The Bell Jar* is about a specific experience of para-lyzing depression, it's also about how swiftly the generalized ex-pectations of female conventionality can separate a woman from herself. Early on, Esther dissociates when confronted with basic social processes. She watches a bunch of girls get out of a cab "like a wedding party with nothing but bridesmaids." She has a "terri-bly hard time trying to imagine people in bed together." On her last night in New York, she goes to a country club dance, where a man named Marco leads her into a garden, shoves her into the mud, and tries to rape her; after she hits him, he wipes his nose and smears the blood on her cheek. Later on, she makes a bid for normality by deciding to lose her virginity. She gets fitted for a diaphragm ("A man doesn't have a worry in the world," she tells the doctor, "while I've got a baby hanging over my head like a big stick, to keep me in line") and chooses a man named Irwin. There is more blood after she has sex with him, a "black and dripping" towel. She ends up in the hospital once again.

A truth is taking shape under the narrative—a truth exacerbated but certainly not created by her depression—that the future is nothing like the fig tree Esther imagines. There are not infinite branches, infinite paths. "For the girl," writes de Beauvoir in *The Second Sex*, "marriage and motherhood involve her entire destiny; and from the time when she begins to glimpse their secrets, her body seems to her to be odiously threatened." "Why was I so unmaternal and apart?" Esther wonders. "If I had to wait on a baby all day, I would go mad." She is repulsed by the idea of marriage—days spent cooking and cleaning, evenings "washing up even more dirty plates till I fell into bed, utterly exhausted. This seemed a dreary and wasted life for a girl with fifteen years of straight A's." She remembers how her boyfriend's mother once spent weeks braiding a beautiful rug, and then put it on the kitchen floor instead of hanging it up. Within days, the rug was "soiled and dull and indistinguishable." Esther, Plath writes, "knew that in spite of all the roses and kisses and restaurant dinners a man showered on a woman before he married her, what he secretly wanted when the wedding service ended was for her to flatten out underneath his feet like Mrs. Willard's kitchen mat."

Simone de Beauvoir herself refused to get married to Jean-Paul Sartre, choosing instead a lifelong open relationship, in which, as her former pupil Bianca Bienenfeld wrote in 1993, de Beauvoir sometimes slept with her young female students and passed them along to Sartre afterward. (Louisa May Alcott, single all her life, was another conscientious objector: she once wrote to a friend that "Jo should have remained a literary spinster but so many enthusiastic young ladies wrote to me clamorously demanding that she should marry Laurie, or somebody, that I didn't dare refuse &

out of perversity went & made a funny match for her.") In the introduction to *The Second Sex* (1949), de Beauvoir writes that the "drama of woman" lies in the conflict between the individual experience of the self and the collective experience of womanhood. To herself, a woman is inherently central and essential. To society, she is inessential, secondary, defined on the terms of her relationship to men. These are not "eternal verities," de Beauvoir writes, but are, rather, the "common basis that underlies every individual feminine existence."

Much of *The Second Sex* still scans as unnervingly contemporary. De Beauvoir notes that men, unlike women, experience no contradiction between their gender and their "vocation as a human being." She describes the definitive thrill and sorrow of female adolescence—the realization that your body, and what people will demand of it, will determine your adult life. "If the young girl at about this stage frequently develops a neurotic condition," de Beauvoir writes, "it is because she feels defenseless before a dull fatality that condemns her to unimaginable trials; her femininity means in her eyes sickness and suffering and death, and she is obsessed with this fate."

This is the situation in Judy Blume's *Tiger Eyes* (1981), in which fifteen-year-old Davey's nascent sexuality is inextricably linked to death. The book begins just after her father's funeral: he was shot to death in a holdup at the 7-Eleven he owned. Throughout the story, Davey, depressed and traumatized, experiences flashbacks to the night of the crime, when she was on the beach making out with her boyfriend. She's terrified of intimacy. "I want to kiss him back but I can't," she thinks. "I can't because kissing him reminds me of that night. So I break away from him and run."

And then there's *The Virgin Suicides* (1993), by Jeffrey Eugenides, which tells the story of the Lisbon sisters, five teenagers from Grosse Pointe, Michigan, who are so confined by their religious parents—and by other mysterious inner forces—that they find themselves gravitating toward the hideous freedom unlocked in death. The first Lisbon girl to attempt suicide is Cecilia, the youngest, who slits her wrists in the bathtub. Newly adolescent, she sees futility everywhere. She stands on her curb, looking at fish flies, talking to a neighbor. "They're dead," she says. "They only live twenty-four hours. They hatch, they reproduce, and then they croak." After her suicide attempt, a doctor chides her: she isn't old enough to understand how bad life really gets, he says. "Obviously, Doctor," says Cecilia, "you've never been a thirteen-year-old girl."

The Virgin Suicides was Eugenides's debut novel, and although his dramatization of the Lisbon sisters' existence—"the imprisonment of being a girl, the way it made your mind active and dreamy"—captures something vivid and undeniable about female adolescence, a distinctly male consciousness is threaded through the book. Eugenides accounts for the ubiquity of male pressure in teenage girls' lives by narrating the book in first-person plural, from the tender, disturbing, attentive "we" of an amorphous group of teen boys. The boys speak of the Lisbons with a damp, devotional fervor—a tone that crosses the religious pilgrim with the peeping Tom. They are obsessed with the dirty miracle of the teenage-girl body, hoarding artifacts (a prized Lisbon thermometer is "oral, alas"), trawling for old photos, interviewing key players as the years go by.

The Lisbon daughters—Therese, Mary, Bonnie, Lux, and Cecilia—occupy the bulk of the teenage life cycle, spaced out evenly in the years between thirteen and seventeen. As a group, they form a case study in the female body's transformation from child to sex object—a fact that is multiplied in this case, freakishly, by a factor of five, and exaggerated by the nature of the Lisbon household, which is puritanical to a near-occult degree. When the narrators catch a glimpse of the Lisbons' faces in school, they look "indecently revealed," they write, "as though we were used to seeing women in veils." Because the girls are not allowed to socialize, the boys observe them not as peers but as dolls in a display case, prostitutes in a window. Behind double layers of glass—their parent-jailers, their boy-observers—the Lisbons intensify into myth. They appear in tragic, glorified states of recombination: they are innocent and arousing ("five glittering daughters in their homemade dresses, all lace and ruffle, bursting with their fructifying flesh," or Cecilia in her wedding dress and soiled bare feet); they are animals and saints ("in the trash can was one Tampax, spotted, still fresh from the insides of one of the Lisbon girls"). The Lisbons' bodies are the rubric through which all else in the town is interpreted. The boys think the smell around the house is "trapped beaver." The air that summer is "pink, humid, pillowing"—the atmosphere is fecund and doomed.

The heroine of *The Virgin Suicides* is playful, enigmatic Lux, whom the high school heartthrob Trip Fontaine refers to as "the most naked person with clothes on he had ever seen." For a while, it seems possible that Lux might get around the Lisbon predicament. She can't be trapped—not Lux, who radiates "health and mischief," who gets Trip to persuade her parents to let the sisters go to prom; who stays out too late after prom having sex with him on the football field; who then, after the girls are collectively grounded, starts having sex with random men on the roof. (For the narrators, this image sticks; as adults, they say, it is Lux they think about when they're fucking their wives, "always that pale wraith we make love to, always her feet snagged in the gutter.")

But Lux doesn't actually ride her adolescence to glory. The night that the Lisbon sisters seem ready to fulfill their observers' fantasies—inviting them into the house in the middle of the night, asking them to get a car ready so that they can all run away—Lux, in the darkened house, undoes one of the boys' belts, leaves it hanging. The boys freeze, ready for all their desires to be realized. Lux goes to the garage, switches the engine on, and lets the carbon monoxide suffocate her. Therese takes a fatal dose of sleeping pills. The boys run out of the house after seeing Bonnie hanging from a rope.

The teenage girl, wrote de Beauvoir, is bound up in a "sense of secrecy," a "grim solitude." She is "convinced that she is not understood; her relations with herself are then only the more impassioned: she is intoxicated with her isolation, she feels herself different, superior, exceptional." So it goes with a certain type of blockbuster YA heroine—the series protagonist who either doubles down on her sense of isolated exceptionalism, if she's in a dystopian universe, or superficially attempts to reject it before acquiescing, if she's in a romantic one.

These teenagers, like their depressed counterparts, cannot conceptualize the future. In the dystopian stories, the reason for this is built right in. Suzanne Collins's *The Hunger Games* (2008) is set in a futuristic totalitarian version of North America called Panem, in which a wealthy Capitol is surrounded by thirteen Districts populated by serfs who are required, every year, to send two human tributes to fight to the death. Our heroine, Katniss Everdeen, volunteers as her district's tribute after her younger sister's name is called at the lottery. Katniss is brave in a grim, fatalistic way: her courage comes from her certainty that the future is a nightmare, and her romantic decisions are driven by her sense that everything has already been lost. *Divergent* (2011), by Veronica Roth, uses a similar frame. The books in the *Divergent* and *Hunger Games* series have collectively sold over a hundred million copies.

In the best-known romance series, the future's opacity (and subsequent inevitability) is a matter of the heroine's personality—these girls are as passive and blank as tofu, waiting to take on the pungency of someone else's life. Bella Swan, the heroine of *Twilight*, and Anastasia Steele, the heroine of *Fifty Shades of Grey*, form a neat bridge between YA and adult commercial fiction: in a sense, they're the same character, as E. L. James wrote *Fifty Shades of Grey* (2011) as fan fiction after Stephenie Meyer's *Twilight* (2005). Bella and Anastasia are both so paper-doll-like that they can barely make choices; they are certainly unable to grasp the romantic fates they're walking into. They are blind to this blindness, just as the dystopian heroines are blind to their own bravery, and all of them are in turn magically blind to the fact that they're very beautiful. (To the male characters in these books who fall in love with Katniss and Anastasia and Bella—as with the pop singers who praise girls for not knowing they're pretty—these blinders form a crucial part of their appeal.) And so Bella gets involved with a vampire, and Anastasia with a damaged, BDSM-fixated billionaire. Both characters balk a little when they get a sense of what might be coming: Edward eventually bites Bella and turns her into a vampire, and Ana's life becomes a vortex of unresolved trauma and high-stakes helicopter incidents. But they have been absolved, by romance, from having to forge a path into the future. Their futures have been predetermined for them by the extreme problems of the men they love.

As is probably clear already, I could never stand a *Twilight* type of story. (It doesn't help that the writing in those books, and in the Fifty Shades series, is amazingly wooden, reiterating the idea that a young woman's story can be perfunctory nonsense as long as she's linked to an interesting man.) Even Francine Pascal's Sweet Valley High series, first published in the eighties, revolved too much around romantic intrigue for me. My relationship to female protagonists changed sharply in adolescence: childhood heroines had shown me who I wanted to be, but teenage heroines showed me who I was afraid of becoming—a girl whose life revolved around her desirability, who was interesting to the degree that her life spun out of control.

There were a few exceptions, of course: I loved Phyllis Reynolds Naylor's Alice series, whose first book came out in 1985, and Sarah Dessen's *Keeping the Moon* (1999), and the Judy Blume books. This was kind, thoughtful, everyday YA literature in which the main characters rarely believed themselves to be exceptional; their ordinariness was a central part of the story's appeal. But during the stretch when I'd outgrown chapter books but couldn't quite process literature, I mostly read commercial fiction that I found on sale at Target, or at my tiny local branch library: Mary Higgins Clark paperbacks that scared the shit out of me, or book-club weepers like Billie Letts's *Where the Heart Is* (1995), or Jodi Picoult novels about amnesia or medical emergencies—stories so dramatic that I felt relieved to have nothing to relate to at all.

If the childhood heroine accepts the future from a comfortable distance, and if the adolescent is blindly thrust toward it by forces beyond her control, the adult heroine lives within this long-anticipated future and finds it dismal, bitter, and disappointing. Her situation is generally one of premature and artificial finality, in which getting married and having children has prevented her from living the life she wants.

That our heroine would have gotten married and had kids in the first place mostly goes without saying: even today, the expectation holds, regardless of the independence a woman demonstrates. In the title essay of *The Mother of All Questions* (2017), Rebecca Solnit writes about being asked, in the middle of a talk she was giving on Virginia Woolf, if she thought the author should have had children. Solnit herself had been asked that question onstage, about her own life, some years earlier. There were any number of ready answers about Woolf's decisions or her own, Solnit writes: "But just because the question can be answered doesn't mean that I ought to answer it, or that it ought to be asked." The interviewer's question "presumed that women should have children, and that a woman's reproductive activities were naturally public business. More fundamentally, the question assumed that there was only one proper way for a woman to live."

We know what that one way looks like: marriage, motherhood, grace, industriousness, mandatory bliss. Prescriptions about female behavior, Solnit notes, are often disingenuously expressed in terms of happiness—as if we really want women to be beautiful, selfless, hardworking wives and mothers because that's what will make *them* happy, when models of female happiness have always tended to benefit men and economically handicap women (and are still, as with the term "girlboss," often defined in reference to male power even when theorized in an ostensibly emancipatory way). But even when women get married, look beautiful, have children, et cetera, they are still often found deficient, Solnit writes, launching into an unforgettable sentence: "There is no good answer to being a woman; the art may instead lie in how we refuse the question." It is a literary statement of purpose, and later, Solnit wonders if the reduction of women to their domestic decisions is, effectively, a literary problem. "We are given a single story line about what makes a good life, even though not a few who follow that story line have bad lives," she writes. "We speak as though there is one good plot with one happy outcome, while the myriad forms a life can take flower—and wither—all around us."

The problem is literary in another way, too. In the late eighteenth century, the middle class, the love-based marriage, and the novel all blossomed into being. Before this point, wealth had come from land and inheritance rather than wage-based work and specialized production, and in marriage, women had served as vehicles for families to transfer and retain wealth. They had also mostly worked alongside their husbands to keep their preindustrial household running. But in a time of rapidly changing economic structures that allowed for individualism and leisure, marriage began taking on a very personal dimension. It *had* to— the new market economy had rendered certain domestic duties redundant, and created, for middle-class women, an occupational void. And so the narrative that framed marriage as a deeply personal achievement, as well as an existentially freighted decision, took shape for women both on and off the page.

The idea of marriage as a totalizing American institution peaked in the years around World War II. Then came second-wave feminism, with *The Second Sex*, and Betty Friedan's *The Feminine Mystique* (1963), which built on de Beauvoir and made it respectable for middle-class white women to question social expectations. "We can no longer ignore that voice within women that says: 'I want something more than my husband and my children and my home,'" Friedan wrote. Ever since then, women have been negotiating down the inflated value of marriage, pushing back against the historical reality of marriage as a boon for men and a regulatory force for women—a problem that was exposed in literature long before political will addressed it. Two of our greatest nineteenth-century heroines, Emma Bovary and Anna Karenina, find themselves locked in unhappy marriages, mothers to young children, with no possibility of respectable escape. They face their own literary problem: what they want is impossible in their society, and characters—people—have to want something to exist.

Adult heroines commit suicide for different reasons than teenage heroines do. Where the teenagers have been drained of all desire, the adults are so full of desire that it kills them. Or, rather, they live under conditions where ordinary desire makes them fatally monstrous. This is the case in Edith Wharton's *The House of Mirth* (1905), where Lily Bart's empty purse and unmarried status is, at twenty-nine, enough to drive her out of respectable society and into an overdose on chloral hydrate. Society breaks poor Tess, too, in Thomas Hardy's *Tess of the D'Urbervilles* (1891). Tess is a teenage milkmaid who experiences the worst of both the adolescent and adult heroine conventions. She is raped and impregnated by her cousin; she falls in love with a man who abandons her after he finds out she isn't a virgin. After she kills her rapist and runs away with her former lover, she is cornered by the police, lying on the rocks of Stonehenge like a sacrifice, her body and life an offering to the world of men.

In Gustav Flaubert's *Madame Bovary* (1856), Emma, a pretty and suggestible farmer's daughter with a taste for romance novels, gets married to a doctor named Charles Bovary and finds herself confused. Marriage is much more dull than she'd expected. "Emma tried to figure out," Flaubert writes, "what one meant exactly in life by the words *felicity, passion, rapture,* that had seemed to her so beautiful in books." She "longed to travel or to go back to her convent. She wished at the same time to die and to live in Paris." She cannot stagnate comfortably, as is expected of her. ("It is very strange," she thinks, about her baby, "how ugly this child is!") "She was waiting for something to happen," writes Flaubert. "Like shipwrecked sailors, she turned despairing eyes upon the solitude of her life, seeking afar off some white sail in the mists of the horizon."

This longing drives Emma to her love affairs—first with Rodolphe, who ditches her the night before their planned elopement, and then with Leon. Their attention is not enough. (She wonders, "Whence came this insufficiency in life—this instantaneous turning to decay of everything on which she leant?") Emma has been perfectly socialized into the idea that female happiness exists in the form of romance and consumer purchases. When romance fails, she goes deep into debt, attempting to excite herself. She begs her lovers for money; she finds out that affairs almost inevitably get as tedious as marriages; finally she takes arsenic, dying a drawn-out, painful death. As with so many other nineteenth-century novels, the main narrative engine is the inability of a woman to access economic stability without the protection of a man.

Leo Tolstoy's protagonist in *Anna Karenina* (1878) is an entirely different sort of woman than Emma—she is intelligent, capable, perceptive—but nonetheless follows the same trajectory. The novel begins with an affair and a possible suicide: two chimes on a clock, telling the reader what time the story's set to. Anna has come to visit her brother, Stiva, who has been cheating on his wife, Dolly. At the train station, the two of them run into Vronsky, an army officer, and Anna is instantly electrified. Then a man either falls or throws himself on the train tracks. "It's an omen of evil," Anna says. During her visit, she urges Dolly to forgive Stiva, and the love between her and Vronsky starts to burn. When she returns to St. Petersburg, the sight of her husband and child disappoints her. She's only in her late twenties, but she's trapped: unlike Stiva, she will be cast out of society if she has an affair. She has a recurring dream about what seems like a threesome, her husband and lover "lavishing caresses on her" simultaneously. "And she was marveling that it had once seemed impossible to her," Tolstoy writes, "was explaining to them, laughing, that this was ever so much simpler, and that now both of them were happy and contented. But this dream weighed on her like a nightmare, and she awoke from it in terror."

Anna gets pregnant with Vronsky's child and confesses to her husband. She can't bring herself to end the affair, and she can't get a divorce without ruining her social standing. She starts to unravel. "She was weeping that her dream of her position being made clear and definite had been annihilated forever . . . everything would go on in the old way, and far worse, indeed, than in the old way . . . she would never know freedom in love," Tolstoy writes. Formerly poised and vivacious, Anna dissolves rapidly—struggling to interact with people, taking morphine to sleep. She turns on Vronsky, becoming erratic and manipulative, the way women do when the only path to power involves appealing to men. She is aware that "at the bottom of her heart was some obscure idea that alone interested her," and suddenly realizes that "it was that idea that alone solved all." The idea is dying. She throws herself in front of a train.

Within the text of *Madame Bovary*, the blame seems to fall mainly on flighty, foolish Emma. In *Anna Karenina*, our heroine is noble and tragic, a victim of the irrationality of desire. By the time Kate Chopin wrote her feminist version of this plot, in *The Awakening* (1899), the affairs were more explicitly a tool through which the heroine, Edna Pontellier, could fumble toward independence and self-determination. But Edna, too, commits suicide, walking into the Gulf of Mexico close to the end of the novel, the waves curling like snakes around her ankles. She "thought of Leonce and the children. They were a part of her life. But they need not have thought that they could possess her, body and soul." Chopin configures Edna's death as a gorgeous, synesthetic moment of freedom and absolution: "There was the hum of bees, and the musky odor of pinks filled the air."

Why all the affairs? De Beauvoir, who famously stated that "most women are married, or have been, or plan to be, or suffer from not being," writes that "there is a hoax in marriage, since, while being supposed to socialize eroticism, it succeeds only in killing it." A husband gets to be "first a citizen, a producer, secondly a husband," where a wife is "before all, and often exclusively, a wife." Her conclusion is that women are destined for infidelity. "It is the sole concrete form her liberty can assume," she writes. "Only through deceit and adultery can she prove that she is nobody's chattel and give the lie to the pretensions of the male." (In 2003, in her polemic *Against Love*, Laura Kipnis argued that adultery was "the sit-down strike of the love-takes-work ethic.")

Perhaps now is a good time to acknowledge the fact that I'm using "heroine" very casually. The feminine of "hero" was first used in the Greek Classical period, and was applied to women who acted within a chaste version of the heroic tradition—women like Joan of Arc, or Saint Lucy, or Judith, the widow who saved her city by decapitating a man. But in the eighteenth century, the conception of the heroine started shifting; novels featured women that were less extraordinary than they were representative, and literature created what the literary scholar Nancy Miller calls the "heroine's text," an overarching composite narrative of how a woman negotiates a world set up for men.

In 1997, the psychologist and theorist Mary Gergen wrote about the contrast between the two gendered narrative lines. On the one hand, there's the "autonomous ego-enhancing hero single-handedly and single-heartedly progressing toward a goal," and on the other, the "long-suffering, selfless, socially embedded heroine, being moved in many directions, lacking the tenacious loyalty demanded of a quest." De Beauvoir glossed this as transcendence versus immanence: men were expected to reach beyond their circumstances, while women were expected to be defined and bounded by theirs. Kate Zambreno, in *Heroines* (2012), nods to de Beauvoir while writing about the existential horror of traditional gender roles—"the man allowed to go out into the world and transcend himself, the woman reduced to the kind of work that will be erased and forgotten at day's end, living invisible among the vestigial people of the afternoon."

Traditionally, male literary characters are written and received as emblems of the human condition rather than the male one. Take Stephen Dedalus, Gregor Samsa, Raskolnikov, Nick Adams, Neddy Merrill (better known as the Swimmer), Carver's blind man, Holden Caulfield, Rabbit Angstrom, Sydney Carton, Karl Ove Knausgaard, et cetera: they are not all exactly acting out the traditional hero's journey, in which the hero ventures forth into the world, vanquishes some foe, and returns victorious. But the hero's journey, in all these stories, nonetheless provides the grammar to be adhered to or refuted. Self-mythologization hovers regardless of the actual plot.

Female literary characters, in contrast, indicate the condition of being a *woman*. They are condemned to a universe that revolves around sex and family and domesticity. Their stories circle questions of love and obligation—love being, as the critic Rachel Blau DuPlessis writes, the concept "our culture uses [for women] to absorb all possible Bildung, success/failure, learning, education, and transition to adulthood." And so I'm using the term "heroine" simply for the women whose version of literary femininity has stuck. Sometimes they repudiate attachments, like the suicidal characters, or Maria Wyeth, losing her mind on the highway in *Play It as It Lays* (1970). Sometimes they turn subjugation into an origin story, like Lisbeth Salander, the titular character of *The Girl with the Dragon Tattoo* (2005), or Julia from *The Magicians* (2009), dark heroines scarred by rape. (I'll note that both of these series were written by male authors; although men quite obviously can produce and have produced magnificently perceptive novels about women, they also seem prone enough to using rape in a reductive, utilitarian way.) Sometimes these characters manipulate the expected narratives to their advantage, as with Becky Sharp in *Vanity Fair* (1848), Scarlett O'Hara in *Gone with the Wind* (1936), or Amy Dunne, the sociopath who narrates *Gone Girl* (2012). (De Beauvoir again: "Woman has been assigned the role of parasite, and every parasite is an exploiter.") All of these women are in pursuit of basic liberty. But our culture has configured women's liberty as corrosion, and for a long time, there was no way for a woman to be both free and good.

The marriage-plot heroines—Jane Eyre, the Jane Austen women— are the major exception. They are good and whole and steady in a way that does not interfere with psychological complexity. Elizabeth Bennet is such a wonderful and acutely perceptive observer *because* she is, all things considered, so cheerful and conventional and well-liked. The timeline plays a role, too, just like in a children's series: *Pride and Prejudice* (1813) cuts out on the high note of new love, with a final chapter that telescopes into Elizabeth's happy future with Mr. Darcy. You wonder about her mood if the novel had started ten years later. Would Elizabeth be happy? Would there be a book if she was? Has anyone ever written a great novel about a woman who is happy in her marriage? Of course, most protagonists are unhappy. But heroes are mostly unhappy for existential reasons; heroines suffer for social reasons, because of male power, because of men.

There are female protagonists who negotiate marital compromise without bitterness, like Dorothea Brooke in *Middlemarch* (1871) and Isabel Archer in *The Portrait of a Lady* (1881). Dorothea and Isabel are smart, thoughtful, independent-minded characters, and uncertainty rules their stories: Dorothea ends her novel in a second, happier marriage after her stultifying union with Casaubon is cut short by his death, and we finish *Portrait* thinking that Isabel will go back to the pompous, insufferable Osmond—but also knowing that she might not stay in Rome for long. Marriage is the animating question, but not the ending. Theirs is the third way, the one in which marriage neither destroys nor completes you, the one that leads most clearly to the present day.

What it means to be a woman has changed immensely in the past half century, and life and literature have shifted hand in hand. In Eugenides's *The Marriage Plot* (2011), a college student takes in her English professor's point of view on the subject:

> In the days when success in life had depended on marriage, and marriage had depended on money, novelists had had a subject to write about. The great epics sang of war, the novel of marriage. Sexual equality, good for women, had been bad for the novel. And divorce had undone it completely. What would it matter whom Emma married if she could file for separation later? How would Isabel Archer's marriage to Gilbert Osmond have been affected by the existence of a prenup? As far as [the professor] was concerned, marriage didn't mean much any-

more, and neither did the novel. Where could you find the marriage plot nowadays? You couldn't.

And yet not as much has been upended as the college professor
thinks. The heroines of the past few decades have been concerned
with the same questions of love and social constriction; it's just
that they answer these questions in a different way. Contemporary fiction about women doesn't reflect or subvert the heroine's
text as much as it explodes the concept, re-creating and manipulating the way that narrative construction influences a woman's
sense of self. Today's best-known heroines are often also writers—
giving them a built-in reason to be hyperconscious of the story
lines at play in their lives.

Chris Kraus, the narrator of Chris Kraus's metafictional *I Love
Dick*, published in 1997 and reissued in 2006, begins the novel as
a failed filmmaker in a sexless marriage to a man named Sylvère.
She develops an all-consuming crush on a shadowy figure named
Dick, and begins sending him obsessive letters. In a previous century, this sort of transgression might have destroyed our heroine's
trajectory. But in *I Love Dick*, the letters rejuvenate Chris's marriage and turn her into the artist she always wanted to be. She and
Sylvère start writing to Dick together. "We've just had sex and
before that spent the last two hours talking about you," she tells
him. Then, through the letters, Chris's sense of self starts to
sharpen. She leaves Sylvère, and continues writing to Dick. "Why
does everybody think that women are debasing themselves when
we expose the conditions of our own debasement?" she asks him,
explaining her desire to be a "female monster." I can't stand this
book, personally—I find it almost radically tedious—but the au-
dacity of Kraus's project is undeniable. Rather than have her protagonist attempt to solve the problem of her social condition, her
protagonist *became* that problem, pursued the problem as an identity in itself, an artistic discipline, a literary form.

Jenny Offill's brilliant *Dept. of Speculation* (2014) is narrated
by a writer in her thirties, a young mother who, echoing Kraus,
wants to be an "art monster," but who also craves domesticity. She
loves and despises her self-directed constraints. "Is she a good
baby? People would ask me. Well, no, I'd say," Offill writes, adding, "That swirl of hair on the back of her head. We must have
taken a thousand pictures of it." The narrator is brutal and dead-
pan; she thinks of a "story about a prisoner at Alcatraz who spent
his nights in solitary confinement dropping a button on the floor
then trying to find it again in the dark. Each night, in this manner,
he passed the hours until dawn. I do not have a button. In all
other respects, my nights are the same." This is all much funnier
and darker, because Offill's narrator, in a way that is world-
historically unprecedented, is genuinely free to leave. Shortly before the novel's revelation that the husband is having an affair, the
narration switches from first to third person: the "I" becomes "the
wife." It's an acknowledgment, from both the narrator and Offill,
of the way that social conventions can become fundamental to
our selfhood—and sometimes by our own design.

And then there's Elena Ferrante, who has accomplished what
no other writer has been able to do at such blockbuster scale. She
instilled her stories about women with an unmistakable shimmer
of universal significance *through* overt feminist specificity; she created a concrete universal that was dominated by women, defined
by what the feminist philosopher Adriana Cavarero calls "existence, relation and attention," that stood in shattering contrast to
the abstract universal dominated by men. Her body of work—
Troubling Love, The Days of Abandonment, The Lost Daughter, and
the four Neapolitan novels—constructs a postwar Italian world
populated by men who hold external power and women who set
the terms of consciousness and identity. Women are haunted by
memories and stories of one another—shadow selves, icons, ob-
sessions, ghosts. It is transcendent, in the way de Beauvoir meant
it, to watch Ferrante's narrators triangulate themselves from these

images, in their emotional and intellectual project of asserting selfhood and control.

Olga, the protagonist of *The Days of Abandonment* (2002), is afraid of becoming the *poverella*, a decrepit figure from her childhood who was spurned by her husband and subsequently lost her mind. Olga has found herself in a similar marital situation. "What a mistake it had been to entrust the sense of myself to his gratifications, his enthusiasms, to the ever more productive course of his life," she thinks, lamenting her forgotten writing career. She remembers, years ago, scoffing at stories of educated women who "broke like knick-knacks in the hands of their straying men. . . . I wanted to be different, I wanted to write stories about women with resources, women of invincible words, not a manual for the abandoned wife with her lost love at the top of her thoughts." But though the abandoned-wife plot was the one that Olga was handed, it is not exactly the one she partakes in. In a phenomenal *n+1* essay on Ferrante, Dayna Tortorici writes that *The Days of Abandonment* "captures the double consciousness of a destroyed woman who doesn't want to be 'a woman destroyed.'" Olga passes through the story of the *poverella* "like a crucible: become the *poverella*, and then become Olga again." In Ferrante's work, a controllable self emerges through communion with an uncontrollable one.

The Neapolitan novels, which begin with *My Brilliant Friend* (2011), trace the story of two friends, Elena (called Lenu) and Lila, from childhood into their sixties. On this expansive timeline, Ferrante's concern with identity formation through women's narratives plays out at extraordinary depth and length. Lenu and Lila define themselves through and against each other, each like a book that the other is reading, each representing an alternate story of what life might be. *My Brilliant Friend* begins with half of this structure suddenly vanishing: Lenu, now an old woman, finds out that Lila has disappeared. She turns on her computer and starts writing down their lives from the beginning. "We'll see who wins this time," she thinks.

As children in a poor, rough neighborhood in Naples, Lenu and Lila were doubles and opposites. They were the smartest in their class, with different types of intelligence—Lenu diligent and tentative, Lila brilliant and cruel. When Lila can't pay for the entrance exam to middle school, their stories start to diverge: Lila, who tutors Lenu as she continues her education, marries the grocer's son at sixteen. On her wedding day, Lila asks Lenu to promise she'll continue studying. She'll pay for it, she says. "You're my brilliant friend, you have to be the best of all, boys and girls," Lila says.

Lila becomes alienated by Lenu's life at university, mocking her for hanging around pretentious socialist writers. Lenu publishes her first novel, and then discovers that she unconsciously plagiarized an old story of Lila's from elementary school. When Lenu hears that Lila has organized a strike at her workplace, she imagines Lila "triumphant, admired for her achievements, in the guise of a revolutionary leader, [telling] me: You wanted to write novels, I created a novel with real people, with real blood, in reality." The struggle and correspondence between the two friends— the mirroring, the deviation, the contradiction, the cleaving, all enacted simultaneously—reflects, more precisely than anything I have ever encountered, the negotiations between various forms of female authority, which themselves negotiate a structure of male authority. Lenu and Lila enact the endlessly interweaving relationship between the heroines we read about, the heroines we might have been, the heroines we are.

In 2015, in an interview with *Vanity Fair*, Ferrante cited as inspiration the "old book" *Relating Narratives*, by Adriana Cavarero: a dense and brilliant tract, translated into English in 2000, that argues for identity as "totally expositive and relational." Identity, according to Cavarero, is not something that we innately possess and reveal, but something we understand through narratives provided to us by others. She writes about a scene in *The Odyssey* where Ulysses sits incognito in the court of the Phaeacians, listening to a blind man sing about the Trojan War. Having never heard his own life articulated by another person, Ulysses starts to weep. Hannah Arendt called this moment, "poetically speaking," the beginning of history: Ulysses "has never wept before, and certainly not when what he is now hearing actually happened. Only when he hears the story does he become fully aware of his significance." Cavarero writes, "The story told by an 'other' finally revealed his own identity. And he, dressed in his magnificent purple tunic, breaks down and cries."

Cavarero then expands the Ulysses story into a third dimension, in which the hero suddenly becomes aware not just of his own story but also of his own *need to be narrated*. "Between identity and narration . . . there is a tenacious relation of desire," she writes. Later in the book, she provides the real-life example of Emilia and Amalia, two members of the Milan Women's Bookstore Collective, a group that also powerfully influenced Ferrante. As part of the consciousness-raising process, Emilia and Amalia told each other their life stories, but Emilia could not make hers sound coherent. So Amalia wrote her friend's story down on paper. By that point, she'd memorized it, having heard it so many times. Emilia carried around the story in her handbag, reading it over and over—"overcome by emotion" at the fact of understanding her life in story form.

The anecdote is different from the one in *The Odyssey*, Cavarero notes, because, where the blind man and Ulysses were strangers to each other, Amalia and Emilia were friends. Amalia's narrative was a direct response to Emilia's need to be narrated. The two women were acting within the framework of *affidamento*, or "entrustment," that the Milan Women's Bookstore Collective developed in the seventies. When two women "entrusted" themselves to each other, they prioritized not their similarities but their differences. They recognized that the differences between their stories were central to their identities, and in doing this, they also *created* these identities and affirmed this difference as strength. (Audre Lorde had made this argument in 1979, framing difference as something not just to be "merely tolerated," but a "fund of necessary polarities, between which our creativity can spark like a dialectic.") In the 1990 book *Sexual Difference*, the Milan women wrote, "Attributing authority and value to another woman with regard to the world was the means of giving authority and value to oneself." Entrustment was a framework that not only allowed them to understand themselves as both woman and human, but consciously predicated the second identity on the first. It was "the form of female gendered mediation in a society which does not contemplate gendered mediations, but only male mediation endowed with universal validity." Given the reality of a world, a language, a literary tradition shaped by male power, these women attempted to remake all three things simultaneously by passing their stories through one another—just as Emilia was able to use Amalia's narrative consciousness to access and create her own.

As part of the work of entrustment, the Milan Women's Bookstore Collective read books by women, whom they called the "mothers (of us all)." They imagined themselves in the place of the novelists, in the place of their heroines, attempting to see what they could learn by this exchange of roles. The result, they wrote, was "to wipe out boundaries between life and literature." The hope was that, somewhere in the midst of all these characters, somewhere within this grand experiment of identification, they might access an original source of authority. They might find a female language that could "speak starting from itself."

You'll have noticed—surely you'll have noticed, although I don't want to be too generous—that all the characters in this essay are white and straight. (Harriet the Spy, resplendent in her baggy jeans and tool belt, may be an exception.) This, perhaps, is the heroine's subtext: the presumed universality of her own straight whiteness is the literary heroine's shallow revenge. There is another tradition, one of deprivation and resistance and beauty, that connects *Walk Two Moons* (1994) and *Julie of the Wolves* (1972) to Jamaica Kincaid's "Girl" (1978) and Esperanza from *The House on Mango Street* (1984) to Janie Crawford from *Their Eyes Were Watching God* (1937) and Sethe from *Beloved* (1987) and Celie from *The Color Purple* (1982) and *The Woman Warrior* (1976) and *Love Medicine*'s Fleur (1984). There is a conversation between *Nightwood* (1936) and *The Price of Salt* (1952) and *Stone Butch Blues* (1993). But these stories are, in every case, animated by very particular modes of socially imposed difference. They do not cohere into an ur-narrative. Just as the heroine's text is constrained by cultural inequities that the unmarked male experience can never speak to, nonwhite and nonstraight literary women are constrained in a way that the heroine's text can never account for or reach.

Here, once again, I feel the numbing sense of asymmetry that has lurked inside me since the day that Power Rangers roleplay taught me about the phenomenological Other. The unspoken flip side of my friend Allison's argument that I couldn't play the Pink Ranger was worse, in part because she would likely never be conscious of it: it wasn't that she *couldn't* play the Yellow Ranger but that, more precisely, she wouldn't ever think to. My hesitation, as an adult, to find myself within the heroine universe has been rooted in a suspicion that that identification would never be truly reciprocal: I would see myself in Jo March, but the world's Jo Marches would rarely, if ever, be expected or able to see themselves in me. Over lazy dinner conversations, my white friends would be able to fantasy-cast their own biopic from an endless cereal aisle of nearly identical celebrities, hundreds of manifestations of blonde or brunette or redhead selfhood represented with Pantone subtlety and variation—if, of course, hardly any variation

in ability or body type—while I would have no one to choose from
except about three actresses who'd probably all had minor roles in
some movie five years back. In most contemporary novels, women
who looked like me would pop up only occasionally, as a piece of
set decoration on the subway or at a dinner party, as a character
whose Asian ethnicity would be noted by the white author as diligently as the whiteness of his or her unmarked protagonist was
not. If women were not allowed to be seen as emblematic of the
human condition, I wouldn't even get to be seen as emblematic of
the *female* condition. Even worse was the fact that the female condition in literature—one of whiteness and confinement—remains
so unsatisfying. I was shut out of a realm that I didn't even really
want to enter. The heroine's text tells us that, at best, under a minimum of structural constrictions, women are still mostly pulver-
ized by their own lives.

But if this text exists to demonstrate that reality, then both
things can always still be rewritten. The heroine's journey, or her
lack of one, serves as a reminder that whatever is dictated is not
eternal, not predestined, not necessarily *true*. The trajectory of
literary women from brave to blank to bitter is a product of material social conditions. The fact that the heroine's journey is framed
as a default one for women is proof of our failure to see, for so
long, that other paths were possible, and that many other ones
exist.

In writing this I've started to wonder if, through refusing to
identify with the heroine, I have actually entrusted myself to
her—if, by prioritizing the differences between us, as the Milan
women did with one another, I have been able to affirm my own
identity, and perhaps hers, too. In *Sexual Difference*, the Milan
women write about a disagreement they had while discussing
Jane Austen, during which one woman said, flatly, "We are not all
equal here." The statement "had a horrible sound, in the literal
sense of the term: sour, hard, stinging," the women wrote. But "it
did not take long to accept what for years we had never regis-

tered. . . . We were not equal, we had never been equal, and we immediately discovered that we had no reason to think we were." Difference was not the problem; it was the beginning of the solution. That realization, they decided, would be the foundation of their sense that they were free.

I cling to the Milan women's understanding of these literary heroines as mothers. I wish I had learned to read them in this way years ago—with the same complicated, ambivalent, essential freedom that a daughter feels when she looks at her mother, understanding her as a figure that she simultaneously resists and depends on; a figure that she uses, cruelly and lovingly and gratefully, as the base from which to become something more.

Ecstasy

The church I grew up in was so big we called it the Repentagon. Its campus was spread across forty-two acres in a leafy, rich, white neighborhood ten miles west of downtown Houston. There was a dried-out field with bleachers, and next to it, a sprawling playground; during the school year, the hypnotic rutting rhythm of football practice bled into recess cacophony through a porous border of tattered, mossy oaks. A circular drive with a fleur-de-lis fountain in the middle led up to a bone-white eight-hundred-capacity chapel; next to it sat a smaller chapel, modest and humble with pale-blue walls. There was a restaurant, a bookstore, four basketball courts, a full exercise center, and a cavernous mirrored atrium. You could spend your whole life inside the Repentagon—starting at the nursery school, continuing through twelfth grade, getting married on the campus, structuring your adult life around this town-size church.

At the middle of everything was an eight-sided, six-story corporate cathedral called the Worship Center. It contained two huge seated balconies, a jumbotron, enormous columns, a glowing baptismal font (my mom sometimes worked as a camerawoman for church services, filming every backward dip into the water like it was a major-league pitch), a pipe organ with nearly two hundred stops and more than ten thousand pipes, tiered seating for the Baby Boomer choir that sang at the 9:30 service, a performance area for the Gen X house band at eleven, and sky-high stained-glass windows depicting the beginning and end of the world. The Worship Center sat sixty-five hundred people. Twenty thousand passed through it each weekend. Around it, mall-size parking lots circled the campus: on Sundays, the church looked like a car dealership, and during the week, like a fortress, surrounded by an impersonal asphalt moat.

The church was founded in 1927, and the school was formed two decades later. The $34 million campus where I spent all my time was built in the eighties, and by the time I got there, in the mid-nineties, Houston was emerging into an era of glossy, self-satisfied power—the dominance of Southern evangelicals and extractive Texan empires, Halliburton and Enron and Exxon and Bush. Through fundraising campaigns flogged by associate pastors during church services, the considerable wealth of the church's tithing population was regularly converted into ostentatious new displays. The church imported piles of fake snow at Christmas. When I was in high school, they built a fifth floor for children with a life-size train you could play inside of, and a teen youth group space called the Hangar, featuring the nose of a big plane half crashed through one wall.

My parents hadn't always been evangelical, nor had they favored this tendency toward excess. They had defected from Catholicism at some point, growing up in the Philippines, and then had begun attending a small Baptist church in Toronto before I was born. But then they moved to Houston, an unfamiliar expanse of looping highway and prairie, and this one pastor's face was everywhere, smiling at commuters from the billboards that studded I-10. My parents took to his kind, civilized, compelling style of preaching—he was classier than your average televangelist, and much less greasy than Joel Osteen, the better-known Houston pastor, famous for his cheap airport books about the prosperity gospel and his chilling marionette smile. Osteen's children attended my school, which my parents persuaded to accept me within a few months of us moving to Texas—and to place me in first grade, even though I was four years old.

I would regret this situation when I was twelve and in high school. But as a kid, I was eager and easy. I made friends, pointed my toes in dance class, did all of my homework. In our daily Bible classes I made salvation bracelets on tiny leather cords—a black bead for my sin, a red bead for the blood of Jesus, a white bead for purity, a blue bead for baptism, a green bead for spiritual growth, a gold bead for the streets of heaven that awaited me. During the holidays, I acted in our church's Christian musicals: one, I remember, was set at CNN, the "Celestial News Network," where we played reporters covering the birth of Jesus Christ. On Wednesday nights, at choir practice, I memorized hymns for prizes. In elementary school, my family moved farther west on I-10, to a place in the new suburbs where model homes rose out of bare farmland. On Sundays, I sat quietly in the back seat, creeping through gridlock as we drove east into the city, ready to sit in the dark and think about my soul. Spiritual matters felt simple and absolute. I didn't want to be bad, or doomed (the two were interchangeable). I wanted to be saved, and good.

Back then, believing in God felt mostly unremarkable, sometimes interesting, and occasionally like a private, perfect thrill. Good and evil is organized so neatly for you in both childhood and Christianity. In a Christian childhood, with all those parables and psalms and war stories, it's exponentially more so. In the Bible, angels came to your doorstep. Fathers offered their children up for mutilation. Fishes multiplied; cities burned. The horror-movie progression of the plagues in Exodus riveted me: the blood, the frogs, the boils, the locusts, the darkness. The violence of Christianity came with great safety: under a pleasing shroud of aesthetic mystery, there were clear prescriptions about who you should be. I prayed every night, thanking God for the

wonderful life I had been given. I felt blessed all the time, instinctively. On weekends I would pedal my bike across a big
stretch of pasture in the gold late-afternoon light and feel holy. I
would spin in circles at the skating rink and know that someone
was looking down on me.

Toward the end of elementary school, the impression of wholeness started slipping. We were told not to watch Disney movies,
because Disney World had allowed gay people to host a parade. In
fifth grade, my Rapture-obsessed Bible teacher confiscated my
Archie comics and my peace-sign notebook, replacing this hea-
then paraphernalia with a copy of the brand-new bestseller *Left
Behind*. A girl at our school died by electrocution when a pool
light blew out into the water, and the tragedy was deemed the
absolute will of the Lord. This was around the time that television
screens were installed all over campus, and the face of our folksy,
robotic pastor bobbed around on them, preaching to no one. At
chapel, we were sometimes shown religious agitprop videos, the
worst of which featured a handsome dark-haired man bidding his
young son farewell in a futuristic white chamber, and then, as
violins swelled in the background, walking down an endless hall
to be *executed*—martyred for his Christian faith. I cried, because—
please—I wasn't heartless! Afterward we all sang a song called "I
Pledge Allegiance to the Lamb."

In middle school, I became aware of my ambivalence—just distant enough to be troubled by the fact that I felt distant. I started
to feel twinges of guilt at the end of every church service, when
the pastor would call for people to come forward and accept Jesus:
what if this feeling of uncertainty meant that I needed to avow
Him again and again? I didn't want to be a bad person, and I especially didn't want to spend eternity in hell. Evangelicals aren't like
Calvinists. You aren't chosen, or elected—God will forgive you,
but you have to work. I started getting agoraphobic in the Worship Center on Sundays. Thinking about these intimate matters
in such a crowded public place felt indecent. I took breaks from

services, sometimes curling up on the couches in the corridor outside where mothers shushed their infants, or walking up to the
highest balcony to pass the time reading the psychedelic book of
Revelation in the blissfully unsupervised pews.

One Sunday, I told my parents I needed a sweater from the car.
I walked out across the big, echoing atrium with the keys jangling
from my hand and our pastor's voice ringing through the empty
space. In the parking lot, the asphalt festered, softening; the sun
burned out my eyes. I got into the passenger seat of our powder-
blue Suburban and put the key in the ignition. The Christian
radio station was playing—89.3 KSBJ, with its slogan "God listens." I mashed the Seek button, hitting country, alt-rock, the
Spanish stations, and then something I had never heard before. It
was the Box, Houston's hip-hop radio station, playing what they
always played on Sundays—chopped and screwed.

Houston, like its megachurches, is unfathomably sprawling. Even
from an airplane it's impossible to clock the whole city at once.
It's low and flat, just a few dozen feet above sea level, and its endless freeways—the two huge concentric loops of 610 and Beltway
8, and the four highways that intersect at the center, slicing the
circle into eighths—trace nineteenth-century market routes,
forming the shape of a wagon wheel around downtown. The
Greater Houston Area covers ten thousand square miles—that's
as big as New Jersey—and contains six million people. The city is
less than an hour from the Gulf Coast, with the alien-civilization
oil refineries of Port Arthur and the ghost piers that rise out of
Galveston's dirty water, and there's a certain irradiated spirit to
everything, a big-money lawlessness that bleaches in the heat.

The weather in Houston is frequently scorching, and as with
much of Texas, an undercurrent of proud, ambitious independence thrums through the air. As a result, there isn't much of a
true public sphere in Houston. Even the thriving arts scene, alter-

nately gala-esque or grungy, is mostly known to itself. Our ideas of the collective are limited by what our minds can see and handle: this is part of the reason Houstonians gravitate to megachurches, which provide the impression of living in a normal-size town. By some metrics, Houston is the most diverse city in America, and it's expanding at a dizzying pace—an estimated thirty thousand new houses are built every year. But the interchange between its many populations is acknowledged mostly in matters of unspoken structure. There are no zoning laws, which means that strip clubs sit next to churches, gleaming skyscrapers next to gap-toothed convenience stores. The freeways are, in effect, the only truly public space in the city—the only arena where people come out of their enclaves to be next to one another, sitting in the prodigious traffic, riding the spokes of Houston's big wheel.

At the same time that I was making salvation bracelets on the floor of Bible class, a universe was coming into being on the south side of town. In the mid-eighties, the Texas Southern University radio station started airing a show called *Kidz Jamm*, where high school students played Afrika Bambaataa and Run-DMC. In 1986, James Prince founded Rap-A-Lot Records, Houston's first hip-hop label, and developed the Geto Boys, a gangster rap group that was hometown loyal ("Today's special is Geto Dope, processed in Fifth Ward Texas") and psychotically game. (The cover of the Geto Boys' 1991 album *We Can't Be Stopped* features a real photo of one of its members, three-foot-eight Bushwick Bill, on a gurney with his eye missing. Bushwick Bill had done PCP, decided to commit suicide so his mom could collect life insurance, and goaded his girlfriend—or, in some versions of the story, his mom—to shoot him in the face; he was pronounced dead at the hospital, but then, according to legend, *came back to life in the morgue*, reportedly due to the blood-flow-slowing effects of the PCP. A later Geto Boys album would be titled *The Resurrection*.)

The Houston sound that took over the city in the nineties and later altered the national hip-hop landscape was developed in nondescript suburban houses, cheap bungalows behind patchy lawns and wire fences, in a handful of harshly bland neighborhoods— Sunnyside, South Park, Gulfgate—south of 610 and west of 45. Most of the original guard of Houston rappers came out of the south side, though a smaller north-side scene would soon develop, and UGK, possibly the best-known Houston act, came out of Port Arthur, which is an hour east. UGK had a kinetic country sophistication, agile and authoritative. Houston rappers like Z-Ro, Lil' Keke, Lil' Troy, Paul Wall, and Lil' Flip patented a flossy, up-front, narcotized, ominous sort of bang and sparkle—it all sounded like an Escalade vibrating, like someone pulling up in a car with spinners and rolling down the window really slow. But if the Houston sound belongs to anyone, it's not to a rapper. It's to Robert Earl Davis Jr., better known as DJ Screw.

DJ Screw was born in 1971, in a town outside Austin, to a trucker father and a mother who held three cleaning jobs and bootlegged cassette tapes from her record collection for extra cash. Like a lot of Houston rappers, Screw played an instrument as a kid—piano, in his case. He taught himself how to DJ with a cousin, who observed his habit of physically scratching up records and gave him the name DJ Screw. He moved to Houston, dropped out of high school, and started DJing at a south-side skating rink. (Skating rinks served, in Houston, as one of many junior iterations of the club.) Screw, quiet and private, round-faced in oversize T-shirts with a guarded look in his eyes, made mixtapes obsessively. The first time he slowed the tempo down to his signature wooze, it was an accident; it was 1989, and he'd hit the wrong button on the turntable. Then a friend gave him $10 to record an entire tape at that sludgy tempo, and Screw did it again and again. The sound caught. He started recording Houston rappers over his mixtapes—directing their long, fluid sessions as he mixed, and then slowing the whole tape down, making it skip beats and stutter, making it sound like your heart was about to stop. Screw made copies of his mixtapes on gray bulk cassettes from Sam's

Club, which he labeled by hand and sold out of his house. To get on a Screw tape was to be knighted; Screw's collective, the Screwed Up Click, quickly became a local hall of fame.

Soon everyone wanted Screw tapes. People started coming to his house from all over the city, then all over the state, then beyond. Neighbors assumed Screw was a drug dealer. The police swooped in a few times, performing mostly fruitless raids. There were any number of better ways for Screw to get his music to people—a local hip-hop distribution company called Southwest Wholesale had sprung up to take advantage of the thriving independent market that Houston provided for its artists—but Screw insisted on this inefficient hand-to-hand, doing everything in cash with no bank account, hiring friends as security, selling cassettes for two hours each night in his driveway with cars lining up around the block. He could never meet the demand for his music. According to Michael Hall's intensively reported chronicle in *Texas Monthly*, frustrated record-store owners started buying directly from bootleggers in bulk. In 1998, Screw finally set up a semi-official shop, establishing Screwed Up Records behind bulletproof glass in a house near South Park. Nothing was for sale except those cassettes.

By this point, a decade into Screw's career, he was famous outside Houston. Chopped and screwed, the style he invented, had permeated the scene. Michael "5000" Watts, a north-side producer and cofounder of Swishahouse Records, adopted the sound; his Swishahouse partner OG Ron C picked it up, too. Watts DJed on Sundays for 97.9, the Box, the hip-hop station that had taken over in the nineties, leaking chopped and screwed to a wider Houston audience. By then, Screw's prodigious output was flagging. He was getting heavier and slower, as if his body had started working at his signature tempo. He had become addicted to codeine cough syrup, also known as lean.

Lean is now permanently associated with rappers, partly because of the Houston scene at its most flamboyant—the grills, rims, and sizzurp aesthetic—and partly because of notable aco-

lytes of the substance, like Lil Wayne. But drugs are always demographically flexible. Townes Van Zandt, the melancholy country
blues artist who got his break in Houston, loved cough syrup so
much that he called it Delta Momma (DM, as in Robitussin) and
sang one song (1971's "Delta Momma Blues") from the genial
point of view of the drug itself. Chopped and screwed mimics the
lean feeling—a heady and dissociative security, as if you're moving
very slowly toward a conclusion you don't need to understand. It
induces a sense of permissive disorientation that melds perfectly
to Houston, a place where a full day can pass without you ever
seeming to get off the highway, where the caustic gleam of day-
time melts into a fluorescent polluted sunset and then into a long
and swampy night. Chopped and screwed picked up something
about Houston that connects impurity to absolution. It was its
own imaginary freeway, oozing with syrup, defining the city's
limits, bounding it like the Loop.

In the blistering hot parking lot of the megachurch, on the old
seats of my parents' powder-blue Suburban, chopped and screwed
sounded right to me as soon as I heard it, even though it would be
years before I began to understand the context in which it was
produced. Like religion, it provided both ends of a total system.
Its sound entangled sin and salvation; it held a tug of unease, a
blanket of reassurance. It was as ominous and comforting as a
nursery rhyme, this first taste of the way that an open acknowledgment of vice can feel as divinely willed, as spiritual—even
more so—than the concealment often required to be good.

Or maybe Houston just crossed too many of my signals. It
wasn't long until the city's music permeated even my sheltered
environment. There was a lack of zoning in our cultural lives, too.
I first learned about twerking when I was thirteen, at cheerleading
camp, where we got measured for navy bell skirts with high slits
that barely cleared our underwear, which we were required to
wear on football game days to our modesty-preaching Christian
school. At camp we prayed that Jesus would keep us safe during

practice, and then we threw one another, with sloppy abandon, ten feet into the air. Southern rap was rising: we dropped to the floor, mimicked the motions that were spreading like a virus, clapping for the girls who could do it best. We still went to church twice a week, and it all started to seem interchangeable. Some nights I went with my girlfriends to youth group and sang about Jesus, and sometimes I would go with them to the club on teen night, driving past the Repentagon into the thicket of liquor stores and strip clubs a mile up on Westheimer, entering another dark room where all the girls wore miniskirts and everyone sought amnesty in a different form. Sometimes a foam machine would open up in the ceiling and soak our cheap push-up bras, and we'd glue ourselves to strangers as everyone chewed on the big mouthfuls of Swishahouse in the room.

We had been taught that even French kissing was dangerous—that anything not marked by rich white Christianity was murky and perverse. But eventually, it was the church that seemed corrupted to me. What had been forbidden began to feel earnest and clean. It was hot out the first time I tasted cough syrup, on a night when everyone had come home from college. I drank it from a big Styrofoam cup with ice, booze, and Sprite. Soon afterward I was in my friend's pool, wading through hip-high water. "Overnight Celebrity" was playing, a song that always made me emotional— Miri Ben-Ari replaying the strings from that tender soul song, Twista yammering on with an auctioneer's devotion. Suddenly the song sounded like it would never end—like it had been screwed down to the Sunday tempo, like it was thick enough to carry me. The water felt like I could grab it. The sky was enormous, eternal, velvet. I looked up, the stars blanketed by the perpetual glow of pollution, and felt as blessed as I ever did when I was a child.

I have been walking away from institutional religion for a long time now—half my life, at this point, fifteen years dismantling what the first fifteen built. But I've always been glad that I grew up the way I did. The Repentagon trained me to feel at ease in odd, insular, extreme environments, a skill I wouldn't give up for anything, and Christianity formed my deepest instincts: it gave me a leftist worldview, an obsession with everyday morality, an understanding of having been born in a compromised situation, and a need to continually investigate my own ideas about what it means to be good.

This spiritual inheritance was, in fact, what initially spurred my defection: I lost interest in trying to reconcile big-tent Southern evangelicalism with my burgeoning political beliefs. I hated the prosperity gospel, which had taught many rich white Christians to believe—albeit *politely*, and with generous year-end donations to various ministries—that wealth was some sort of divine anointment, that they were genuinely worth more to God and country than everyone else. (Under this doctrine, as in Texas in general, inequality is framed as something close to deliberate: if you're poor, that's unfortunate, because God must have ordained that, too.) People at my school were so cocooned within whiteness that they often whispered the words "Mexican" and "black," instinctively assuming those descriptions were slurs. I read the Gospel to be constantly preaching economic redistribution—John the Baptist commands, in the book of Luke, "Let him who has two tunics share with him who has none," et cetera—but everyone around me seemed mainly to believe in low taxes and the unconditional righteousness of war. The fear of sin often seemed to conjure and perpetuate it: abstinence education led to abortions, for rich people, and for poor people to children who would be loved and supported until the day they were born. There was so much beatific kindness, and it was so often undergirded by brittle cruelty. (In 2015, the church's longtime pastor spoke out against the "deceptive and deadly" Houston Equal Rights Ordinance, which would have allowed transgender people to use the bathroom that matched their gender identity. After the 2018 midterms, he called the Democratic Party "some kind of religion that is basically god-less." In 2019, the *Houston Chronicle* published an investigation into seven hundred sexual assault cases at Southern Baptist churches over the previous two decades. In the piece, leaders at my church were criticized for allegedly mishandling sexual abuse accusations in two cases that resulted in lawsuits—one in 2010, involving a youth pastor, and the other in 1994, involving a man who was contracted to coordinate youth music productions. In an unrelated affidavit from 1992, our pastor, who at the time was the head of the Southern Baptist Convention, declined to testify in a lawsuit against an admitted child molester who had worked as a youth pastor at a church in Conroe. The SBC, he wrote, had no organizational authority over any of its associated churches, which operated autonomously. He added that he did not "hold an opin-ion as to the proper handling of any claims of sexual abuse by church members against their members," and that any testimony on this subject would "unfavorably affect [his] television ministry, which now is seen on a daily basis in the greater Houston area.") It was impossible to separate the performance of superiority from the public demonstration of virtue or worth or faith. One year, a troupe of Christian bodybuilders regularly appeared at chapel to rip apart phone books as a demonstration of the strength we could acquire through Jesus. At Halloween, the church put on a "Judg-ment House," a walk-through haunted-house play in which the main character drank beer at a party and then kept sinning and wound up in hell.

Severing ties to these theatrics was easy. But for some time af-terward, I retained an intense hunger for devotion itself. For about five years—the end of high school, the beginning of college—I turned my attention inward, tried to build a church on the inside, tried to understand faith as something that could draw me closer to something overwhelming and pure. I kept a devotional journal, producing a record of spiritual longing that was fierce and jagged and dissolving. I pleaded for things I still find very recognizable.

Help me to not put on an act of any kind, I wrote. I told God that I
wanted to live in accordance with my beliefs, that I wanted to diminish my own sense of self-importance, that I was sorry for not
being better, and that I was grateful for being alive. *It's hard to
draw the line between taking pleasure in God's purpose and aligning
God's purpose with what I take pleasure in*, I wrote, between entries
where I tried to understand if it was inherently wrong to get drunk.
(At my school, you could be expelled for character-based spiritual
offenses such as partying, being gay, or getting pregnant.) I stood
between both sides of my life, holding the lines that led to them,
trying to engage with a tension that I stopped being able to feel.
Eventually, almost without realizing it, I let one side go.

Throughout these years of shedding my religion, I read a lot of
C. S. Lewis, the strangest, most reasonable, and most literary of
twentieth-century Christian writers. I reread *The Great Divorce*,
which portrays hell as a drained, gray, hazy town where nothing
happens. I reread his sci-fi novel *Perelandra*, in which Lewis-the-
narrator encounters an extraterrestrial spirit whose color he can't
put a name to: "I try blue, and gold, and violet, and red, but none
of them will fit. How it is possible to have a visual experience
which immediately and ever after becomes impossible to remember, I do not attempt to explain." Lewis goes on to tell a story in
which a linguist named Dr. Ransom travels to Venus, and experiences, on this violently beautiful planet, a "strange sense of excessive pleasure which seemed somehow to be communicated to him
through all his senses at once. I use the word 'excessive' because
Ransom himself could only describe it by saying that for his first
few days on Perelandra he was haunted, not by a feeling of guilt,
but by surprise that he had no such feeling."

Most often I went back to *The Screwtape Letters*, a collection of
fictive missives sent by a bureaucratic demon named Screwtape to
his nephew Wormwood, a "junior tempter" who is trying to lead
his first human subject astray. "The safest road to Hell is the grad-
ual one," Screwtape reminds Wormwood, "the gentle slope, soft

underfoot, without sudden turnings, without milestones, without signposts." When I first came across that sentence, I felt like someone was reading my palm. The book's title, too, with its coincidental echoes, provided a clue to me about my relationship to its central subject—the ordinary temptations, in my case drugs and music, that could lead a person to hell. My road that way has in fact been gentle, although there could have been signposts had I wanted to build them: I could say, without too much oversimplification, that I stopped believing in God the year I first did ecstasy, for one.

I have always found religion and drugs appealing for similar reasons. (*You require absolution, complete abandonment*, I wrote, praying to God my junior year.) Both provide a path toward transcendence—a way of accessing an extrahuman world of rapture and pardon that, in both cases, is as real as it feels. The word "ecstasy" contains this etymologically, coming from the Greek *ek-stasis*—*ek* meaning "out" and *stasis* meaning "stand." To be in ecstasy is to stand outside yourself: a wonderful feeling, one accessible through many avenues. The *Screwtape* demon tells his nephew, "Nothing matters at all except the tendency of a given state of mind, in given circumstances, to move a particular patient at a particular moment nearer to the Enemy or nearer to us."

In other words, the cause matters less than the effect—what matters is not the thing itself, but whether that thing moves you closer to God or closer to damnation. The demon was asking: What are the conditions that make you feel holy, divine? For me, this calculus has been unreliable. I have been overpowered with ecstasy in religious settings, during bouts of hedonistic excess, on Friday afternoons walking sober in the park as the sun turns everything translucent gold. On Screwtape's terms, the fact that everything feels like God to me ensured that I would not remain a Christian. Church never felt much more like virtue than drugs did, and drugs never felt much more sinful than church.

The first woman to ever publish a book in English was a reli-

gious ecstatic—Julian of Norwich, the fourteenth-century ancho-
rite, whose name possibly comes from the St. Julian Church in
Norwich, a town one hundred miles outside London. At age
thirty, Julian became so ill that she experienced sixteen extended
and agonizing visions of God, which she collected later in a book
called *Revelations of Divine Love*. "And our Lord's next showing
was a supreme spiritual pleasure in my soul," she writes. "In this
pleasure I was filled with eternal certainty. . . . This feeling was so
joyful to me and so full of goodness that I felt completely peace-
ful, easy and at rest, as though there were nothing on earth that
could hurt me." The high is then followed by a comedown: "This
only lasted for a while, and then my feeling was reversed and I was
left oppressed, weary of myself, and so disgusted with my life that
I could hardly bear to live."

This type of experience is a human constant, appearing in basically identical phrasing regardless of era or cause. In the sixties,
the British biologist Sir Alister Hardy compiled a database of
thousands of narratives that sound almost exactly like Julian's.
One man writes:

> I was out walking one night in busy streets of Glasgow when,
> with slow majesty, at a corner where the pedestrians were hurry-
> ing by and the city traffic was hurtling on its way, the air was
> filled with heavenly music; and an all-encompassing light, that
> moved in waves of luminous colour, outshone the brightness of
> the lighted streets. I stood still, filled with a strange peace and joy.

Hardy's archive is, technically, a compendium of religious
experiences—in *Aeon*, Jules Evans calls it a "crowdsourced Bible."
But it could easily pass as a series of transcripts from Erowid, the
nonprofit website based in Northern California that catalogs people's experiences with psychoactive substances. The site has more
than 24,000 drug testimonials, and tens of millions of people visit
it each year. The specifics in these accounts vary, of course, but

ecstatic experiences—ones that make you stand outside yourself—are described in a consistent fashion. An Erowid story from a teenage boy doing molly in his basement is not much different from any of the transcripts from the supervised drug sessions conducted in the mid-seventies to mid-eighties, during the brief period when ecstasy and acid could be used in therapeutic trials.

During this period, ecstasy was called Adam for the state of Edenic innocence it induced in users. Accounts from "Adam sessions" were collected in a 1985 book called *Through the Gateway of the Heart*. One rape survivor on ecstasy reports "exceptional presence—a vibrancy and change of color, an expansive quality rather than a fearful, contracted quality—and with a beaming sort of aura. I felt expansive, physically exhausted but full of love and a deep feeling of peace." Another person writes, "I remind myself that I am becoming a home to the indwelling Spirit; it will see out my eyes, and it likes to see beauty, proportion, and harmony. . . . I intend to become a perfect temple for this God-consciousness." Another subject identifies the drug as a religious pathway: "I allow, invite, surrender God into my own body."

Ecstasy, now mostly called molly in the US, is an empathogen, or an entactogen—a category named in the eighties to describe the way these compounds generate a state of empathy, or "touching within." Its technical name is methylenedioxymethamphetamine, or MDMA. It blocks serotonin reuptake, and induces the release of both serotonin and dopamine. (The first mechanism is what you'll find in many antidepressants—SSRIs, or selective serotonin reuptake inhibitors, keep serotonin floating around the brain.) Ecstasy was developed in 1912, by Merck, in Germany, as a compound that could stop abnormal bleeding. In the fifties, the Army Chemical Corps tested it on animals. In the sixties, a related substance called MDA gained popularity as "the love drug." During the seventies, a number of scientists—including Leo Zeff, the one who named the drug Adam—tried the drug, and a network of practitioners of underground MDMA psychotherapy began to grow. In 1978, Alexander Shulgin and David Nichols published the first human study on ecstasy, noting the substance's possible therapeutic effects.

The attainment of chemical ecstasy—empathogenesis—occurs in stages. The drug first places the attention on the self, stripping away the user's inhibitions. Second, it prompts the user to recognize and value the emotional states of others. Finally, it makes the user's well-being feel inseparable from the well-being of the group. It "completely ablates the fear response in most people," writes Julie Holland, in her comprehensive clinical guide to ecstasy. And unlike other drugs that provoke extraordinary interpersonal euphoria—mushrooms or acid—it does not confuse the user about what is occurring. You maintain a sense of control over your experience; your awareness of self and of basic reality is unchanged. It's because of this grounded state that ecstasy can provide a sense of salvation that might be more likely to stick than, say, a hallucinogen epiphany delivered from a face in the clouds. It was "penicillin for the soul," said Ann Shulgin, a researcher and therapist who was married to Alexander. Ecstasy can and generally does make you feel like the best version of the person you would be if you were able to let your lifelong psychological burdens go.

While scientists and doctors were working to document these therapeutic effects, regulators were working to make ecstasy illegal. In the fifties, a participant in a legal MDA trial had died after being given 450 milligrams of the substance; at least eight people died after taking MDMA from 1977 to 1981. (For context, about ninety thousand people die every year in the U.S. from excessive consumption of alcohol, and nearly five hundred thousand people die each year from smoking cigarettes. Ecstasy is in no way a casual drug, but if the substance was legal, its death rate would be dwarfed by that of tobacco or alcohol.) In 1985, the DEA banned ecstasy in a yearlong emergency measure. Researchers protested. In 1986, shortly before the ban ended, one DEA judge recommended that MDMA be placed in the Schedule III category, for drugs that have an accepted medical use and a mild to moderate potential for abuse and addiction—substances like testosterone and ketamine and steroids. He was overruled. MDMA was placed on Schedule I, the category for drugs with high abusive potential, no accepted medical usage, and severe safety concerns. Heroin is in this category, as are bath salts—along with drugs that don't really fit the criteria, like LSD and marijuana.

Around this time, a drug dealer renamed the substance ecstasy. Quoted but not named in Bruce Eisner's 1989 history of MDMA, he says, though I find the neatness of this phrasing dubious: "Ecstasy was chosen for obvious reasons, because it would sell better than calling it empathy. Empathy would be more appropriate, but how many people know what it means?" The drug went global in the nineties, in 5,000- or 15,000-person raves. Huge batches were stamped with the Mitsubishi logo and shipped to New York City, where, at the turn of the century, people took three quarters of a million hits of ecstasy every weekend. The drug was still called ecstasy half a decade later, when I first tried it, in college, shortly before a Girl Talk show in a two-hundred-fifty-capacity room. By the time I came back from the Peace Corps in 2011, ecstasy had been rebranded as molly, and it was once more a mainstream drug, one that had been engineered for the decade of corporate music festivals—both a special-occasion option and no big deal.

A lot of the danger attributed to ecstasy comes from urban legend. For example, the old rumor that ecstasy turns your spine to jelly comes from eighties clinical trials that required participants to receive spinal taps. The idea that it'll put holes in your brain may come from a 1989 *New York Times* article in which a researcher cited brain damage in animals exposed to ecstasy. (It may also just come from the fact that, after you do a lot of drugs, your brain feels like it's full of holes.) Dealer adulteration is now the main thing that makes ecstasy risky—for a while, there was a supply of molly floating around New York so soul-crushingly poisonous that I couldn't even look at the substance for a year—along with the general danger in doing imprecise amounts of any drug in a setting where no one's taking precautions. It's also been documented that ecstasy's magic is strongest at the beginning and worn down through repetition. In my own life I've become careful about using it: I'm afraid that the high will blunt my tilt toward unprovoked happiness, which might already be disappearing. I'm afraid that the low that comes after will leave a permanent trace.

But God knows that it can feel like divinity. It can make you feel healed and religious; it can make you feel dangerously wild. What's the difference? Your world realigns in a juddering oceanic shimmer. You feel that your soul is dazzling, delicate, unlimited; you understand that you can give the best of yourself away to everyone you love without ever feeling depleted. This is what it feels like to be a child of Jesus, in a dark chapel, with stained-glass diamonds floating on the skin of all the people kneeling around you. This is what it feels like to be twenty-two, nearly naked, your hair blowing in the wind as the pink twilight expands into permanence, your body still holding the warmth of the day. You were made to be here. You are depraved, insignificant, measureless; you are gorgeous, and you will never not be redeemed. When I took ecstasy for the first time in my friend's bedroom when I was seventeen and slipped into a sweaty black box of a venue down the street, I felt weightless, like I'd come back around to a truth I had first been taught in church: that anything could happen, and no matter what, a sort of grace that was both within you and outside you would pull you through. The nature of a revelation is that you don't have to re-experience it; you don't even have to believe whatever is revealed to hang on to it for as long as you want. In the seventies, researchers believed that MDMA treatment would be discrete and limited—that once you got the message, as they put it, you could hang up the phone. You would be better for having listened. You would be changed.

They don't say this about religion, but they should.

"What if I were to begin an essay on spiritual matters by citing a poem that will not at first seem to you spiritual at all," writes Anne Carson, in the title essay of her 2005 book *Decreation*. The poem she refers to is by Sappho, the ancient Greek poet who is said to have thrown herself over a cliff in 580 B.C. from an excess of love for Phaon, the ferryman—though this is, for Sapphic reasons, unlikely. In "Decreation," Carson connects Sappho to Marguerite Porete, the French Christian mystic who was burned at the stake in 1310, and then to Simone Weil, the French public intellectual who, during World War II, assumed solidarity with the residents of the German occupation and died from self-starvation in 1943. The spiritual matter in question is mysticism, a strain of thought found in nearly all religious traditions: mystics believe that, through attaining states of ecstatic consciousness, a person can achieve union with the divine.

Carson turns our attention to Sappho's Fragment 31, in which the poet looks at a woman who is sitting next to a man, laughing with him. Sappho describes her feelings as she watches this woman, how the sight makes her speechless—"thin / fire is racing under skin," reads Carson's translation, "and in eyes no sight and drumming / fills ears":

> and cold sweat holds me and shaking
> grips me all, greener than grass
> I am and dead—or almost
> I seem to me.

Fragment 31 is one of the longest extant pieces of Sappho's work, preserved because it was excerpted in Longinus's first-century work of literary criticism *On the Sublime*. In the seventeenth century, John Hall translated Fragment 31 for the first time in English: the "greener than grass" line, in Hall's version, is "like a wither'd flower I fade." In 1925, Edwin Cox translated the line as "paler than grass in autumn." William Carlos Williams's 1958 translation gives it as "paler than grass," too.

The Greek word in question is *chloros*, which is the root of the word "chlorophyll"—a pale yellow-green color, like new grass in spring. As the narrator takes on the quality of that color, a translator could easily imagine her growing paler, fading: the "pale horse" in Revelation is a *chloros* horse. Carson, wonderfully, reaches for the opposite effect. As she stares at the woman she loves, the narrator becomes greener, and the line becomes an expression of ecstasy in its original sense. Sappho steps outside herself; she observes herself ("greener than grass / I am"). Love has caused her to abandon her body, and in this abandonment, to intensify. The green grows greener. Some essential quality deepens as the self is removed.

Seventeen centuries later, Marguerite Porete wrote *The Mirror of Simple Souls*, a book that tracks the human soul on its journey toward ecstasy—a state of voluntary annihilation that brings perfect union with God. Porete, whose biography remains mysterious but who was likely a beguine, a woman who lived in an all-female religious community, "understands the essence of her human self to be in her free will," writes Carson. She believes that her free will "has been placed in her by God in order that she may give it back." So Porete, in her religious devotion, tries to deplete herself. Like Sappho, she pursues love as an "absolute emptiness which is also absolute fullness." She describes this spiritual self-abasement erotically: the soul, Porete writes, is "rendered into the simple Deity, in full knowing, without feeling, beyond thought. . . . Higher no one can go, deeper no one can go, more naked no human can be." Because of this writing, Porete was charged with heresy and imprisoned for a year and a half. When she was burned at the stake, she was reportedly so calm that onlookers were moved to tears.

"Decreation," finally, is a word that comes from Simone Weil— her term for the process of moving toward a love so unadulterated that it makes you leave yourself behind. There is "absolutely no other free act which it is given us to accomplish," Weil writes, except for yielding ourselves to God. Her writing is animated by this compulsive longing to erase herself. "Perfect joy excludes even the very feeling of joy," she writes. "For in the soul filled by the object no corner is left for saying I." She dreams of vanishing completely: "May I disappear in order that those things that I see may become perfect in their beauty from the very fact that they are no longer things that I see."

There's an obvious paradox here, for all three women: their fantasy of disappearance reinscribes the dazzling force and vision of their intellectual presence. It's a "profoundly tricky spiritual fact," Carson writes. "I cannot go toward God in love without bringing myself along." Being a writer compounds the dilemma: to articulate this desire to vanish is always to reiterate the self once again. Greener, not paler. Porete calmly burning in Paris. Weil willing herself, starving and brilliant, toward her end.

Later in Carson's book, in a three-part libretto, the poet imagines Weil in a hospital bed, as "the Chorus of the Void tap-dance around her." Carson's Weil says, in a line that makes me shiver: *"I was afraid this might not happen to me."* She expires in the white space that follows the libretto, reaching the logical endpoint of her philosophy of devotion: reaching toward ecstasy in this way is not so different from reaching toward death. "Our existence is made up only of his waiting for our acceptance not to exist," Weil writes in *Gravity and Grace.* "He is perpetually begging from us that existence which he gives. He gives it to us in order to beg it from us." To grasp at the type of self-erasure that Carson's three women become fixated upon is to approach a cognitive limit, a place of instinct and unconsciousness, a total annihilation that can be achieved only once. I have wondered if this is part of the reason that evangelical Christians often seem so eager for the Rapture, the prophesied end-of-days event in which they'll die and ascend to heaven. When you love something so much that you dream of emptying yourself out for it, you'd be forgiven for wanting to let your love finish the job.

The last time I participated in anything on my forty-two-acre church campus, it was high school graduation. I was wearing a white flowered sundress under a royal-blue robe, and I was on-stage at the Worship Center, looking up at the bright lights, toward the empty balconies, giving the salutatorian's speech. I barely remember what I said—I know I made at least one joke about the Repentagon—but I had turned in a different speech for approval than what I delivered, and though my classmates were whooping, an administrator hissed at me, when I crossed the stage to accept my diploma, that they were tempted not to let me walk. A younger friend told me that the school scrubbed the speech from its official record: in the video archive of graduation proceedings going back decades, whatever I said is no longer there.

The next Christmas, when I came home from college, my church held its holiday service in conjunction with Joel Osteen's enormous megachurch in the Toyota Center, the huge arena in downtown Houston where the Rockets play. Before getting dressed for the evening service, I had spent much of the afternoon getting stoned with my friend Robert, and in the middle of the spectacle, I started to lose it. A man from *Dancing with the Stars* was singing, his face looming huge on the jumbotron. I left my parents, just like I had when I was in middle school, edging my way out of the stadium seating. Outside, on the perimeter of our church service, vendors were selling popcorn and brisket sandwiches and thirty-two-ounce Cokes. I went to the bathroom, overwhelmed, and cried. I was afraid of how distant I felt, how disloyal—I still am. When I sent a draft of this essay to Robert, asking him to check my memory, he told me that he'd noticed, over the years, that I still felt oddly guilty about my graduation speech. "But what you did wasn't a shit-talking mic drop," he wrote. "It felt, in a very particular, human way, like an act of love."

I wonder if I would have stayed religious if I had grown up in a place other than Houston and a time other than now. I wonder how different I would be if I had cleaved to this feeling of devoted self-destruction—or even of solitude and striving, or writing, in the manner of Carson's three women—and only been able to find it through God. I can't tell whether my inclination toward ecstasy is a sign that I still believe, after all of this, or if it was only because of that ecstatic tendency that I ever believed at all.

I wonder, sometimes, if I have continued to do drugs *because* they make me feel the way I did when I was little, an uncomplicated creation, vulnerable to guilt and benevolence. The first time I did mushrooms, I felt perfect and convicted and rescued, like someone had just told me I was going to heaven. I walked down a beach and everything coalesced with the cheesy, psychotic logic of "Footprints in the Sand." The first time I did acid, I saw God again immediately—the trees and clouds around me blazing with presence, like Moses's burning bush. Completely out of my mind, I wrote on a napkin, "I can process nothing right now that does not terminate in God's presence—this revelation I seem ready to have forever in degraded forms."

Recently, I found myself doing this again—this time in the desert, that perennial seat of madness and punishment and epiphany, in a house at the top of a hill in a canyon where the sun and wind were incandescent, white-hot, merciless, streaking and scintillating across the bright blue sky. I left the house and walked down in the valley, and started to feel the drugs kick in when I was wandering in the scrub. The dry bushes became brilliant—greener—

and a hummingbird torpedoed past me so quickly that I froze. I experienced, for the first time, Weil's precise fantasy of disappearance. Each breath I took felt like it was echoing clangorously, an impure reverberation. I wanted to see the landscape as it was when I wasn't there. I had tugged on some fabric and everything was rippling. I had come to that knife-edge of disappearance. For hours I watched the blinding swirl of light and cloud move west and I repented. At sunset, the sky billowed into mile-wide peonies, hardly an arm's length above me, and it felt like a visitation, like God was replacing the breath in my lungs. I sobbed—battered by a love I knew would fall away from me, ashamed for all the ways I had tried to bring myself to this, humiliated by the grace of encountering it now. I dragged myself inside, finally, and looked at the mirror. My eyes were smeared with black makeup, my face was red, my lips were swollen; a thick whitish substance clung stubbornly around my mouth. I looked like a junkie. I found a piece of paper and wrote on it, after attentively noting that the ink seemed to be breathing: "The situations in my life when I have been sympathetic to desperation are the situations when I have felt sure I was encountering God."

I don't know if I'm after truth or hanging on to its dwindling half-life, or if it matters. I might only be hoping to remember that my ecstatic disposition is the source of the good in me—spontaneity, devotion, sweetness—and the worst things, heedlessness, blankness, equivocation, too. I'm trying to rid myself of the delusion that either type of Sunday belongs to me. The sense of something is not its substance. It isn't love, trying to make two things interchangeable, when they are not. In *Revelations of Divine Love*, Julian of Norwich describes sin as "behovely," which translates as "advantageous," even "expedient." "It is no shame to them that they have sinned," she wrote, "any more than it is in the bliss of heaven, for there, the badge of their sin is changed into glory." But then, at the end of the book, she warns the reader that her work "must not remain with anyone that is in thrall to sin and the devil. And beware that you do not take one thing according to your taste and fancy and leave another, for that is what heretics do."

But what are we other than our own version of glory? In the fall of 2000, DJ Screw was found dead, fully dressed, on the bathroom floor at his studio. He was twenty-nine. He had an ice-cream wrapper in his hand. In the autopsy, coroners found that his body was full of codeine; his blood flowed with Valium and PCP. His heart was engorged, enormous. At his funeral in Smithville, writes Michael Hall in *Texas Monthly*, the old folks sang gospel and the rappers nodded quietly along with the hymns. People lined up outside the church the way they'd done outside Screw's house to pick up their tapes, mourning the man the way they had always gotten his music—that sound he'd created that approximated the feel of a drug binge, no matter what Screw told reporters; the sound that mimicked the flow of all these substances, darkening the wide, anonymous, looping highways, a secret and sublime desecration that seeped through the heart and the veins of a city, that set the pace and the rhythm of its people slipping past one another in their cars.

The year of Screw's death, I got on a bus and drove east toward Alabama with a thousand other kids. On a middle-of-nowhere beach, we participated in mass baptisms, put our hands up in huge services where everyone cried in the darkness. We groped one another on the bus afterward and talked all day about being saved. Later on, it was one of the boys from that trip who chopped lines on my friend's kitchen table as I waded through her pool, drunk on sweet syrup, staring at the stars. There are some institutions— drugs, church, and money—that aligned the superstructure of white wealth in Houston with the heart of black and brown culture beneath it. There are feelings, like ecstasy, that provide an unbreakable link between virtue and vice. You don't have to believe a revelation to hold on to it, to remember certain overpasses, sudden angles above and under the cold and heartless curves of that industrial landscape, a slow river of lights blinking white and red into the distance, and the debauched sky gleaming over the houses and hospitals and stadium churches, and your blood thrumming with drugs or music or sanctity. It can all feel like a mirage of wholeness: the ten thousand square miles around you teeming with millions of people who do the same things, drive under the same influences, respect the same Sundays, with the music that sounds like their version of religion. "Our life is impossibility, absurdity," wrote Simone Weil. "Everything we want contradicts the conditions or the consequences attached to it. . . . It is because we are a contradiction—being creatures—being God and infinitely other than God."

The Story of a Generation
in Seven Scams

Billy McFarland started scamming at the age of twenty-two. Born in 1991, to parents who were real estate developers, he spent nine months at Bucknell before getting accepted to a startup accelerator and then dropping out to found a nonsense company called Spling. (Crunchbase describes it as a "tech-driven ad platform helping brands increase media engagement and marketing revenue by optimizing their content presentation." This was 2011, when it was still possible to say that sort of thing straight-faced; it was the year that Peter Thiel, the libertarian venture capitalist and Facebook founding board member who once wrote that women's suffrage had compromised democracy, started offering $100,000 fellowships to dropout entrepreneurs.) In 2013, McFarland founded Magnises, a company that charged upwardly mobile millennials a suspiciously modest $250 a year for VIP event tickets and access to a clubhouse. Magnises gave members a "signature" black card, which duplicated the magnetic strip of an existing credit card but held no other advantages: like the company itself, the card was just for show.

Magnises ("Latin for absolutely nothing," McFarland said) attracted breathless press and a growing membership culled from the boundless cohort of young New Yorkers who are interested in projecting an aura of exclusive cool. "Billy McFarland wants to help you build the perfect network," *Business Insider* wrote, describing Magnises as a "club for elite millennials where everyone gets a black card and parties in a New York City penthouse." The golden phase lasted less than a year. Members purchased expensive theater and concert tickets that would become mysteriously invalid on the day of the show. McFarland text-spammed them with try-hard offers: a "private networking dinner" for $275 per person, hoverboards delivered by courier. "Also, have the Maserati w/ a driver available this weekend. LMK if you're in." Sometimes, oddly, his offers involved the rapper Ja Rule. On New Year's Day in 2016, he texted: "Happy New Year! Ja Rule is working on a new song and can mention your name, nickname, company name, etc in the upcoming hit single for $450. 5 Spots. LMK!" Later on, in the dueling, ethically dubious documentaries about McFarland's demise that were released near-simultaneously by Hulu and Netflix—I appeared in the Hulu one, although I, unlike McFarland, was not paid an enormous sum to do so—former Magnises employees explained the fraudulent pattern of the business: McFarland would make offers he couldn't fulfill, then go into debt while half-trying to fulfill them, and then make more bogus offers to pay off that debt, and on and on.

That January, Magnises settled a $100,000 lawsuit filed by its landlord in the West Village, who complained that McFarland was using a residential space to conduct commercial business, and also that he had trashed the place. No problem. McFarland moved Magnises to the penthouse of the Hotel on Rivington on the Lower East Side. By that point, the company had raised at least $3 million in venture capital, but its customers were getting frustrated. "If you change a couple of words you can define Magnises in a very similar fashion to how one would define a Ponzi scheme," reads one Yelp review of the Magnises Townhouse from 2016. Another: "I implore you to avoid doing business with this company on any level and am completely embarrassed to have been swindled by this myself."

Magnises chugged along in public, but in private, it was collapsing. McFarland boasted that there were 100,000 members; in
reality, fewer than 5,000 people had signed up. He pivoted to a
new venture, Fyre Media, which he envisioned as a platform
where rich people could bid on celebrity appearances for private
events. Ja Rule was involved. Their friendship had blossomed over
a "mutual interest in technology, the ocean, and rap music," he
would later tell reporters. They raised money for Fyre Media together. And then, as 2016 drew to a close, McFarland got one of
the most ill-fated ideas in the history of American scamship. He
would promote his company through a luxury festival in the Bahamas. The first annual Fyre Festival, he decided, would be held
in April 2017.

It would be difficult to plan a medium-size wedding on four
months' notice: this was an objectively impossible timeline for an
all-inclusive music festival for ten thousand people on a remote
beach. McFarland would have likely understood this without a
second thought if he'd ever, for example, had a job performing
actual services of any kind, if he'd ever waited tables or earned
minimum wage working a concession stand—or if he'd ever even
been to a music festival, which, astoundingly, he had not. Instead,
the twenty-five-year-old had been busy building a career on the
principle that a person could front his way into any desired reality,
and he'd also tapped into a deep vein of customers who were
eager to believe the same. McFarland put up a website and started
selling tickets to a once-in-a-lifetime festival on "Fyre Cay," which
he described as a private island formerly owned by the Colombian
drug lord Pablo Escobar. Fyre Festival advertised a slate of major
musical acts, a highly Instagrammable party, and super-deluxe
accommodations. Attendees could choose between tiers of fancy
housing options—the most expensive of which, the "Artist's Pal-
ace," cost $400,000 for four beds in a bespoke, stand-alone beach
house, plus eight VIP tickets and dinner with a performer.

There was never a plan to actually construct these Artist's Pal-

aces. Also, there was no Fyre Cay. (Carlos Lehder, another Me-
dellín kingpin, *had* briefly taken over a tiny Bahamian island
called Norman's Cay, but McFarland's Escobar story was fake.)
Early in 2017, McFarland took a private jet to the Bahamas to film
an expensive promotional video for Fyre Fest, which featured
models frolicking in blue waves and glittering sand. He paid, along
with hundreds of other "influencers," the models Emily Ratajkowski, Kendall Jenner, and Bella Hadid to promote the event on Instagram; Jenner received $250,000 for a single post. But he didn't
pick an actual site until two months before the festival, selecting
a bleak gravel lot next to a Sandals resort on the non-private island
of Great Exuma. (The obvious Hail Mary would have been to just
try to book all the attendees into the Sandals. That's what happened, at least, at Bacardi Triangle, which was the weekend in
2016 when Bacardi inexplicably flew thousands of people to the
Bermuda Triangle to see Calvin Harris and Kendrick Lamar perform on the beach. They put us up—I was there, of course—in a
sprawling resort in Puerto Rico and gave us three days of open
bar. It was just like Fyre Fest, except it worked, and also we were
the ones scamming Bacardi. Anyway, it's hard to account for a
single part of McFarland's reasoning, as he had chosen a festival
date that coincided with the annual George Town Regatta, for
which most island hotels had already hit capacity.)

In March, with Blink-182, Major Lazer, and Disclosure set to
headline Fyre Fest, a production team was flown down to the site.
Chloe Gordon, a talent producer, was a member of the team. "Before we arrived, we were led to believe things had been in motion
for awhile," she wrote at *The Cut* later on. "But nothing had been
done. Festival vendors weren't in place, no stage had been rented,
transportation had not been arranged." Toilets, showers, and housing had not been arranged, either. On site, Bahamian day laborers
were dumping sand on the concrete; McFarland was forging wire
transfer receipts and telling unpaid contractors that the money
was on its way. Gordon quit after realizing that Fyre Media was

planning on stiffing the bands. Before she left the Bahamas, she attended a meeting at which the "bros" in charge were advised to roll everyone's tickets over to 2018 and start over. They rejected that idea. One of the marketing employees, Gordon wrote, said, "Let's just do it and be legends, man."

In the end, of course, Fyre Fest did become legendary. It was the most gleefully covered disaster of 2017. McFarland had continued to push forward with his obviously doomed operation until the very last minute. FuckJerry, the company that handled Fyre Fest's marketing and later produced the Netflix Fyre documentary, mass-deleted Instagram comments from people who wanted to know why they hadn't gotten any flight information and what the tents actually looked like. The week before the festival, when McFarland once again ran out of money, attendees received emails and calls asking them to preload thousands of dollars on wristbands that they would be required to use at Fyre Fest in lieu of cash. But none of the bands got paid, and all of them pulled out just before the festival started. In Miami, charter flights failed to materialize for the attendees. Some festivalgoers made it to the Bahamas, where they were plied with alcohol and then taken to the untransformed site, which featured UNICEF-style disaster-relief tents, loose mattresses that had been soaked in a rainstorm, folding chairs, and shipping containers overflowing with junk. At the empty concierge desks, scraps of branded canvas flapped in the breeze. Instead of gourmet dining, attendees got Styrofoam to-go boxes and infamously sad sandwiches of wilted lettuce and American cheese. The crowd started to panic—and to tweet photos of their gulag Coachella. Chaos ensued. People started hoarding mattresses and toilet paper. McFarland threw his hands up and told everyone to sleep in the first open tent they found. Several dozen people were locked into a room at the Bahamian airport after begging locals to give them rides off the site. The internet snorted each dispatch from Great Exuma like a line of medical-grade schadenfreude.

In June 2017, McFarland was arrested and charged with fraud. Aside from scamming his festival attendees, he had completely falsified Fyre Media's financial position—earlier that year, he'd claimed that the company took in $21.6 million in revenue over a single month, and that it owned land in the Bahamas worth $8.4 million. He had stiffed and cheated a slew of companies and workers, many of them Bahamians who had placed their livelihood in his hands, believing his promises that Fyre Fest would be an enormous annual venture. And still, undaunted, McFarland kept scamming: later that summer, he holed up in a penthouse and sold, through a company called NYC VIP Access, $100,000 worth of fake tickets to exclusive events, some of which he had made up completely. According to a 2018 federal complaint, McFarland actually *retargeted* Fyre Fest attendees from behind the shield of his new venture, drawing from a spreadsheet that identified the customers with the highest annual salaries. When I read that detail, I felt something close to admiration. I thought about how, in the midst of the real-time social media frenzy, Ja Rule had tweeted that Fyre Fest was "NOT A SCAM." The phrase functioned like a ribbon-cutting ceremony. It announced McFarland, whom *The New York Times* described as "Gatsby run through an Instagram filter," as the scammer of his generation, and Fyre Fest as not just a scam, but a definitive one—America's first major all-millennial scam event.

Fyre Fest sailed down Scam Mountain with all the accumulating force and velocity of a cultural shift that had, over the previous decade, subtly but permanently changed the character of the nation, making scamming—the abuse of trust for profit—seem simply like the way things were going to be. It came after the election of Donald Trump, an incontrovertible, humiliating vindication of scamming as the quintessential American ethos. It came after a big smiling wave of feminist initiatives and female entrepreneurs had convincingly framed wealth acquisition as progressive politics. It came after the rise of companies like Uber and

Amazon, which broke apart the economy and then sold it a cheap ride to the duct tape store, all while promising to make the world a better and more convenient place. It came after the advent of reality TV and Facebook, which drew on the renewable natural resource of our narcissism to create a world where our selves, our relationships, and our personalities were not just monetizable but actively in need of monetization. It came after college tuition skyrocketed only to send graduates into low-wage contract work and world-historical economic inequality. It came, finally, after the 2008 financial crisis, the event that arguably kick-started the millennial-era understanding that the quickest way to win is to scam.

The Crash

In 1988, twenty-seven-year-old Michael Lewis quit his job at Salomon Brothers, the investment bank that sold the world's first mortgage-backed security, and wrote a book called *Liar's Poker*. It was a portrait of Wall Street in the years following federal deregulation, a time when the industry blossomed with savvy, cynical, lucky actors who stumbled into a world of extreme manipulation and profit. Lewis, as an inexperienced twentysomething, had found himself in charge of millions of dollars in assets without fully understanding what was going on. Revisiting that period in 2010, he observed, "The whole thing still strikes me as totally preposterous. . . . I figured the situation was unsustainable. Sooner rather than later, someone was going to identify me, along with a lot of people more or less like me, as a fraud." He had thought that *Liar's Poker* would live on as a period piece, a document of how "a great nation lost its financial mind." He didn't expect that, after the 2008 crash, eighties finance would seem almost quaint.

Lewis writes about this crash in *The Big Short*, which chronicles the unspeakably complicated mechanisms that bankers created to inflate the mid-2000s housing market, and then to monetize skyrocketing levels of homeowner liability, until, inevitably, the whole system collapsed. Laws against predatory lending had been overruled in 2004, which allowed mortgages to be extended to people who would never be able to pay them; this, in turn, made the pool of potential homeowners basically endless. Housing prices rose in some markets by as much as 80 percent. People financed their homes with home equity credit, a scheme that worked as long as prices kept rising, which they would as long as people kept buying. To keep the system going, mortgages were granted willy-nilly: it was possible to get a loan without supplying financial documentation, going through a credit check, or putting money down. One type of subprime loan was called the NINJA, which stood for the borrowers having no income, no job or assets. The financial industry disguised the instability of this arrangement with obscure terms and instruments: CDOs, towers of debt that would be recouped through payments on rotten mortgages, and synthetic CDOs, towers of debt that would be recouped through insurance payments on that rotten debt. In *The Big Short*, a young banker tells Lewis, "The more we looked at what a CDO really was, the more we were like, *Holy shit, that's just fucking crazy. That's fraud.* Maybe you can't prove it in a court of law. But it's fraud."

I was in college while the housing bubble was expanding, and everything else about the country seemed to be on the same turbo-powered track. Goldman Sachs and McKinsey came to campus and recruited my most intense classmates to the sort of life that ensures money for down payments and private school. I watched *America's Next Top Model* and *Project Runway*, shows that were all bustle and glitz and giddy-up, and *Laguna Beach*, where the world looked like long granite countertops and lamplit stucco, palm trees and infinity pools. Upward mobility felt like oxygen—unremarkable, ubiquitous. I wrote a thesis proposal about the American Dream. Then, in 2007, home prices started rapidly declining. Homeowners started defaulting in great waves. Every time I passed by the TVs in the student center, they seemed to be broadcasting news footage of families guarding their possessions on the sidewalk outside foreclosed homes. I found myself staring at my laptop late at night, embarrassed, revising. I'd been writing about immigrants, and how uncertainty was central to the magic spell of America. But the backdrop had suddenly changed from prosperity to collapse.

In September 2008, Lehman Brothers became the first to file for bankruptcy. AIG soon followed, and was bailed out with $182 billion of federal money. (Despite posting a $61 billion loss at the end of 2008—the worst quarterly loss for any corporation in history—AIG gave out $165 million in bonuses to its financial services division the next year.) Then came a global recession. Unemployment and economic inequality skyrocketed. From 2005 to 2011, median household wealth would drop 35 percent. Other countries might have jailed the bankers who did this. Iceland sentenced twenty-nine bank executives for misdeeds leading up to the 2008 crisis; one CEO was sent to jail for five years. But in America, all the bankers were bailed out by the government. Many were richer by the end of the ordeal.

The financial crisis was a classic con—a confidence trick, carried off by confidence men. The first person to earn the official con-man designation was William Thompson, sometimes referred to as Samuel, a petty criminal whose misdeeds were reported by *The New York Herald* in the summer of 1849. "For the last few months a man has been traveling about the city, known as the 'Confidence Man,'" the first article begins. Dressed in a respectable suit, Thompson would approach strangers, make polite small talk, then ask, "Have you confidence in me to trust me with your watch until tomorrow?" The *Herald*'s ongoing coverage of Thompson was so entertaining that the "confidence man" epithet stuck. But Thompson, actually, was a pretty bad con man: opportunists by other names had been working better angles for a long time.

Real con men don't have to ask you for your watch, or your confidence. They act in such a way that you feel lucky to give it to them—eager to place a sure bet on a horse race or park your money in an impossibly successful investment fund, eager to fly to the Bahamas for a party that doesn't exist.

In 1849, three days after Thompson was arrested, the *Herald* published an unsigned editorial called " 'The Confidence Man' on a Large Scale," which sardonically expressed condolences that Thompson hadn't gotten the chance to work on Wall Street.

> His genius has been employed on a small scale in Broadway. Theirs has been employed in Wall Street. That's all the difference. He has obtained half a dozen watches. They have pocketed millions of dollars. He is a swindler. They are exemplars of honesty. He is a rogue. They are financiers. He is collared by the police. They are cherished by society. He eats the fare of a prison. They enjoy the luxuries of a palace. . . . Long life to the real "Confidence Man"!—the "Confidence Man" of Wall Street—the "Confidence Man" of the palace up town—the "Confidence Man" who battens and fattens on the plunder coming from the poor man and the man of moderate means!

The op-ed continues, providing Thompson with caustic advice:

> He should have issued a flaming prospectus of another grand scheme of internal improvement. . . . He should have got all the contracts on his own terms. He should have involved the company in debt, by a corrupt and profligate expenditure of the capital subscribed in good faith by poor men and men of moderate means. . . . He should have brought the stockholders to bankruptcy. He should have sold out the whole concern, and got all into his own hands in payment of his "bonds." He should have drawn, during all the time occupied by this process of "confidence," a munificent salary; and, choosing the proper, ap-

propriate, exact nick of time, he should have retired to a life of virtuous ease, the possessor of a clear conscience, and one million dollars!

The con is in the DNA of this country, which was founded on the idea that it is good, important, and even noble to see an opportunity to profit and take whatever you can. The story is as old as the first Thanksgiving. Both the con man and his target want to take advantage of a situation; the difference between them is that the con man succeeds. The financial crisis of 2008 was an extended, flamboyant demonstration of the fact that one of the best bids a person can make for financial safety in America is to get really good at exploiting other people. This has always been true, but it is becoming all-encompassing. And it's a bad lesson to learn the way millennials did—just as we were becoming adults.

The Student Debt Disaster

After the financial crisis, nearly one in four homes with mortgages in the United States were underwater, valued at less than what their owners owed the banks. Sixty-five percent of homes in Nevada were underwater; in Arizona, it was 48 percent; in California, more than a third. (Predictably, most of these borrowers had bought new homes between 2005 and 2008.) Homeowner debt is the biggest source of household debt in America. For a long time, the second biggest source was car debt. But in 2013, student debt—the second generation-defining scam—took car debt's place.

Adjusting for inflation, college tuition at a private university is currently three times as much as it was in 1974. At public schools, tuition is four times as expensive. Car prices, in comparison, have remained steady. Median income and minimum wage have hardly moved. At some point in the mid-nineties, it became mathematically impossible for a student to work her way through college, and financial aid has nowhere near kept up with the disparity between what students need and what they have. Within the life span of the millennial generation, the average debt burden has *doubled:* for the class of 2003, average debt at graduation was around $18,000; for the class of 2016, it was over $37,000. More than two thirds of college graduates have student debt at graduation, and almost a quarter of postgraduate degree holders with debt owe $100,000 or more. The situation often gets so punishing that it seems fit only for an actual crime. If you borrowed $37,000 on a thirty-year Stafford loan, you would end up paying over $50,000 in interest. The Public Service Loan Forgiveness program has rejected 99 percent of applicants. It is very easy, these days, for student borrowers to end up underwater—indebted for a degree that's worth much less than what they paid.

There are lots of similarities between the housing bubble and the tuition bubble. Like subprime mortgages, student loans at for-profit colleges are nearly always extended in bad faith. The Obama administration nationalized most of the student loan industry as part of the 2010 Affordable Care Act legislation, and so this web of securitized debt is government business, and it is expanding rapidly—student debt ballooned to over $1.5 *trillion* in 2018. But there's one major difference between housing debt and education debt: at least for now, if you hope to improve your life in America, you can't quite turn away from a diploma the way you can a white picket fence.

In the meantime, tuition increases have done little to improve the education students receive. Faculty jobs, like most jobs, have become unstable and precarious. Salaries are stagnant. In 1970, nearly 80 percent of college faculty were employed full-time; now less than half are full-time. Colleges, competing for tuition dollars, spend their money on stadiums, state-of-the-art gyms, fancy dining halls—the cost of which is reflected in tuition. The institution's need to survive in the market, in other words, ends up hampering the student's ability to do the same after they graduate.

And, as protections and benefits and security are steadily stripped away from the labor market, it gets correspondingly harder to pay off this sort of debt.

In 2005, 30 percent of American workers were contingent workers—contract employees, or part-time employees, or self-employed. Now the number is 40 percent and rising. From 2007 to 2016, the number of people working involuntarily part-time (meaning that they'd prefer full-time employment) increased by 44 percent. In the years following the recession, I kept hearing the little factoid that people my age would change careers an average of four times in our first decade out of college. Stories about how millennials "prefer" to freelance still abound. The desired takeaway seems to be: Millennials are free spirits! We're flexible! We'll work anywhere with a Ping-Pong table! We are up for anything and ready to connect! But a generation doesn't start living a definitively mercurial work trajectory for reasons of personality. It's just easier, as Malcolm Harris argues in his book *Kids These Days*, to think millennials float from gig to gig because we're shiftless or spoiled or in love with the "hustle" than to consider the fact that the labor market—for people of every generation—is punitively unstable and growing more so every day. I've been working multiple jobs simultaneously since I was sixteen, and I have had an exceptionally lucky professional life, and, like a lot of Americans, I still think of employer-sponsored health insurance as a luxury: a near-divine perk that, at thirty, I have had for only two years in my career—the two years that I was working at *Gawker*, which was sued into the ground by Hulk Hogan, who was funded by the dropout-loving, suffrage-hating, Trump-supporting billionaire Peter Thiel.

In the current economy, for most students, colleges couldn't possibly deliver on providing hundreds of thousands of dollars' worth of anything. Wages aren't budging, even though corporate profits have soared. The average CEO now makes 271 times the salary of the average American worker, whereas in 1965, the ratio was twenty-to-one. Healthcare costs are staggering—per capita health spending has increased *twenty-nine times* over the past four decades—and childcare costs are rising like college tuition, even as the frontline workers in both healthcare and childcare often receive poverty wages. A college degree is no guarantee of financial stability. Today, aside from inherited money, such guarantees barely exist. (Of course, as we saw in 2019's "Operation Varsity Blues" scandal, plenty of exorbitantly wealthy parents still place enough value in a college education that they will commit outright fraud in order to game the already rigged admissions system and give their children an education that they, of all people, do not actually need.) And still, colleges sell themselves as the crucible through which every young person must pass to stand a chance of succeeding. Into this realm of uncertainty has come a new idea—that the path to stability might be a personal brand.

The Social Media Scam

The most successful millennial is surely thirty-five-year-old Mark Zuckerberg, whose net worth fluctuates around the upper eleven digits. Lowballing it at $55 billion means that Zuckerberg has nearly *five million* times as much money as the median American household, which is worth $11,700. He is the eighth-richest person in the world. As the founder of Facebook, he effectively controls a nation-state: with a quarter of the world's population using his website on a monthly basis, he can sway elections, and change the way we relate to one another, and control broad social definitions of what is acceptable and true. Zuckerberg's most prominent characteristic is a lack of a discernible personality. In 2017, he took a tour around America, seeding rumors of a possible presidential run while giving off the aura of an alien trying to learn how to pass as one of us. The dissonance at the heart of Facebook is at least partly due to the fact that it was *this* man, of all people— this man who once said that having different identities showed a "lack of integrity"—who understood better than anyone that personhood in the twenty-first century would be a commodity like cotton or gold.

Zuckerberg's ascendance to the realm of viable presidential candidates began one October night in 2003, when he was a sophomore at Harvard. He was bored, he wrote on his blog, and he needed to take his mind off his "little bitch" of an ex. At 9:49 P.M.:

> I'm a little intoxicated, not gonna lie. So what if it's not even 10 pm and it's a Tuesday night? What? The Kirkland dormitory facebook is open on my desktop and some of these people have pretty horrendous facebook pics. I almost want to put some of these faces next to pictures of farm animals and have people vote on which is more attractive.

By 11:10 P.M., he was pivoting:

> Yea, it's on. I'm not exactly sure how the farm animals are going to fit into this whole thing (you can't really ever be sure with farm animals . . .), but I like the idea of comparing two people together.

"Let the hacking begin," he wrote, just before one A.M.

Zuckerberg created a site called Facemash, which put photos of Harvard undergrads side by side and asked you to vote between them. It wasn't an original concept: the website Hot or Not was founded in 2000 by two recent college graduates who had gotten into a disagreement about the exact fuckability of a woman they saw on the street. (These young people were men, obviously, as are the founders of YouTube, who have also said they originally intended to build a riff on Hot or Not.) But when Facemash went up, 450 people visited the website within the first four hours; the photos were voted on more than 22,000 times. Zuckerberg got in trouble, and students protested the site as invasive, but plenty of them also liked the *idea* of an online directory, which would allow you to compare yourself to your peers in a more acceptable way. The *Crimson* wrote that Facemash provided "clear indicators that a campus-wide facebook is in order." Zuckerberg, understanding that he could build in a month what would take Harvard much longer, launched the first version of Facebook the next February. Four thousand people signed up within the next two weeks.

When I got Facebook (or "thefacebook") at the end of my senior year of high school, I felt like I had stepped into a wonderful, narcissistic dream. At the time, I was at a peak of self-interest, extremely invested in figuring out who I would become when no longer confined to an environment of Republicans and daily Bible class. My friends and I were already used to creating digital avatars—we'd had AIM, Myspace, Xanga, LiveJournal—and Facebook seemed to make the concept clean and official; it felt as if we were going to a virtual City Hall and registering our new, proto-adult selves. (At the time, Facebook was restricted to college students, but in 2006 it would open up to anyone over thirteen who had an email address.) Once I got to college, people joked about coming home drunk and staring at their own Facebook pages—a precursor of today's endless social media scroll. The concept was entrancing from the beginning: a bona fide, aesthetically unembarrassing website, seemingly devoted to a better version of you.

Back then, it seemed that we were all using some new, wonderful product. Now, more than a decade later, it has become an axiom that we, the users, are the product ourselves. Even if Zuckerberg didn't set out to consciously scam the people who signed up for Facebook, everyone who signed up—all two and a quarter billion monthly users (and counting)—has been had nonetheless. It's our attention being sold to advertisers. It's our personal data being sold to market research firms, our loose political animus being purchased by special interest groups. Facebook has outright deceived the public on many occasions: for one, it reportedly inflated viewer statistics for its videos by up to 900 percent, causing nearly every media company to shift its own strategy—and lay off workers—to reflect a Facebook profit strategy that didn't exist. In the months surrounding the 2016 election, Facebook claimed that there had been no significant Russian interference on Facebook, despite the fact that an internal Facebook committee devoted to investigating the subject had already found evidence of this interference. (And *then* Facebook hired a Republican opposition-research firm to discredit the growing opposition to the company.) Facebook has allowed other companies, like Netflix and Spotify, to view its users' private messages. It has tricked kids into spending their parents' money in Facebook games through tactics that the company internally referred to as "friendly fraud."

But even when Facebook isn't deliberately exploiting its users, it is exploiting its users—its business model requires it. Even if you distance yourself from Facebook, you still live in the world that Facebook is shaping. Facebook, using our native narcissism and our desire to connect with other people, captured our attention and our behavioral data; it used this attention and data to manipulate our behavior, to the point that nearly half of America began relying on Facebook for the news. Then, with the media both reliant on Facebook as a way of reaching readers and powerless against the platform's ability to suck up digital advertising revenue—it was like a paperboy who pocketed all the subscription money—Facebook bent the media's economic model to match its own practices: publications needed to capture attention quickly and consistently trigger high emotional responses to be seen at all. The result, in 2016, was an unending stream of Trump stories, both from the mainstream news and from the fringe outlets that were buoyed by Facebook's algorithm. What began as a way for Zuckerberg to harness collegiate misogyny and self-interest has become the fuel for our whole contemporary nightmare, for a world that fundamentally and systematically misrepresents human needs.

At a basic level, Facebook, like most other forms of social media, runs on doublespeak—advertising connection but creating isolation, promising happiness but inculcating dread. The Facebook idiom now dominates our culture, with the most troubling structural changes of the era surfacing in isolated, deceptive specks of emotional virality. We see the dismantling of workplace protections in a celebratory blog post about a Lyft driver who continued to pick up passengers while she was in labor. We see the madness of privatized healthcare in the forced positivity of a stranger's chemotherapy Kickstarter campaign. On Facebook, our basic humanity is reframed as an exploitable viral asset. Our social potential is compressed to our ability to command public attention, which is then made inextricable from economic survival. Instead of fair wages and benefits, we have our personalities and stories and relationships, and we'd better learn to package them well for the internet in case we ever get in an accident while uninsured.

More than any other entity, Facebook has solidified the idea that selfhood exists in the shape of a well-performing public avatar. But Zuckerberg, in picking up on the fact that we would sell our identities in exchange for simply being *visible*, was riding a wave that had been growing for a long time. *The Real World* started airing when Zuckerberg was eight, *Survivor* and *The Bachelor* while he was in high school. Friendster was founded his freshman year of college. Soon after Facebook came YouTube in 2005, Twitter in 2006, Instagram in 2010, Snapchat in 2011. Now children are going viral on TikTok; gamers make millions streaming their lives on Twitch. The two most prominent families in politics and culture—the Trumps and the Kardashians—have risen to the top of the food chain because of their keen understanding of how little substance is required to package the self as an endlessly monetizable asset. In fact, substance may actually be anathema to the game. And with that, the applause roars, the iPhone cameras

start snapping, and the keynote speaker at the women's empowerment conference comes onstage.

The Girlbosses

The superficially begrudging self-styled icon Sophia Amoruso
was born in 1984, the same year as Mark Zuckerberg. She appeared on the cover of her 2014 memoir #*GIRLBOSS* in a black
deep-V dress with structured shoulders, short hair blown back by
a wind machine, hands planted on her hips. She was the CEO of
Nasty Gal, an online fashion retailer that she'd started in 2006 as
a shoplifting anarchist who sold thrift-store clothes out of her San
Francisco apartment. Eight years later, Nasty Gal was doing hundreds of millions of dollars in sales, and Amoruso, who had man-
aged, impressively, to build the business without taking on debt,
was being hailed as the "Cinderella of tech."

#*GIRLBOSS* is an extended exercise in motivational personal
branding, in which Amoruso strives to idealize herself while de-
nying that she's interested in any such thing. "I don't want to be
put on a pedestal," she writes. "Anyway, I'm way too ADD to stay
up there. I'd rather be making messes, and making history while
I'm at it. I don't want you to look up, #GIRLBOSS, because all
that looking up can keep you down. The energy you'll expend
focusing on someone else's life is better spent working on your
own." The book was marketed with the language of pop feminism—
Amoruso was successful, her readers wanted to be successful, and
becoming successful was a feminist project—but Amoruso dis-
owns the label: "Is 2014 a new era of feminism where we don't
have to talk about it? I don't know, but I want to pretend that it is."

#*GIRLBOSS* pays enjoyable and genuine tribute to the value of
menial employment: during her crust-punk period, Amoruso
worked at a plant store, an orthopedic shoe store, a Borders book-

store, an outlet mall, a Subway. Briefly, she worked as a land-scaper. But she approached the jobs as if they were a "big, fun experiment," she writes; deep down, she knew that something great was around the corner. The story does have an odd Cinder-ella aspect to it, with money replacing magic. "I entered adult-hood believing that capitalism was a scam, but I've instead found that it's a kind of alchemy," Amoruso writes. (Scams, of course, are also a kind of alchemy, spinning horseshit into gold.) For a while, she stole to support herself, because her political ethos "didn't really jibe with working for the Man." Her first eBay sale was a shoplifted item. What magic! That sale turned into a dozen more, then hundreds, then thousands, and then, soon enough, Amoruso stopped seeing money as a "materialistic pursuit for ma-terialistic people. . . . What I have realized over time is that in many ways, money spells freedom."

Upon release, #GIRLBOSS received reflexive hosannas. Amoruso was profiled in New York. Billboards and taxis adver-tised the book with a cute slogan: "If this is a man's world, who cares?" A few months later, Amoruso's company laid off twenty employees. The next January, she stepped down as CEO. In 2015, a handful of ex-employees sued her and Nasty Gal; several claimed that they had been fired because they were pregnant, and one woman claimed she had been fired because she was laid up with kidney disease. In June 2016, Amoruso was named to Forbes's second-annual list of America's Richest Self-Made Women. In November 2016, Nasty Gal filed for bankruptcy. In 2017, the TV adaptation of #GIRLBOSS premiered on Netflix. Amoruso had thought the series would be free marketing for her brand and her company, she told Vanity Fair. She clarified: "It still benefits me, of course." #GIRLBOSS was canceled during its first season. By then, Amoruso had already left Nasty Gal, cruising away like a shuttle detaching itself from a burning space station. She'd started a new company, called Girlboss, whose slogan was "redefining success for ourselves."

Girlboss is "a community of strong, curious, and ambitious women," the site announces—a company that's "unapologetic in our beliefs and values of supporting girls and women who are chasing dreams both big and small in a shame-free, lame-free zone." Its website features blog posts like "4 Things I Learned as a Millennial Workaholic" and "How Rupi Kaur Built a Career on the Relentless Pursuit of Creativity," but the company is geared toward events: Girlboss holds conferences, or "Girlboss Rallies," which sell VIP tickets for $700 and digital access for $65. "Part conference part experiential inspiration wonderland," the website proclaims, "the Girlboss Rally has taken the tired conference world by storm, creating a space for the next generation of entre-preneurs, intrapreneurs, and thought leaders to meet, hatch plans, and thrive together."

The basic idea here is that, for women, photogenic personal confidence is the key to unlocking the riches of the world. In her memoir, Amoruso writes, "In the same way that for the past seven years people have projected themselves into the looks I've sold through Nasty Gal, I want you to be able to use #*GIRLBOSS* to project yourself into an awesome life where you can do whatever you want." The Girlboss Rallies are supposed to work the same way: you pay to network, to photograph yourself against millennial-pink and neon backdrops, to take the first step toward becoming the sort of person who would be invited to speak onstage. This is meant to scan as a deeply feminist endeavor, and it generally does, at least to its participants, who have been bombarded for many years with the spurious, embarrassing, and limitlessly seductive sales pitch that feminism means, first and foremost, the public demonstration of getting yours. (Later on, The Wing, the wildly successful and meticulously branded women-only coworking space founded by Audrey Gelman and Lauren Kassan, would simultane-ously harvest this acquisitive, performative energy and attempt to make it ineligible for criticism through its self-aware membership, savvy branding, and stated commitments to inclusion, commu-

nity, and safe space. In December 2018, The Wing, by then operating in five locations, raised $75 million, bringing its funding to a
total of $117.5 million. Many investors were female—venture cap-
italists, actresses, athletes. "This round is proof positive that
women can be on both sides of the table," Gelman said.)

The ever-expanding story of Girlboss feminism really begins
with *Lean In*, Sheryl Sandberg's 2013 manifesto, co-written with
Nell Scovell. *Lean In* was sharp, sensible, and effective, urging
women to take ownership of their ambition. Sandberg was the
chief operating officer of Facebook, and, writing years before the
Facebook backlash, she had impeccable mainstream credibility:
she was a powerful, graceful, rich, hardworking, married white
woman, making an argument about feminism that centered on
individual effort and hard work. Early in the book, she acknowledges that her approach presents a partial, private solution to a
huge collective problem. She believes that women should demand
power as a way to tear down social barriers; others believe that
barriers should be torn down so that women can demand power.
Both approaches are "equally important," Sandberg writes. "I am
encouraging women to address the chicken"—the individual
solutions—"but I fully support those who are focusing on the
egg."

Unfortunately, the chicken also happens to taste better. Provided with a feminist praxis of individual advancement and
satisfaction—two concepts that easily blur into self-promotion and
self-indulgence—women happily bit. A politics built around getting and spending money is sexier than a politics built around politics. And so, at a time of unprecedented freedom and power for
women, at a time when we were more poised than ever to understand our lives politically, we got, instead of expanded reproductive protections and equal pay and federally mandated family leave
and subsidized childcare and a higher minimum wage, the sort of
self-congratulatory empowerment feminism that corporations can
get behind, the kind that comes with merchandise—mugs that

said "Male Tears," T-shirts that said "Feminist as Fuck." (In 2017, Dior sold a "We Should All Be Feminists" shirt for $710.) We got conferences, endless conferences—a *Forbes* women's conference, a Tina Brown women's conference, a *Cosmopolitan* Fun Fearless Females conference. We got Arianna Huffington's Thrive Global, which aims to end the "stress and burnout epidemic" through selling corporate webinars and a $65 velvet-lined charging station that helps you keep your smartphone away from your bed. We got Miki Agrawal, who was regularly given media tongue-baths on the subject of Thinx, her line of period panties, until it was alleged that Agrawal, who proudly called herself a "She-E-O," was abusive to her employees and didn't know much or care about feminism at all. We got, instead of the structural supports and safety nets that would actually make women feel better on a systematic basis, a bottomless cornucopia of privatized nonsolutions: face serums, infrared saunas, wellness gurus like Gwyneth Paltrow, who famously suggested putting stone eggs in one's vagina, or Amanda Chantal Bacon, whose company Moon Juice sells 1.5-ounce jars of "Brain Dust" for $38.

On the wings of market-friendly feminism, the idea that personal advancement is a subversive form of political progress has been accepted as gospel. The trickiest thing about this idea is that it is incomplete and insufficient without being entirely wrong. The feminist scammer rarely sets out to scam anyone, and would argue, certainly, that she does not belong in this category. She just wants to be successful, to gain the agency that men claim so easily, to have the sort of life she wants. She should be able to have that, shouldn't she? The problem is that a feminism that prioritizes the individual will always, at its core, be at odds with a feminism that prioritizes the collective. The problem is that it is so easy today for a woman to seize upon an ideology she believes in and then exploit it, or deploy it in a way that actually runs counter to that ideology. That is in fact *exactly* what today's ecosystem of success encourages a woman to do.

I know this because my own career has depended to some significant extent on feminism being monetizable. As a result, I live very close to this scam category, perhaps even inside it—attempting to stay on the ethical side, if there is one, of a blurry line between "woman who takes feminism seriously" and "woman selling her feminist personal brand." I've avoided the merchandise, the cutesy illustrated books about "badass" historical women, the coworking spaces and corporate panels and empowerment conferences, but I am a part of that world—and I benefit from it—even if I criticize its emptiness; I am complicit no matter what I do.

The Really Obvious Ones

What a relief, within this world of borderline or inadvertent or near-invisible scamming, to have a category delineated by egregiousness: the obvious, unmistakable scams. One such scam surfaced in the brief Silicon Valley interest in "raw water," which is untreated and unfiltered spring water—teeming with bacteria, and free from all the tooth-strengthening minerals that come out of the tap. In 2017, the *Times* Styles section ran a piece on the Bay Area raw-water enthusiasts:

> Mr. Battle poured himself a glass. "The water from the tap just doesn't taste quite as refreshing," he said. "Now is that because I saw it come off the roof, and anything from the roof feels special? Maybe."

Gale-force ridicule followed. Stories like this—and the gleeful scorn they engender—are ostensibly a sort of scammer prophylaxis. Those idiots, we think, those morons drinking their tapeworm water: *we* would never be so dumb as to buy *that*. These stories crop up often in the food space, where it is easy for entrepreneurs to capitalize on the endless well of magical thinking that surrounds health and authenticity in our deeply unhealthy and inauthentic environment. Then, once they cross some line of absurdity or ineptitude, we get to make fun of the suckers who fell for the pitch.

Before raw water, there was Juicero, the company that raised nearly $120 million to manufacture $700 juicers. In Juicero's model, fruits and vegetables would be individually packaged in Los Angeles and shipped to Juicero customers, who would put the packs into the Juicero machine, which would scan the packs, cross-check them against a database, and then, finally, make a cup of juice. A Google Ventures partner told the *Times* that the company was "the most complicated business that I've ever funded." The company's founder boasted that his juicers were made out of aircraft-grade aluminum, that they contained ten circuit boards, that they could deploy thousands of pounds of force. But soon after Juicero's machines went on the market, Bloomberg reported that you didn't actually need them. If you squeezed the Juicero packs by hand, you could make juice even *faster* than the juicer. The company became an immediate laughingstock and, within a few months, shut down.

It can be hard, of course, to draw a precise line between a scam and a product with a highly exaggerated sales pitch. One of the only ways to do so is finding a concrete misrepresentation—as a food blogger did in 2015 with Rick and Michael Mast. The Masts were two bearded brothers who lived in Brooklyn, dressed like they were in Mumford & Sons, and made $10 artisan chocolate bars. The Mast Brothers had always advertised themselves as "bean-to-bar" chocolatiers who processed all their cocoa beans in-house. But then a Dallas blogger named Scott Craig exposed the Mast Brothers for being "remelters," meaning that they had melted down and remolded industrial bulk chocolate, wrapped it up in Italian paper, and called it a day. The story broke in another enormous schadenfreude tsunami, with the joke falling first on the Mast Brothers and then, ultimately, as it always does, on the dummies who bought their product. *This is what you gentrifiers get with your hard-ons for artisanal garbage!* the tweets and blog posts cackled. *This is what you Instagram addicts get for paying three months' rent money for a festival no one had ever heard of! This is what you get for being so rich that you need a QR code to make a glass of fucking juice!*

Right around this vicious and satisfying point in the scam news cycle, popular identification often begins to slide toward the scammer, who, once identified, can be reconfigured as a uniquely American folk hero—a logical endpoint of our national fixation on reinvention and spectacular ascent. Stories about blatant con artists allow us to have the scam both ways: we get the pleasure of seeing the scammer exposed and humiliated, but also the retrospective, vicarious thrill of watching the scammer take people for a ride. The blatant scammers make scamming seem simultaneously glorious and unsustainable. (In reality, the truly effective ones, like the prophets of the anti-vaccination movement, can keep going indefinitely, even after they get caught.) In 2016, news broke of a Florida teenager named Malachi Love-Robinson, who had been arrested for posing as a doctor and opening his own medical practice, and then for using false credentials in an attempt to buy a Jaguar, and then for *pretending to be a doctor again.* In 2018, Jessica Pressler at *New York* wrote the definitive story on Anna Delvey, the so-called Soho Grifter, a broke young woman with a mysterious European accent who effortlessly convinced hotels, private jet companies, and a bunch of vacuous art-world scenesters that she was a millionaire heiress who just needed to hold a couple grand. On today's terms, figures like Malachi Love-Robinson and Anna Delvey are highly inspirational. As women's conference after women's conference might have told me had I attended them, it's precisely that kind of self-delusion—deciding beyond all reason that you should have something, and then going for it—that will get you somewhere in this world.

That was, anyway, the preferred tactic for Elizabeth Holmes, the thirty-five-year-old CEO and founder of Theranos, a health technology company that was once valued at $9 billion despite the fact that its revolutionary blood-test technology did not actually exist. A maniacally disciplined blonde with stressed-out hair, a Steve Jobs obsession, and a voice that sounded like it was being disguised to preserve her anonymity, Holmes had become fixated, at age nineteen, on the idea of a machine that could perform a vast array of blood tests from a pin prick. (She had a lifelong fear of needles: this was central to her personal myth.) She founded Theranos in 2004, raised $6 million by the end of the year, and began stacking her board of directors with big names: Henry Kissinger, James Mattis, Sam Nunn, David Boies. She had Rupert Murdoch and Betsy DeVos as investors. Her TED Talk went viral. She got a *New Yorker* profile and a *Glamour* Woman of the Year award; she spoke at Davos and the Aspen Ideas Festival; *Forbes* labeled her the world's youngest self-made female billionaire. And then, in 2015, John Carreyrou published an article in *The Wall Street Journal* exposing Theranos as a shell game. The company, which by then had contracted with Walgreens and Safeway, was performing most of its blood tests using other companies' machinery. Its pin-prick technology had never worked as advertised. Its executives had been cheating proficiency tests.

At first, Holmes resisted the story. In a company meeting, she suggested generating sympathy for herself by revealing that she had been sexually assaulted at Stanford. She went on CNBC and said, "First they think you're crazy, then they fight you, and then all of a sudden you change the world." But Carreyrou was right about everything. For years, Holmes and her boyfriend, Sunny Balwani, had been firing or silencing anyone who knew the truth. In 2016, the Centers for Medicare & Medicaid Services gave Holmes a two-year ban on owning or operating a diagnostic lab. In March 2018, the Securities and Exchange Commission sued her; in return, she consented to return her Theranos shares, give

up voting control, and be barred from serving as an officer of a
public company for the next ten years. In May 2018, Carreyrou
published *Bad Blood*, a book-length investigation of the rise and
fall of Theranos, in which Holmes's belief in her own significance
appears to border on sociopathic zealotry: at one point she proclaims, at a company party, "The miniLab is the most important
thing humanity has ever built." In June 2018, Holmes was in-
dicted by a federal grand jury on nine counts of fraud.

Holmes, unlike Billy McFarland and Anna Delvey, never became the subject of ironic celebration. This is partly because she
did more than scam a bunch of rich assholes. (Americans like it
when this happens, in part because many of us feel, instinctively
and accurately, that rich assholes have generally benefited from
the scams that pushed the rest of the country down.) Holmes
went further: she knowingly toyed with the health of strangers for
the sake of her own wealth and fame. Mostly, though, the scale of
Holmes's fraud is too horrifying to be funny. She was toppled
eventually, but for years, she was one of the biggest success stories
in the world. The absurd length of time that it took for Holmes to
be exposed illuminates a grim, definitive truth of our era: scammers are always safest at the top.

The Disruptors

Amazon, a company now worth $1 trillion, was originally going to
be called Relentless. Jeff Bezos's friends told him that the name
sounded too aggressive, but he hung on to the URL anyway—if you
type in relentless.com, you'll find yourself on Amazon, at which you
can buy almost anything you could think of: an 1816 edition of the
Bible ($2,000); a new hardcover copy of #*GIRLBOSS* ($15.43); a
used paperback #*GIRLBOSS* ($2.37); paranormal romance ebooks
published by Amazon itself (prices vary); a Goodyear SUV tire
($121 with Amazon Prime); a Georgia-Pacific automated paper-

towel dispenser ($35 with Prime); 3,000 Georgia-Pacific paper tow-els (also $35 with Prime); more than 100,000 different cellphone cases under $10; 5,000 pens customized with your name and logo ($1,926.75); a jar of face mask made from sheep placenta and em-bryo ($49); a bunch of bananas ($2.19); a forty-pound bag of Dia-mond Naturals Adult Real Meat dog food ($36.99); voice-controlled Amazon hardware that will tell you the weather, and play you Tchaikovsky, and turn over evidence to the police if it needs to ($39.99 to $149.99); a stream of the 1942 movie *Casablanca* ($3.99 to rent); two seasons of the Amazon show *The Marvelous Mrs. Mai-sel* (free if you're a Prime member, which more than half of Ameri-can households are); a wide variety of data storage and cloud computing services (prices vary, but the quality is unbeatable—Amazon is used by the CIA). My Amazon homepage is advertising two-hour grocery delivery. Fifty-six percent of online retail searches now begin at Amazon.com.

Amazon is an octopus: nimble, fluid, tentacled, brilliant, poi-sonous, appealing, flexible enough to squeeze enormous bulk through tiny loopholes. Amazon has chewed up brick-and-mortar retail: an estimated 8,600 stores closed in 2017, a significant in-crease from the 6,200 stores that closed in 2008, at the peak of the recession. The company has decimated office-supply stores, toy stores, electronics stores, and sporting goods stores, and now that it owns Whole Foods, grocery stores will likely be next. Amazon, which spent years taking huge venture-backed losses so that it could lower prices enough to kill off all the competition, is now, as writers have argued in the *New York Times* and *New York Magazine*, a ques-tionably legal monopsony. (In a monopsony, a single buyer pur-chases goods from the vast majority of sellers; in a monopoly, it's the opposite.) And all of this began when Bezos was working at a hedge fund in the nineties and got the idea to sell books online.

Bezos chose books because they presented a unique market opportunity: whereas physical bookstores could stock and sell only a tiny fraction of all the books that were on the market, an online bookstore could keep a basically unlimited inventory. Books also gave Bezos a way to track the habits of "affluent, educated shoppers," wrote George Packer in 2014, in a *New Yorker* piece detailing Amazon's takeover of the book industry. With this data, Amazon could figure out what else it could sell the way it sold books—at artificially low prices, with razor-thin margins. As long as the company kept growing, "investors would pour in money and Wall Street wouldn't pay much attention to profits." Amazon didn't get out of the red until 2001, seven years after Bezos started the company—at which point it was well on its way to effectively synthesizing human instinct with its consumer interface. Buying something on Amazon, Packer wrote, feels instinctive, reflexive, much like scratching an itch.

Efficiency at this scale requires extreme devaluation. To use Amazon—which I did regularly for years, with full knowledge of its labor practices—is to accept and embrace a world in which everything is worth as little as possible, even, and maybe particularly, people. Its corporate culture is notoriously hellish. In 2015, the *Times* published a story that described Amazon as "conducting a little-known experiment in how far it can push white-collar workers, redrawing the boundaries of what is acceptable." A former employee told them, "Nearly every person I worked with, I saw cry at their desk." Treatment is far worse at the warehouse level, and until recently, the pay was inexcusable: Bezos is the richest man in the world, but his warehouse employees often made just enough to clear the federal poverty line. (Of course, this is part of the reason he's the richest man in the world.) Amazon warehouse workers, unlike most other warehouse workers, are unprotected by unions and often classified as temps, which for years allowed the company to avoid providing benefits and to skirt workers' compensation claims for people who were injured, sometimes seriously, on the job. They enter through metal detectors and spend the day strapped to Amazon-patented monitoring equipment, speed-walking in circles around an enormous, airless, fluorescent-lit warehouse, expected to pack and complete new packages every thirty seconds. (The new Amazon trackers even vibrate to warn workers that they're moving too slow.) As Mac McClelland detailed in her 2012 undercover investigation at *Mother Jones*, managers time their workers' toilet breaks—there are many stories of workers peeing in water bottles to avoid punishment—and if they don't consistently adhere to what Mc-Clelland described as a "goal-meeting suicide pace," they're fired.

Until the company became a target of sustained criticism for its labor practices, in no small part due to a series of worker strikes, Amazon warehouses were often unheated in winter and sweltering in summer: during one heat wave in Pennsylvania, rather than bring in AC units, Amazon chose the solution of parking ambulances outside the doors to collect the people who collapsed. Exhausted workers sometimes passed out on the warehouse floor. It's because of this approach—treating everything, including labor, as maximally disposable—that Amazon has been so successful; it was like Walmart, except beloved even by the wealthy, in large part because the degraded conditions that the company both created and depended on were conveniently concealed behind computer screens. When, in 2018, the company finally responded to public pressure by raising minimum wage for its warehouse workers to $15, it made these changes at the expense of those very workers, taking their holiday bonus incentives and potential stock grants away.

The model of business success in the millennial era is that of dismantling social structures to suck up cash from whatever corners of life can still be exploited. Uber and Airbnb have been similarly "disruptive." Where Amazon worked to avoid state sales taxes, Uber ignored local transportation regulations, and Airbnb ignored city laws against unregulated hotels. With Uber and Airbnb, the aesthetic of rapid innovation—and, crucially, the sense of relief these cheap experiences provide to consumers who are experiencing an entirely related squeeze—obscures the fact

that these companies' biggest breakthroughs have been successfully monetizing the unyielding stresses of late capitalism, shifting the need to compete from the company itself to the unprotected
individual, and normalizing a paradigm in which workers and
consumers bear the company's rightful responsibility and risk.
Airbnb didn't tell its New York City users that they were breaking
the law by renting their apartments. Uber, like Amazon, has been
artificially holding down prices to take over the market, at which
point the prices will almost certainly go up. Driver pay, in the
meantime, has been declining sharply. "We are living in an era of
robber barons," said John Wolpert, in Brad Stone's *The Upstarts*.
(Wolpert was the CEO of Cabulous, an Uber-esque company
that had tried to work with San Francisco's taxi commission instead of against it.) "If you have enough money and can make the
right phone call, you can disregard whatever rules are in place and
then use that as a way of getting PR."

At the other end of the venture-capital disruption spectrum
are a bunch of companies that raked in heaps of money for doing
nothing at all. A company called Twist raised $6 million to build
an app that would text your friends when you were late to something. A social network for people with curly hair, called Natural-
lyCurly, raised $1.2 million. DigiScents, which promised to build
a device that would perfume your home with scents attuned to
your internet browsing, raised $20 million. Blippy, which adver-
tised all your credit card purchases publicly—that was it—raised
$13 million. Wakie, which set people up with human alarm
clocks, strangers who would call them at whatever time they
wanted, raised $3 million. The most infamous of all, maybe, was
the app Yo, whose exclusive function was allowing users to send
the word "Yo" to one another, and which raised $1.5 million in
2014. These companies represent a socially approved version of
millennial scamming: the dream of being a "founder" who gets a
dumb idea, raises a ton of money, and sells the company before he
has to do too much work.

Configured this way, success is a lottery—just as survival today can look like a lottery, too. If you're super lucky, if everyone likes you, if you've got hustle, you might end up making millions. Similarly, if you're super lucky, if everyone likes you, if you can get that GoFundMe to go viral, you might end up being able to pay for your insulin, or your leg surgery after a bike accident, or your $10,000 hospital bill from giving birth. In any case, everything is so expensive that you might find yourself reading about the recent rash of suicides among New York taxi drivers as you take a slightly cheaper VC-subsidized ride from the company that has destroyed the taxi industry. You might find yourself routinely taking advantage of warehouse workers who have to pee in water bottles to get two-day shipping on a box of doggie poop bags you could've bought down the street. This is, in any case, mostly how things have worked out for me, even though my life is so easy, relatively speaking: I don't have dependents, I don't live with a disability— I never needed the reliability of Amazon to do what our current social contract won't.

Aside from this dead-end sense of my own ethical brokenness, what bothers me most about this situation is the idea that our cut-out-the-middleman era has somehow made everyone more equal—that a lack of technological barriers and a surplus of hustle have ushered in a fairer world. But venture capital is social capital, doled out according to networks and affinity and comfort. Seventy-six percent of venture capital partners are white men. Only 1 percent are black. In 2017, 4.4 percent of all VC deals went to companies founded by women, which was the highest percentage since 2006. Until now, only white men have been able to boldly stride forward the way Amazon and Uber did—on a business model of sidestepping regulations, cutting out protections, shoving off liability, and siphoning as much money as possible away from the people who physically do the work. Whenever this changes, whenever women and minorities are allowed to be their own Bezos, it will hardly be a victory for anyone at all.

The Election

The final, definitive scam for the millennial generation is the election of an open con artist to the presidency in 2016. Donald Trump is a lifelong scammer, out and proud and seemingly unstoppable. For decades before he entered politics, he peddled a magnificently fraudulent narrative about himself as a straight-talking, self-made, vaguely populist billionaire, and the fact that the lie was always in plain sight became a central part of his appeal. In his 1987 ghostwritten business book *The Art of the Deal*, Trump—surrounded then, as now, with an aura of cheap skyscraper glitz—coined the phrase "truthful hyperbole," which he called a "very effective form of promotion." Flogging the book on *Late Night with David Letterman*, he refused to clarify the actual extent of his net worth. In 1992, he made a cameo in *Home Alone 2*, giving Macaulay Culkin directions while standing in the Plaza Hotel lobby, surrounded by marble columns and crystal chandeliers. (This was a condition of filming at a Trump hotel: you were required to write him a walk-on part.) That same year, he went bankrupt for the second time. In 2004, the year of his third bankruptcy, he started hosting *The Apprentice*, in which he, the brilliant businessman, got to fire people on TV. It was a gigantic hit.

But Trump's con artistry runs much deeper than false advertising. He has always wrung out his profits through exploitation and abuse. In the seventies, he was sued by Richard Nixon's Department of Justice after crafting policies to keep black people out of his housing projects. In 1980, he hired two hundred undocumented Polish immigrants to clear the ground for Trump Tower, putting them to work without gloves or hard hats, and sometimes having them sleep on-site. In 1981, he bought a building on Central Park South, hoping to convert rent-controlled apartments into luxury condos; when the tenants wouldn't leave, he issued illegal eviction notices, cut off their heat and hot water, and placed newspaper ads offering to house the homeless in the building. He has a long history of stiffing his waiters, his construction workers, his plumbers, his chauffeurs. He once rented out his name to a couple of scammers named Irene and Mike Milin, who ran the Trump Institute, a "wealth-creation workshop" that plagiarized its materials and declared bankruptcy in 2008. He spent tens of thousands of dollars buying his own books to inflate sales numbers. His charitable foundation, which has given almost no money to charity, has repeatedly been found in violation of laws against self-dealing. The approach is hideous even when rendered in miniature: in 1997, Trump played principal for the day at a Bronx elementary school where the chess team was trying to raise $5,000 to go to a tournament. After publicly handing them a fake million-dollar bill and taking photos, he later sent them $200 in the mail.

Prior to his presidential career, Trump's most appalling scam was Trump University, the scheme in which he promised to teach people his get-rich-quick real estate secrets. As soon as the company was operational, in 2005, the New York attorney general's office sent a notification that Trump University, which falsely advertised itself as a "graduate program," was breaking the law for using the word "University" when it wasn't. The company changed its branding slightly and continued on its merry way of convincing people to pay $1,500 to attend three-day seminars, which promised invaluable tricks of the trade but actually delivered trips to Home Depot, basic drivel about time-shares, and sales pitches for the *real* Trump University programs, which would cost them as much as $35,000 up front. In one of the eventual class-action lawsuits, a former salesman testified:

> While Trump University claimed it wanted to help consumers make money in real estate, in fact Trump University was only interested in selling every person the most expensive seminars they possibly could. . . . Based upon my personal experience and employment, I believe that Trump University was a fraudulent scheme, and that it preyed upon the elderly and uneducated to separate them from their money.

Three days before his inauguration, Trump paid out $25 million to settle fraud claims related to Trump University. The settlement was finalized by Gonzalo Curiel, a judge who Trump suggested had overseen an unfair trial for reasons of personal bias—Curiel was Mexican, he noted, and so must hold a grudge against him because he was planning to build a wall.

As president, Trump receives his daily briefings on large note cards printed with information reduced to, as a White House aide put it, "See Jane Run" diction. He became president despite not really wanting to be president, and as the fumes of our young but rapidly sundowning country propelled him to the Oval Office, he made dozens of outlandish empty promises along the way. He promised to prosecute Hillary Clinton, to drop Bowe Bergdahl out of an airplane without a parachute, to make Nabisco produce Oreos in America, to make Apple produce iPhones in America, to bring back all the jobs to America, to get rid of gun-free zones in schools, to give everyone who killed a police officer the death penalty, to deport all the undocumented immigrants, to spy on mosques, to defund Planned Parenthood, to "take care of women," to get rid of Obamacare, to get rid of the EPA, to make everyone say "Merry Christmas," to build an "artistically beautiful" wall between the United States and Mexico that would be the "greatest wall that you've ever seen," to make Mexico pay for that wall, and—funniest of all, sort of—to *never take a vacation as president.* (In his first 500 days in office, he golfed 122 times.) He did all this out of a sort of demented, maniacal salesman's instinct, grabbing rough handfuls of all the things that half-secretly thrilled his base most—violence, dominance, the disowning of the social contract—and tossing them at crowds that roared and roared. When the map started turning red on election night and the dread *Times* meter swung in the opposite direction, I got a nauseating flash-forward to what it might be like, at the end of Trump's presidency, with immigrant families ripped apart, Muslims shut out of the country, refugees denied shelter, trans people stripped of the protections they had just barely begun to come into, poor children with no healthcare, disabled kids without aid, low-income women who couldn't access life-saving abortions—what it might be like when people who subconsciously don't think any of that stuff is personally *too* important start to say, as I'm sure they will, that the Trump era really wasn't all that bad. All politicians are crooks. What's the difference? Why not lend him our country until tomorrow, when everything is already crumbling, and anyway we have so little idea what tomorrow will bring? And here one of the most soul-crushing things about the Trump era reveals itself: to get through it with any psychological stability—to get through it without routinely descending into an emotional abyss—a person's best strategy is to think mostly of himself, herself. As wealth continues to flow upward, as Americans are increasingly shut out of their own democracy, as political action is constrained into online spectacle, I have felt so many times that the choice of this era is to be destroyed or to morally compromise ourselves in order to be functional—to be wrecked, or to be functional for reasons that contribute to the wreck.

In January 2017, Trump held a press conference surrounded by huge, apparently blank stacks of paper. These, he said, were all the documents he had signed to rid himself of conflicts of interest; this was all the paperwork that turned the family business over to his sons. (Naturally, reporters were not allowed to actually examine these papers.) By January 2018, Trump had spent a third of his first year in office at his commercial properties. He had publicly referred to his businesses at least thirty-five times. More than one hundred members of Congress and executive branch officials had visited Trump properties; eleven foreign governments had paid money to Trump companies; political groups had spent $1.2 million at Trump properties. Mar-a-Lago's revenues spiked by $8 million. Profit is Trump's end goal, his singular ambition. He won't fulfill any of his promises—he can't drop Bowe Bergdahl out of a helicopter, or make Mexico pay for a wall, or bring back the postwar economic boom, or quell the nontraditional idea that women and minorities deserve equal rights—but it doesn't matter. As long as he's rich and white and male and bigoted and rapacious, to many people he represents the most quintessentially American form of power and strength. He was elected for the same reason that people buy lottery tickets. It's not the actual possibility of victory that you pay for; it's the fleeting vision of victory. "We're selling a pipe dream to your average loser," Billy McFarland said, on camera, while he was in the Bahamas filming the video ad for Fyre Fest. The pipe dream is becoming the dominant structure of aspiration, and its end-stage shadows—cruelty, carelessness, nihilism—are following close behind. After all, in becoming party to a scam, we access some of the hideous glory of scamming: we get to see, if not to actually experience, what it might be like to loot the place and emerge unscathed.

It would be *better*, of course, to do things morally. But who these days has the ability or the time? Everything, not least the physical world itself, is overheating. The "margin of refusal," as Jenny Odell puts it, is shrinking, and the stakes are getting higher. People are so busy just trying to get back to zero, or trying to build up a buffer against disaster, or trying to enjoy themselves, because there's so little else to count on—three endeavors that could contain the vast majority of human effort until our depleted planet finally ends it all. And, while we do this—*because* we do this—the honest avenues keep contracting and dead-ending. There are fewer and fewer options for a person to survive in this ecosystem in a thoroughly defensible way.

I still believe, at some inalterable level, that I can make it out of here. After all, it only took about seven years of flogging my own selfhood on the internet to get to a place where I could comfortably afford to stop using Amazon to save fifteen minutes and five dollars at a time. I tell myself that these tiny scraps of relief and convenience and advantage will eventually accumulate into something transformative—that one day I will ascend to an echelon where I won't have to compromise anymore, where I can *really* behave thoughtfully, where some imaginary future actions will cancel out all the self-interested scrabbling that came before. This is a useful fantasy, I think, but it's a fantasy. We are what we do, and we do what we're used to, and like so many people in my generation, I was raised from adolescence to this fragile, frantic, unstable adulthood on a relentless demonstration that scamming pays.

We Come from Old Virginia

I wasn't planning on going to the University of Virginia for college. I applied mostly to schools in New England and California; at the time, having spent twelve years in a cloistered, conservative, religious environment, I wanted to get as far away from Texas as I could. For most of my senior year, I dreamed about living in a mysterious future in which I would wear wool sweaters and write for a newspaper and spend my free time in coffee shops cultivating a rigorous life of the mind. But then my guidance counselor nominated me to compete for a scholarship at UVA, insisting that the school would suit me. In the spring, I flew to Charlottesville for the final round of the scholarship competition, which began with the current scholars taking us to a house party, where I sat on a kitchen counter, drank keg beer, and started to feel the dazzle. It felt like cherry bombs were going off outside in the darkness; a strain of easy, fancy Southernness was in the air. The next day, when I walked through campus, the sun was warm and golden, and the white-columned brick buildings rose into a bluebird sky. The students lounged on the grass, glowing with conventional good looks. West of town, the Blue Ridge Mountains raised the horizon in layers of dusk and navy, and the lacy dogwood trees were flowering on every street. I stepped onto the Lawn, UVA's centerpiece—a lush, terraced expanse lined with prestigious student rooms and professors' pavilions—and felt an instantaneous, overpowering longing. At this school, I thought, you would grow like a plant in a greenhouse. This dappled light, the sense of long afternoons and doors propped open and drinks poured for strangers, the grand steps leading up to the Pantheon dome of the Rotunda—this was where I wanted to be.

Charlottesville sells itself this way, effortlessly, as a sort of honey-eyed Eden, a college town with Dixie ease and gracefulness but liberal intellectual ideals. UVA's online guide to Charlottesville opens with an illustration of a hazy golden sunset, the mountains turning purple in the sun's last flare. "A Place Like No Other," the illustration states. "This is a place where the world spins as it should," the narrator in a promotional video says. As UVA's website informs you, Charlottesville has been named the happiest city in America by the National Bureau of Economic Research, the best college town in America by *Travelers Today*, and the number-five US community for well-being, according to a Gallup index. The *Fiske Guide to Colleges* writes that "students nationwide go ga-ga for UVA" and quotes a student who calls Charlottesville "the perfect college town." Another student observes, "Almost everything here is a tradition." A comment on UVA's College Confidential message board reads, "Girls here dress very well and are very physically attractive. The key to get them is alcohol."

When I moved to Charlottesville in 2005, I was sixteen, and nothing about that comment would have seemed off-color to me. I'd spent my whole life in a tiny evangelical school where white male power was the unquestioned default, and UVA's traditionalism, in matters of gender or anything else, did not immediately register. (In fact, on that first visit, I found it comforting. I wrote approvingly in my journal that the political atmosphere felt "moderate, not extremely liberal.") Sure, there were boys double-majoring in history and economics who half-jokingly referred to the Civil War as "the War of Northern Aggression," but this still

seemed like a major leap forward from the outright racism I had
known. UVA was like a live-action recruitment brochure: everyone was always ostentatiously "finding their people," carrying
stacks of books around green expanses, moving from picnics to
day parties in packs of best friends. Classes were just the right
kind of difficult; people were sharp, but generally too basic, myself included, to be pretentious. On weekends, students dressed
up in sundresses and ties to get drunk at football games, and I
liked this air of debauched Southern etiquette, the sweet generic
quality of mid-Atlantic preppy life. For four years I cranked out
papers at the library; I wrapped myself around a boyfriend; I volunteered and waited tables and sang in an a cappella group and
pledged a sorority and sat on my rooftop, smoking spliffs and
reading, as the kids at the elementary school across the road
shrieked. I graduated in 2009, and afterward didn't think much
about Charlottesville. I had loved my time there easily and auto-
matically. Then, in 2014, *Rolling Stone* dropped its bomb.

The feature story, "A Rape on Campus," written by Sabrina
Rubin Erdely, was, now infamously, a graphic account of a gang
rape at Phi Kappa Psi, the UVA fraternity whose white-columned
house looms at the top of a big field off Rugby Road. "Sipping
from a plastic cup, Jackie grimaced, then discreetly spilled her
spiked punch onto the sludgy fraternity-house floor," Erdely
began. It was Jackie's first frat party, and the line sent me into a
wormhole. My first frat party had been at Phi Psi, too: I could see
myself with messy long hair, wearing flip-flops, overwhelmed by
a drinking game and spilling my own cup of punch on the floor.
I'd left soon afterward, crossing the train tracks in hopes of finding a better party. In the *Rolling Stone* story, Jackie was shoved
into a pitch-black bedroom, slammed through the glass of a coffee
table, pinned down, and beaten. " 'Grab its motherfucking leg,'
she heard a voice say. And that's when Jackie knew she was going
to be raped." Erdely wrote that Jackie endured "three hours of
agony, during which, she says, seven men took turns raping her."

One of them hesitated, then shoved a beer bottle into her as the rest of them cheered. After the attack, Jackie ran away from the house, shoeless, with bloodstains on her red dress. She called her friends, who cautioned her against reporting it to the police or the university: "We'll never be allowed into any frat party again." Later on, Jackie disclosed her assault to UVA dean Nicole Eramo. Then, a year later, she told Eramo that she knew two other women who had been gang-raped at Phi Psi. Both times, according to Erdely, Eramo laid out the options available to Jackie, who declined to pursue further action, and the school left it at that. This was unforgivable, Erdely argued, given what the dean had heard.

There was a precedent at UVA for all of this—both this specific crime and the reality of institutional dismissal. In 1984, a seventeen-year-old UVA freshman named Liz Seccuro was brutally gang-raped at Phi Psi, and, by her account, when she reported the crime, a UVA dean asked her if she'd just had a rough night. In 2005, Seccuro received a traumatic validation of her memory when one of her assailants wrote her an apology letter as part of his Alcoholics Anonymous recovery process. (The school had actually given him her address.) UVA's cycle of rape and indifference was such, Erdely wrote, that only fourteen people had ever been found guilty of sexual misconduct in the school's history, that *not a single person* at UVA had ever been expelled for sexual assault, and that UVA's fetishized honor code—in which single acts of lying, cheating, or stealing will trigger expulsion—did not consider rape to be a relevant offense. Erdely noted that the school didn't put Phi Psi under investigation until it learned that she was writing her piece.

When the *Rolling Stone* story came out, I had just moved to New York to take a job as the features editor of the feminist site *Jezebel*. When I got to our dim, brick-walled blog factory in Soho that morning, my coworkers were giving off an odd and heavy silence, reading Erdely's article on their computer screens. I saw the illustration of Phi Psi and realized what was happening. I sat down in my swivel chair and pulled up the story, feeling the call-is-coming-from-inside-the-house nausea that sets in when the news cycle focuses on something that feels private to you. By the time I finished reading, I was dizzy, thinking about my four years in Charlottesville, what I'd been blind to, what I'd chosen to see and not to see. I pictured my college self, never signing up for a women's studies class, funneling my waitressing money toward sorority dues. I remembered that, whenever a classmate in one of my seminars prefaced a statement with "As a feminist," my internal response was "All right, girl, *relax*." I had never attended a Take Back the Night march. Though Liz Seccuro had brought her rapist to trial while I was in college—there's no statute of limitations for rape in Virginia—it had barely crossed my radar at school. (Her rapist was sentenced to eighteen months, ultimately serving six.) I myself had been roofied by a grad student at Georgetown during my first semester at college, while on a weekend trip with a UVA group. Blaming myself for accepting drinks from strangers, and thanking my luck that I'd gotten violently sick shortly after he started touching me, I'd barely talked about the incident, dismissed it as no big deal.

This was a different era. In the five years since my graduation, feminism had become a dominant cultural perspective. Title IX, the 1972 civil rights law that had at first been invoked in service of equal-opportunity college athletics, was now being applied to sexual assault and harassment cases. In a 2011 "Dear Colleague" letter from the Office of Civil Rights, the Obama administration proclaimed, "The sexual harassment of students, including sexual violence, interferes with students' right to receive an education free from discrimination and, in the case of sexual violence, is a crime." There had been several high-profile news stories about college assault and harassment. In 2010, Yale suspended the fraternity Delta Kappa Epsilon for five years after their pledges chanted "No means yes, yes means anal!" in front of the school's

Women's Center. In 2014, Emma Sulkowicz started carrying their mattress across Columbia's campus in protest of the administration finding their alleged rapist not responsible. (They continued carrying the mattress until graduation.) In 2015, two Vanderbilt football players were found guilty of raping an unconscious woman. The struggle to adjudicate campus rape was nationwide news. The *Rolling Stone* article went viral within an hour of being posted, and would end up being the most-read non-celebrity story in the magazine's history. I had changed, too. I was working at *Jezebel*. I felt almost disembodied by dread, in my office chair, thinking about how many women would read the piece and feel the need to compare their stories to Jackie's—to play down the harm they'd faced, to preface their own experiences, as we already do, with "It wasn't that bad."

At UVA and within the school's network, the story was explosive. Reactions were mostly supportive, but they were mixed. My Facebook feed flooded with messages from UVA alumni expressing outrage and recognition; for my boyfriend, a former UVA fraternity member, a number of his college acquaintances expressed a stiff, suspicious distance or disbelief. In Charlottesville, the police department opened an investigation into Jackie's assault. Phi Psi was vandalized. There was an emergency Board of Visitors meeting. Bright Post-it notes and posters—"Expel Rapists," "Harm to One Is Harm to All"—covered the brick walls and buildings surrounding the Lawn. Protesters walked Rugby Road with signs that said "Burn Down the Frats." ("Nobody wants to rape you!" a few people yelled back.) *The Cavalier Daily*, the campus newspaper, overflowed with responses from both students and alumni. Letter writers acknowledged the insidious leeway given to the Greek system on campus; they criticized the school's history of suppressing victims and accusers; they questioned *Rolling Stone*'s intentions and Erdely's cherry-picked account of UVA life. "It feels immensely frustrating to be singled out, when inaction on

rape and sexual assault cases persists across the country," one student wrote. The newspaper's managing board ran an op-ed acknowledging the mood of "anger, disgust, and despair."

A couple of days after the piece went up, Emma, my editor in
chief, asked me if the reporting seemed right. Some details were
off, I said. But people who knew the school recognized what Erdely was talking about. She was right that UVA had a systemic
problem—that the school believed in itself as an idyll, a place of
genteel beauty and good citizenship, and that this belief was so
seductive, so half true, and so widely propagated, that the social
reckonings that had come elsewhere had been suppressed and delayed.

At this point, I had never reported a story or edited a reported
story—Emma had brought me to *Jezebel* from my first job in
media, at *The Hairpin*, a small blog where I mostly edited and
wrote essays. I didn't understand that it *did* matter that the details
were off: that the piece's epigraph came from what Erdely called
a "traditional University of Virginia fight song," which I had never
heard, and which she said was in the standing rotation of an a
cappella group called the Virginia Gentlemen, whose repertoire I
knew from top to bottom because they were the brother group to
my own. If I'd been more experienced, I would have known that
it was actually suspicious, not just a matter of writerly flourish,
that she described Phi Psi as "upper tier." (Phi Psi was, at best,
somewhere in the nondescript middle of UVA's rigid fraternity
caste system—a hard social fact that would have been easy to
check.) I would've noticed the absence of disclosures and paren-
theticals telling the reader how the people in the story—the seven
men who raped Jackie, or the friend who said, as if reading aloud
from a bad screenplay, "Why didn't you have fun with it? A bunch
of hot Phi Psi guys?"—responded to the allegations. I would have
noticed that there was no way, within the story, to tell exactly
how Erdely knew what she knew.

At twenty-five, I was closer to my time at UVA than I was to the age I am now—closer to the idea of being the subject than the idea of being the writer. I didn't know how to read the story. But a lot of other people did.

It didn't take long for journalists to start pulling apart "A Rape on Campus." At first, it seemed possible that the doubters had some ideological motivations. Richard Bradley, who'd previously edited the fabulist Stephen Glass, wrote in his blog that the lede "boggle[d] the mind," and required a reader to "indulge your pre-existing biases" against "fraternities, against men, against the South," as well as "about the prevalence—indeed, the exis-tence—of rape culture." Robby Soave, a blogger at the libertarian site Reason, who had previously written that the movement against campus rape was a large-scale criminalization of campus sex, wondered if the whole story was a hoax.

Then *The Washington Post* interviewed Erdely, who declined to disclose whether she knew the names of Jackie's attackers, or if she had contacted "Drew," the man who had taken Jackie to Phi Psi. Erdely went on the *Slate* podcast *Double X* and skirted the same questions. Then she and her editor, Sean Woods, confirmed to the *Post* that they'd never talked to any of the men. "I'm satis-fied that these guys exist and are real," Woods said. Erdely told the *Post* that by dwelling on these details, "you're getting side-tracked."

Soon afterward, the *Post* reported that Phi Psi had not held a party on the night in question. *The Washington Post* found con-vincing evidence that "Drew" did not exist, at least not as the person Jackie had described. CNN interviewed the friends quoted in the article, who detailed major discrepancies in what Jackie told Erdely and what Jackie had told them. Late at night on De-cember 4, Erdely received a phone call from Jackie and Jackie's friend Alex, who had, apparently, spoken to Jackie about her sto-ry's inconsistencies.

At 1:54 A.M. on December 5, Erdely emailed her editor and her publisher: "We're going to have to run a retraction. . . . Neither I, nor Alex, find Jackie credible any longer." That day, *Rolling Stone* put up a statement, explaining that Jackie had requested that they not contact "Drew" or any of the men who raped her. They had honored this request, as they found her trustworthy, and took seriously her apparent fear of retaliation. But "there now appear to be discrepancies in Jackie's account, and we have come to the conclusion that our trust in her was misplaced." (Later on, that last unfortunate clause, about trust, disappeared.) As I read the note, my eyes kept flicking to one sentence, about how Jackie's friends on campus had "strongly supported" her story. Those friends had supported her emotionally; they'd offered sympathy for the experience she told them about. But they had not *corroborated* her story, or supported it the way a journalist should have been obligated to—the way that walls support a house.

The following March, the Charlottesville police department issued a statement saying that there was no evidence to back up Jackie's account of her assault. Later on, the *Columbia Journalism Review* published an extensive report laying out exactly how Erdely and her editors erred. Jackie and Erdely were subsequently deposed in *Eramo v. Rolling Stone*, a lawsuit lodged by Dean Eramo, who was portrayed as discouraging Jackie from reporting the alleged assault and had been quoted, on Jackie's word alone, worrying that no one would want to send their kids to "the rape school." (In November 2016, a jury found both Erdely and *Rolling Stone* responsible for defamation. Eramo was awarded $3 million in compensatory damages.) Through *CJR*'s report and the court documents, a story behind the story assembles itself.

Something likely happened to Jackie on September 28, 2012. Late that night, she called her friends, distraught. She met them outside freshman dorms, with no visible injuries, and told them that something bad had happened. Soon afterward, she told her roommate that she'd been forced to perform oral sex on five men.

On May 20, 2013, she reported the assault to Dean Eramo and declined to pursue action. A year later, in May 2014, she went back to Eramo to report an act of retaliation—someone had thrown a bottle at her on the Corner, the main social drag, she said—and asserted that she knew two other women who'd been gang-raped at the same frat. Eramo, by her account, encouraged Jackie to report the alleged assault to the authorities and arranged for Jackie to meet with the Charlottesville police; she said that Jackie had two such meetings in the spring of 2014.

Erdely confirmed her assignment around the same time. She was an experienced journalist in her early forties who had recently been given a star contract at *Rolling Stone:* she was set to receive $300,000 for filing seven feature stories over two years. She had written about sexual abuse before. Her 1996 *Philadelphia* article about a woman who had been raped by her gynecologist was nominated for a National Magazine Award, and at *Rolling Stone*, she had recently published two consequential exposés about sexual abuse in the Catholic Church and the US Navy. (In December 2014, *Newsweek* noted that Erdely's reporting on the Catholic Church story was also remarkably flawed.) Her intent, with this new *Rolling Stone* piece, was to follow a single assault case on a "particularly fraught campus," she wrote, in a memo—she wasn't sure which one. But she talked to rape survivors at a few Ivy League schools and was unsatisfied with the stories that turned up. She came down to Charlottesville in the summer of 2014, and heard about Jackie from a former student named Emily, who had met Jackie in a sexual assault prevention group. "Obviously," Emily told Erdely, "her memory may not be perfect." A few days later, Erdely sat down with Jackie, whose story had changed: on September 28, she told the reporter, she had met her friends outside Phi Psi, bloody and bruised and shoeless, after escaping an hours-long gang rape at the hands of seven men. She declined to provide the names of those friends, or the name of the boy who took her to the frat.

The two of them kept talking. In September, Jackie and her boyfriend had dinner with Erdely, who asked about the scars from the shattered glass. "I haven't really seen any marks on your back," the boyfriend said. Jackie told Erdely, "When you've come from a background where you're always told that you're worthless . . . it's like you're an easy target . . . like I was easily manipulated because I didn't have the self-esteem to—I don't know." A week later, Jackie texted a friend, "I forgot to tell you that Sabrina [Erdely] is really nice, but you have to choose your words really carefully because she's taken some things I've said out of context and skewed them a little." She started to get cold feet. In October, one of her friends texted Erdely, "I'm talking to Jackie right now, and she's telling me she 100 percent doesn't want her name in the article." Erdely replied that she was "up for discussing whether she wants to discuss changing her name, et cetera, but I need to be clear about this. There's no pulling the plug at this point." Erdely emailed her photo editor, writing, "Yeah, unfortunately, I would say Jackie is not in great mental shape right now and won't be for a long while." At the end of October, Jackie stopped answering Erdely's calls and texts, but Erdely coaxed her back into the process for fact-checking. In final edits, two all-important disclosures—that Jackie had refused to provide the name of the boy who had taken her to the frat party and that the magazine had not contacted her friends to corroborate her story—disappeared.

The piece came out in mid-November. Erdely gave her suspiciously vague interviews to *Double X* and *The Washington Post*. The day before Thanksgiving, Erdely called Jackie and pressed her for the name of the boy who brought her to Phi Psi, and Jackie said that she wasn't sure how to spell it. In public, the story started to fall apart. In early December, Jackie texted a friend, "I'm so scared. I never even wanted to do this article when it became about my rape. I tried to back out of it, but she said I couldn't." A few days later, she and Erdely had the late-night phone call that triggered *Rolling Stone*'s note from the editor. A week or so after that, Erdely emailed Jackie, finally asking her to explain her changing story. She also asked for the name of someone who had ever seen the scars on Jackie's back.

Under oath, in her deposition testimony, Jackie doesn't admit outright to lying. She is an unreliable narrator, and to some degree, so is Erdely. (And, given that here I'm choosing to see certain things and discard others, as a person does anytime she tells a story, so am I.) But what strikes me in reading the two women's testimonies is the way that the structure of the original violation, the language of force and betrayal, filters into the way that they interacted with each other—in the same way that Title IX procedures often end up replicating the patterns of invasion they set out to address and negate. Jackie remembers Erdely telling her "that there was no way . . . to pull out at that point." She tells the court, "I was under the impression that [the details of my assault] were not going to be published. . . . I wasn't—you know, I was 20 years old. I had no idea that there was an off the record or on the record. I—I was naïve." In her own deposition, Erdely says, "I mean, she was aware it was entirely up to her whether she was going to participate."

What should have been reportorial red flags, too, were passed over as normal parts of the rape recovery process. When Erdely asked to speak to the two women Jackie knew who'd also been gang-raped at Phi Psi, Jackie insisted on serving as a go-between. (She most likely fabricated the texts attributed to them that she eventually showed Erdely.) Erdely believed, reasonably enough, that Jackie only hoped to spare them further trauma. She wasn't too concerned that Jackie's story had changed. "I do know that [rape victims'] stories do sometimes morph over time as they come to terms with what happened to them," she says in her deposition. In this, Erdely replicated the mechanism of self-delusion that's embedded at UVA: she acted as if the story she believed in, that she thought she was working for, was already real.

I have sympathy for the experience of being fooled by what you want to believe in. Good intentions often produce blind spots. It's hard to blame Erdely for believing that Jackie's memory had initially been obscured by trauma. It's easy to understand how a college administrator might believe in her institution's moral progress despite evidence to the contrary, or how a reporter would believe that stories tend to shift in the direction of truth. This is, after all, what happened with Liz Seccuro, the woman who was gang-raped at Phi Psi in 1984. When her rapist, William Beebe, wrote her an apology twenty-one years later, she asked him— having been haunted by an unplaceable feeling—if he was the only one who raped her. Yes, he said. And also, he didn't remember the night the same way she did. In his original letter, he hadn't used the word "rape." He had written, "Dear Elizabeth: In October 1984 I harmed you. I can scarcely begin to understand the degree to which, in your eyes, my behavior has affected you in its wake." In the follow-up letter to Seccuro, he wrote, "There was no fight and it was all over in short order."

"I awoke wrapped naked in a bloody sheet," Seccuro wrote back.

"I am sincere in my recollection," Beebe replied, "though it may not be the whole truth of what happened to you that night."

In her memoir *Crash into Me*, Seccuro writes that she had been a virgin when she was assaulted, and that her dean told her, "Well, you know these parties can get out of control. . . . Are you sure you didn't have sex with this young man and now you regret it? These things happen." Her story was squashed by the school, the police department, and the era she lived in—there were no rape kits at the UVA hospital when she dragged herself there after her assault. Out of options, Seccuro eventually went to a reporter and told her story under a pseudonym: a man had raped her at a frat one night, she said.

Two decades later, after she had Beebe's apology letter, the Charlottesville police began reinvestigating and interviewing witnesses. An officer called her one day. "Liz, you were right," he said. "Beebe was one of three. Three men raped you that night and Beebe was the last. I am so sorry to be the one to tell you this." One of the men "had allegedly been seen digitally raping me," Seccuro writes, "with four men witnessing and cheering as he hiked my sweater above my neck and my skirt above my waist." Another one had left her bleeding and unconscious, and walked to the frat's communal showers, "naked except for a towel, high-fiving friends along the way." Beebe had been seen dragging Seccuro into his room while she was screaming; afterward, he had dragged her body into the bathroom and tried to clean her up. *His* story had become less true with time, and monstrously so: he had come to believe that there was "no fight," that there was plenty of ambiguity, that it was just a confusing, ungentlemanly night.

It seems possible that Beebe, honing the trajectory of his life in recovery, genuinely convinced himself of this over the ensuing decades, and that he contacted Seccuro in part to validate his altered narrative. Conversely, I've always thought that Jackie must have believed, at some deep and bizarre level, in the truth of her imagined story. If she hadn't, she wouldn't have been able to consistently fool Erdely and the fact-checker. I wonder if she thought that a written record, a big-deal *Rolling Stone* piece, would enshrine the narrative she wanted as the truth.

Seccuro published her memoir in 2012, five years after her court case concluded. She suggests in the book that gang-raping a freshman girl might have been some Phi Psi rite of passage, "a tradition of sorts." This is what Jackie suggested to her friends, as well as to Erdely—who, when Jackie noted the similarities between her story and Seccuro's, responded, according to the tape transcripts read aloud in the deposition, "Holy shit. Every hair on my arm is standing up. Seems like more than a coincidence." In her own deposition, Jackie states that a professor assigned *Crash into Me* in a class that she took in 2014. She read only a portion of it, she says—the portion describing Seccuro's assault.

The most generous way to describe Jackie's sense of reality is to say that it was porous. She could lie wildly even in cases where the stakes were low. One of her friends, Ryan, had once received an email from a guy named Haven Monahan—the guy who Jackie later said took her on a date on the night of her rape. (In *Rolling Stone*, Haven was the person identified as Drew.) "Haven," a composite figure whose purported email account was likely controlled by Jackie, forwarded Ryan an email that Jackie had supposedly sent him. It was a love letter about Ryan, and it was lifted almost word-for-word from *Dawson's Creek*. All of this—the fake persona, the dummy email account, the plagiarized letter—was Jackie's casually deranged way of expressing a crush.

Jackie also told Erdely, during one of their interviews, about a *Law & Order: Special Victims Unit* episode that, she said, portrayed a situation like her rape. Erdely admits in the deposition that she never watched the episode. It was called "Girl Dishonored," a lawyer tells her. In it, a young woman is gang-raped at a fraternity, and one of the perpetrators says, "Grab her leg."

At one point during the proceedings, Erdely reads aloud a statement, written the morning that *Rolling Stone* posted its mea culpa, in which she explains that Jackie's "case seemed to get to the heart of the larger story I sought to tell."

"Were you sincere when you wrote those words?" the lawyer asks her.

"Was I sincere?" Erdely replies.

"Were you making that up, or were you being sincere when you wrote those words?" asks the lawyer.

"I don't make anything up," says Erdely.

"Were you being sincere, then, when you wrote those words? Did you believe that statement when you wrote it?" the lawyer asks.

Erdely says yes. But the choice is not always between being sincere and untruthful. It's possible to be both: it's possible to be

sincere and deluded. It's possible—it's very easy, in some cases—to believe a statement, a story, that's a lie.

In April, after *Rolling Stone* retracted the story, UVA's president,
Teresa Sullivan, issued a statement slamming the magazine for
what they had published. "Irresponsible journalism unjustly damaged the reputations of many innocent individuals and the University of Virginia," she wrote. "Sexual violence is a serious issue
for our society, and it requires the focus and attention of all in our
communities. Long before *Rolling Stone* published its article, the
University of Virginia was working to confront sexual violence.
And we will continue to implement substantive reforms to improve culture, prevent violence, and respond to acts of violence
when they occur."

Just like that, we were back to the old story. *Rolling Stone* was
the problem, and the problem had been nullified, and UVA could
continue on as it was. I remembered a late night a few years prior.
In the back corner of a bar after a wedding reception, a woman
told me that she knew a couple of the boys who had played Duke
lacrosse during the 2006 scandal. The boys had been injured permanently, she said—scarred forever, along with their families, by
some whore's disgusting lie. Her anger was raw, palpable, bloom-
ing. It cowed me, and reminded me that most people still find
false accusation much more abhorrent than rape. In 1988, the
Cav Daily published a piece by a student who wrote, "Don't ask
for increased prosecution of allegations of rape until women who
falsely accuse men of rape and attempted rape are investigated
with similar intensity, prosecuted with equal vigor, and jailed for
a greater length of time."

In the Bible, Potiphar's wife tries to seduce Joseph, who has
been enslaved by her rich husband, and cries rape after Joseph
resists her advance. In Greek mythology, Phaedra, the wife of

Theseus, does the same to Hippolytus. These stories, and the many others like them, are framed as obscene anomalies. Rape itself, though, is sanctioned in the same texts. In Numbers, Moses commands his army to kill all the men and the nonvirgin women, and save all the virgin women for themselves. In Greek myth, Zeus rapes Antiope, Demeter, Europa, and Leda. Poseidon rapes Medusa. Hades rapes Persephone. For centuries, rape was viewed as a crime against property, and offenders were often punished by the imposition of a fine, payable to the victim's father or husband. Until the 1980s, most rape laws in America specified that husbands could not be charged with raping their wives. Rape, until very recently, was presented as a norm.

This extends to UVA, which for many decades expelled students for plagiarism while refusing to consider rape a serious offense. From 1998 to 2014, 183 students were kicked out of UVA for honor code violations: one of them had, for example, cribbed three phrases from Wikipedia while on study abroad. When, in the late nineties, a student was found guilty of sexually assaulting another student, named Jenny Wilkinson, UVA punished him by adding a letter of reprimand to his record, which could be removed after a year if he completed an assault education program. Because of student privacy laws, Wilkinson could not protest this outcome in public. "In fact, in a crazy twist, I could have faced charges from the university if I had talked about them," she wrote in the *Times* in 2015. Her assailant, meanwhile, was allowed to keep one of UVA's top honors: he lived on the Lawn.

In the decades that followed, things got microscopically better. After Erdely's story was published, I interviewed one of my former UVA classmates at *Jezebel*, referring to her with the pseudonym Kelly. In 2006, Kelly filed university charges against the student who sexually assaulted her. After ten months, UVA found him guilty. (Again, the rarity of a guilty finding can't be overstated: at the time when I interviewed Kelly, there were only thirteen other guilty findings in the school's history—one of whom was Wilkinson's assailant.) Kelly was assaulted, as many college women are, in the fall of her first semester: she went to a frat party, where a guy she knew poured her drinks until she passed out. In the university's investigation, it came out that a witness had seen Kelly's limp body being carried up the stairs. A nurse visiting her younger brother in the frat that night testified that Kelly's pulse had been "low, in the 20s and 30s." At the hearing, a male faculty member asked Kelly if she'd ever cheated on her boyfriend. But her assailant was found guilty, and suspended for three years.

This was, in the context of UVA's long record of apathy and in-action, an extreme success story. In the year prior to the *Rolling Stone* piece, thirty-eight students had reached out to Dean Eramo to report being sexually assaulted. Only nine of those incidents re-sulted in formal complaints, and only four resulted in misconduct hearings. And, as at most colleges, those thirty-eight reports were the visible fraction of a vast and unseen iceberg. Though I rarely back away from difficulty, I feel sure that, if I had been traumati-cally assaulted in college, I wouldn't have had the courage—or the stamina for the inevitable bureaucratic humiliation—to report.

Erdely noted, in her piece, that "genteel University of Virginia has no radical feminist culture seeking to upend the patriarchy." And it's true that the school is far from radical. But, though I never thought to learn about this while I was on campus, UVA's women have been agitating to change the institution ever since it went coed. "The fact that none of us here are afraid to pursue the truth wherever it may lead," a woman wrote in the *Cav Daily* in 1975, referencing a much-used Thomas Jefferson quote, "pales alongside the fact that many of us have good reason to fear pursu-ing a midnight snack on the Corner." That fall, a local committee surveyed the local statistics—rape was almost twice as prevalent in the town as in Virginia as a whole—and labeled Charlottesville "rape city" in a widely shared report. At the same time, a Jack the Ripper–themed Corner bar called the Minories English Pub put up a sign featuring a nude female corpse dangling from a lamp-post. In the *Cav Daily*, another student wrote, "People are now tired of the rape issue coming up time again and in the news. Well, I'm tired, too; more than you could ever fathom." She had been raped, she wrote, six weeks before. That year, UVA's president, Frank Hereford, sent a letter to a Virginia delegate assuring him that there was no rape problem on campus. He provided ten pieces of evidence that the school was being proactive. Number six was that the student council sold women "alarm devices" at "well below cost." Number nine was that women were locked inside their dorms at midnight.

During this period, UVA's default assumption of male dominion over women became more strident in response to the rise of two student demographic groups that inherently challenged this idea: women and gay men. In 1972, the *Cav Daily* ran a disgusted "humor piece" envisioning a sissy new fraternity called Gamma Alpha Yepsilon, or GAY. The same year as the "rape city" report, the Virginia Alcoholic Beverage Control Authority passed a ruling "prohibiting homosexuals from alcohol-serving restaurants," and UVA used the rule to bar gay people from a pavilion on the Lawn. Hereford, as president, attempted to remove a student named Bob Elkins from his RA position because he was a "professed homosexual." In 1990, a student publication ran a satire piece called "Great to Be Straight," laying out a schedule for a week of heterosexual pride and celebration that included a "Take Back the Bathrooms" march. When I went to football games in college, people would sing UVA's "The Good Old Song," to the tune of "Auld Lang Syne," after every touchdown. After the line "We come from old Virgin-i-a, where all is bright and gay," a huge portion of the crowd always screamed "*Not gay!*"

In the nineties, student conversation started to sharpen around the role that fraternities—a source of violence against women, against gay men, and against their own members—played in the prevalence of sexual assault at UVA. "The only first-week social option is attending Rugby Road fraternity parties," wrote a *Cav Daily* editor in 1992. "Intimidating for some and dangerous for others, the Rugby option is simply not an adequate answer to initial social needs of first-year students." That same year, at Pi Lambda Phi, another UVA fraternity, an eighteen-year-old woman was trapped in a storage room, pinned down on a mattress, raped, and beaten.

In his 2009 history of white fraternities, *The Company He Keeps*, Nicholas Syrett writes, "Fraternities attract men who value other men more than women. The intimacy that develops within fraternal circles between men who care for each other necessitates a vigorous performance of heterosexuality in order to combat the appearance of homosexuality." (The chair of the UVA women's studies department gave a similar statement after the 1992 rape at Pi Lamb: "Fraternities and sororities reinforce the subordinate position that women hold in general," she said. "Men experience a sense of male identity by abusing women and hazing each other.") Syrett writes that fraternity men prove their heterosexuality through "aggressive homophobia and the denigration of women"— through using homoerotic hazing rituals to humiliate one another, and through framing sex with women as something engaged in "for one's brothers, for communal consumption by them."

White fraternities have historically existed for the purpose of solidifying elite male power and entitlement. In the nineteenth century, wealthy men separated themselves from their poorer classmates through the frat system. In the twentieth century, men used frat houses to preserve an exclusively male space in an "increasingly mixed-gender world," Syrett writes. As the idealism of the earliest frats was subsumed, in the twentieth century, by a changing idea of masculinity that increasingly allowed high-class status and low-class behavior to coexist in a single individual, fraternity members "used their status as self-proclaimed gentlemen to justify their less-savory antics. . . . In performing gentlemanliness in public, they justified their existence. What they did behind closed doors was then supposed to be their business alone."

Universities have a tendency to overlook fraternity violence in part because fraternities are a significant source of institutional capital. Frats funnel enormous amounts of alumni money back toward universities, and free them from the obligation to provide housing for their most privileged students. In return, frats enjoy a built-in leeway. Boys who join frats today are mostly conscious of wanting good parties, funny friends, hot girls around every weekend. Underneath this lies the thrill of group immunity, of being able to, on the wholesome end, throw a sink out the window without being written up for property destruction. On the unwholesome end, frats provide social cover to engage in extraordinary interpersonal violence, through the hazing process; to purchase and consume as much alcohol and as many drugs as one wants to; and to throw parties at which everyone is there at the pleasure of the "brothers"—particularly the girls.

As early as the 1920s, Syrett writes, fraternity culture started to explicitly invoke sexual coercion. "If a girl don't pet, a man can figure he didn't rush 'er right," a fraternity member says in the 1923 novel *Town and Gown*. In 1971, William Inge wrote a novel called *My Son Is a Splendid Driver*, based on his experience in a University of Kansas frat in the twenties. The characters go on dates with sorority girls, take them home, and then go back out to solicit sex from prostitutes. One night they participate in a "gangbang" in the frat basement. "I felt that to have refused," the narrator thinks, "would have cast doubts upon my masculinity, an uncertain thing at best, I feared, that daren't hide from any challenge." The woman at the center of the event yells, resigned and aggressive, "Well, go on and fuck me. . . . That's what I'm here for."

Thirty-five percent of UVA students belong to a fraternity or sorority. When I was on campus, people outside the Greek system were referred to as goddamn independents, or GDIs. Because first-year students live in dorms, and mostly can't buy alcohol or throw parties, a huge amount of partying at UVA takes place in frat houses, on frat terms. (Due to the Greek system's dogged adherence to gender traditionalism, sororities aren't allowed to throw parties at all.) There is as much individual variance within the Greek system as within any other: I was welcomed into it despite being openly averse to many of its central features, and Andrew, my partner of a decade, lived in his UVA frat house for two years, volunteered at the daycare across the street on Tuesdays and Thursdays, and remains a sweeter, more sincere person than I am. But it's been well documented that men in fraternities have a higher perpetration rate than college men in general. A recent study at Columbia showed that they are victimized more often, too. The fraternity environment doesn't create rapists as much as it perfectly obscures them: every weekend is organized around men giving women alcohol, everyone getting as drunk as possible, hookups as the performative end goal, and a lockable bedroom only a handful of steps away.

Jackie's false accusation, in this context, appears as a sort of chimera—a grotesque, mismatched creation; a false way of making a real problem visible. In 2017, in a beautiful piece for *n+1*, Elizabeth Schambelan wrote about her own lingering obsession with Jackie's story, which she observed, in retrospect, was guided by a sort of fairy-tale inevitability: a girl in a red dress walked into a wilderness and encountered a pack of wolves. "In retrospect, the failures of its naturalism seem so clear," she writes. "The dark chamber, the silhouetted attackers. . . . But most of all, it's the table, the crystalline pyrotechnics of its shattering. That's the place where the narrative strains hardest against realism, wanting to move into another register altogether." Jackie had woven another version of "Little Red Riding Hood," which Susan Brown-miller once argued was a "parable of rape." A girl is intercepted on her journey by a wolf, a violent seducer, who then disguises himself, and falls upon her, and eats her up.

Schambelan quotes two anthropologists, Dorcas Brown and David Anthony, who in 2012 wrote an article tracking the association of wolf symbols with "youthful war-bands" in ancient Europe "that operated on the edges of society, and that stayed together for a number of years and then were disbanded when their members reached a certain age." These war-bands were "associated with sexual promiscuity," Brown and Anthony write. They "came from the wealthier families . . . their duties centered on fighting and raiding . . . they lived 'in the wild,' apart from their families." In Germanic legend, this organization is called the Männerbund, a word that means "men-league." The men disguised themselves with animal skins, which allowed them to break social restrictions without guilt until their time in the Männerbund was over. "At the end of four years," Brown and Anthony write, "there was a final sacrifice to transform the dog-warriors into responsible adult men who were ready to return to civil life. They discarded and destroyed their old clothes and dog skins. They became human once again." In her piece, Schambelan wonders: once you have formed leagues of men, isolated from their wealthy families, trained for collective wildness—"once you make that choice, as a society, to create that institution, how do you keep the chaos at bay? How do you make sure it never turns against *you*?"

Schambelan suggests that "Little Red Riding Hood" could be a "parable of rape, yes, of rape and murder and the most extravagant transgression imaginable."

But possibly it was less a warning than a ritualized mnemonic. Maybe its function, or one of them, was to ensure that no one could forget or deny the price they had agreed to pay, the price of maintaining a Männerbund, an institution of wolfishness.

There is no darkly romantic teleology here, no unbroken chain of historical inheritance linking wolf boys to frat boys, just as there is no primordial wellspring of masculine violence that forces wolf boys to kill or frat boys to rape. There are two institutions, two leagues of young men, one belonging to an archaic and semi-mythic past, the other flourishing here and now. Institutions, by definition, are not natural or primal. They are not what just happens when you let boys be boys. They are created and sustained for a reason. They do work.

Rape is an inescapable function of a world that has been designed to give men a maximal amount of lawless freedom, she argues. It "cannot, logically, be just a vile anomaly in an ethical system otherwise egalitarian and humane." Writing six months before the Harvey Weinstein revelations and everything that followed, she goes on: "There is, as yet, nothing and no one to make us know [the injustice of rape], nothing to make it public knowledge, knowledge that we all share and that we all *acknowledge* that we share. To create that kind of knowledge, you must have more power than whatever forces are working to maintain oblivion." Perhaps, she suggests, it was in some misguided attempt to claim this power that Jackie told her lie.

In January 2015, in the aftermath of the *Rolling Stone* story, I went back to Charlottesville to write about fraternity rush. It was the first story I'd ever reported, and I was nervous, looking at UVA, feeling my vantage point change from participant to observer. On my first night back, I sat in a booth in the Virginian and drank beer with my friend Steph to calm my jitters, listening for the tone of the chatter in a sea of khaki-and-North-Faced fraternity hopefuls, sorority rushees with tall boots and curled hair.

It quickly became apparent that there was a much larger and deeper story transpiring than what Erdely had captured. The *Roll-*

ing Stone story had arrived in the midst of a season of shocking local brutality, bookended by the death of a young woman named Yeardley Love in 2010 and the fatal white-power rally in 2017. Love, whom I'd met during sorority rush, was murdered in her bedroom by her ex-boyfriend George Huguely, who kicked down her door and brutalized her until her heart stopped. In 2014, a second-year student named Hannah Graham disappeared from downtown. Later, a cab driver named Jesse Matthew was charged with murdering Graham, as well as Morgan Harrington, a girl who'd disappeared five years earlier. He, like Huguely, had a history of violence. He pled guilty in both cases, to murder and to "abduction with intent to defile."

Charlottesville is a small community: it takes just fifteen minutes on the old-fashioned trolley to go from the UVA chapel to the pedestrian mall downtown. These crimes reverberated. One of my best friends from college—a girl named Rachel, blond and white and beautiful, as all these girls had been—was the last passenger Matthew drove in his cab before he abducted and murdered Morgan Harrington, a fact she found out from police much later, in the midst of the intensive Hannah Graham investigation. And yet, at the same time, other young women disappeared and hardly anyone noticed. When Sage Smith, a black trans woman, went missing in the fall of 2012, the police department waited eleven days before requesting external support. In contrast, as Emma Eisenberg noted in a piece for *Splinter*, nearly every law enforcement agency in Virginia knew Graham's name and face within forty-eight hours, with the FBI and a slew of volunteer search groups following close behind. Coverage of Graham was inescapable; coverage of Smith was nonexistent. (Eisenberg told me that she tried twenty-eight outlets before finding one that would publish the piece.) Alexis Murphy, a seventeen-year-old black girl who went missing near Charlottesville in 2013, also received a minimum of press coverage. When a white man named Randy Taylor was found guilty of murdering her, his pale, gaunt face was mostly absent from the news. But Matthew—his dark skin, his full lips, his thick locs—was everywhere you looked.

Charlottesville's history of gendered violence and its history of racial violence, long intertwined, were emerging. A vast undercurrent of trauma and inequity was welling up. Women's bodies have always been test sites upon which governing hierarchies are broken down and reiterated. In the nineteenth century, black men convicted of rape in Virginia got the death penalty, where white men were imprisoned for ten to twenty years. In the first half of the twentieth century, Virginia citizens became very concerned about the rape of white women—but almost exclusively in cases when the accused were black.

Violence against women is fundamentally connected to other systems of violence. Though Erdely tried, it's not possible to capture the reality of rape—or even of fraternities—at UVA without writing about race. When I left Charlottesville that January, I kept thinking about a damning fact that a grad student named Maya Hislop had told me, a fact that had not surfaced either in *Rolling Stone* or in the exhaustive coverage that followed it: UVA's first reported sexual assault occurred in 1850, when three students took an enslaved girl into a field and gang-raped her.

UVA was founded in 1819, by a seventy-six-year-old Thomas Jefferson, who retired from politics to Monticello, his Virginia plantation, and dedicated himself to what at the time was a radical vision: a secular public university that would be accessible to all white men, regardless of whether they were rich or poor. Today, the Thomas Jefferson cult is intrinsic to the UVA experience. Jefferson is frequently, and creepily, referred to as "TJ," or as "Mr. Jefferson." My full ride to UVA came from the Jefferson Scholars Foundation. The school enthusiastically celebrates Jefferson's ingenuity, his integrity, his rebelliousness, his vocabulary. When I was in college, every Valentine's Day, flyers blanketed the campus with Jefferson and his slave Sally Hemings depicted in cameo silhouette, and the cutesy slogan "TJ ♥s Sally" below that.

Sally Hemings was thirty years younger than Jefferson, and she was an infant when she became his property, courtesy of his wife, Martha. Hemings was Martha's slave, and her half sister; she was three quarters white. When she was fourteen, she was put in charge of one of Jefferson's daughters on an overseas voyage. Jefferson met them in Paris, and by the time he left, Hemings was sixteen and pregnant. (At the time, the age of consent in Virginia was ten.) Hemings considered staying in Paris, where the French freedom principle had emancipated her by default. But, according to her son Madison, Jefferson persuaded her to return by promising her "extraordinary privileges," and assuring her that he would free her children once they turned twenty-one.

In "Notes on the State of Virginia," Jefferson muses that blacks are "much inferior" to whites in their critical capacities, and that the obvious inferiority of black people is "not the effect merely of their condition of life." It may have been *because* of these views, not in spite of them, that Hemings, a light-skinned ladies' maid, appeared particularly attractive. The relationship was an open secret. In 1818, the *Richmond Recorder* wrote, "It is well known that the man, whom it delighteth the people to honor, keeps, and for many years past has kept, as his concubine, one of his own slaves. Her name is SALLY." But Jefferson never commented, and so the story was suppressed. (One of his grandchildren wrote in a letter, "I would put it to any fair mind to decide if a man so admirable in his domestic character as Mr. Jefferson . . . would be likely to rear a race of half-breeds. . . . There are such things, after all, as moral impossibilities.") He did free Hemings's children before he died, but not Hemings herself, who was freed by Jefferson's daughter in 1834. In 1835 she died, and was buried in an unmarked grave that likely lies under a parking lot near the Hampton Inn in downtown Charlottesville. Jefferson, of course, is buried at Monticello, along with his descendants—the white ones.

In 1987, Monticello was designated, along with the UVA campus, as a UNESCO World Heritage Site. It remains a popular tourist destination in Charlottesville, and it has been steadily altering its programming to acknowledge the lived reality of Jefferson's slaves. In 2018, Monticello finally mounted an exhibit about Hemings, which depicted her in silhouette—there is no record of what she looked like—and noted, "Enslaved women had no legal right to consent. Their masters owned their labor, their bodies, and their children." Annette Gordon-Reed, whose 1997 book on Jefferson and Hemings cemented the truth about their relationship, points out that Martha had no legal right to refuse her husband, either. (Spousal rape was not criminalized in Virginia until 2002, and the state senator Richard Black is still fighting to decriminalize it.) A *Times* piece about the Monticello exhibit mentions the inevitable backlash, quoting a woman in the Thomas Jefferson Heritage Society, which is dedicated to disputing the narrative that Jefferson fathered Hemings's children. "Some nights I just curl up in the semidark and just read his letters," the woman said. "He just doesn't seem to be a person who would do this."

This tension between honorable appearances and unsavory reality was embedded at UVA in the nature of its founding. "The school was new and experimental, unsure of the public's support and uncertain of its own future," write Rex Bowman and Carlos Santos in *Rot, Riot, and Rebellion*, their 2013 history of UVA in its infancy. "No powerful church denomination backed the university, no well-connected alumni group stood ready to come to its defense. Its leaders understood that student drunkenness, violence, and rebellion could result in the university's ruin." The students, drawn from the Southern slave-owning class, were uncontrollable nonetheless. In the classroom, they displayed an "exaggerated sense of self-importance." Outside class, they drank and fought. A teacher in Fredericksburg called the school "a nursery of bad principles." A student wrote, "Here nothing is more common than to see students so drunk as to be unable to walk." Bowman and Santos note that Jefferson believed that "pride, ambition, and morality would lead students to behave. . . . Students' honor would make strict rules unnecessary." But the concept of honor, particularly where white men and the South are concerned, is inextricably tied to violence. UVA's greatest self-designated virtue served, from the beginning, as cover and fuel for its greatest sins.

From even these early days, administrators feared student violence primarily as a publicity problem. "A murdered student would bring unwanted attention to the students' widespread lawlessness," write Bowman and Santos, as well as "bad publicity to a university bent on protecting a fragile image as a quiet 'academical village.'" The school suppressed compromising information: after a typhoid outbreak in 1828 that killed three students, UVA failed to officially record the deaths or report them to the state, as was required by law. After a resurgence of typhoid the next year, students began withdrawing. Robley Dunglison, UVA's first professor of medicine, suggested that these students were spreading "an alarm throughout the Country highly calculated to injure the institution."

All of this has been swept behind the curtain of Thomas Jefferson's reputation. UVA boosters point out that he wrote legislation opposing slavery, even though he also brought slaves to the White House, and used them as human collateral for the debts he accrued while turning Monticello into a future UNESCO landmark. On UVA's opening day, enslaved people—construction workers, cooks, laundresses—outnumbered the students. There are very few traces left of the lives of enslaved women at UVA, and yet it was on these women's perceived lack of personhood that the personhood of UVA students was established. The first recorded sexual assault on campus took place seven months after the school opened, when two students stormed into a professor's house and stripped an enslaved woman of her clothes. The men who studied medicine under the supervision of Robley Dunglison owed their education in part to the work of one enslaved woman named Prudence, who cleaned blood off the floors of the Anatomical Hall.

UVA didn't go coed until 1970. Before that, on the terms of the university, women were fundamentally other. Women were prohibited from walking on the Lawn when school was in session—an "unwritten rule," the *Cav Daily* notes, that was enforced until the twenties. In 1954, in response to a proposal that "house moms" be installed in dormitories, one student joked to the paper, "I think housemothers would be fine if they were deaf, dumb, and blind, their arms and legs cut off, and would be contented with bread and water while being chained to the basement furnace." In April of the same year, a nineteen-year-old girl was brutally gang-raped in a Lawn room. She was brought there by a date just before two in the morning; she emerged, dazed and beaten, at ten A.M.

The girl, who was from a well-connected family, went to her parents soon afterward. Her parents went directly to Colgate Darden, UVA's president at the time. Darden expelled or suspended all twelve men who were involved in the gang rape, a move that provoked widespread anger on campus. Three of the accused wrote a letter to the *Cav Daily* saying that they were "charged only with a failure to put a halt to the actions of others." Darden stuck to his convictions, and the students rose up, submitting a sixteen-page formal complaint to the university. A hundred men showed up at a faculty meeting to protest. Soon afterward, students lobbied to change the structure of the university's government. They formed a student judiciary committee that would, the *Cav Daily* noted, "return the disciplinary power of the President's Office to the student body with a machinery vastly different from that of previous years." Student self-governance is a Jeffersonian ideal, and it remains one of UVA's proudest practices. The Office of the Dean of Students lists it first in a line of traditions that make the school a "special place."

A month after the 1954 gang rape, the Supreme Court handed

down *Brown v. Board of Education*. Harry F. Byrd, the senator who controlled Virginia politics, began promoting the program known as Massive Resistance—a group of laws that would reward students who opposed integration and close any public school that complied. In 1958, Charlottesville closed down its schools for five months rather than admit black students. In 1959, a federal judge overruled this, ordering that nine black students be admitted to Venable Elementary—the school on Fourteenth Street, whose shrieking recess breaks I used to observe with a beer on my roof. My friend Rachel, the one who rode in Jesse Matthew's cab just before he killed Morgan Harrington, now sends her own daughters to Venable. The girls are twins, gorgeous and funny and brilliant; Andrew and I are their godparents. Some days I feel crazed with hope and certainty that the world they grow up in will be unrecognizably different. And yet, on the day of the Unite the Right rally, David Duke and his band of white supremacists marched right by Rachel's house.

College towns, which turn over their population every four years, are suffused with a unique and possibly necessary sort of amnesia. If you know the history, you have to remake it, or at least believe that remaking it is possible. You have to believe that there is a reason *you* are there now, not the people who got it all so wrong before. More likely, though, you feel like you're the only person who's ever stepped on campus. Most likely you have no tangible sense of historical wrongdoing. The ugliness, the trauma, of UVA's past half decade is related to how intensely and consistently the school has tried to suppress the idea that it could ever be ugly or traumatic. (The same is true of America under Trump.) The school's self-conception will never become completely true until it can admit the extent to which it has always been false: that its fetishized campus was built by slave laborers; that it has, in fact, a long history of gang rape; that Alderman Library, where I spent so many nights writing terrible papers, was named after a staunch eugenicist who, as president of the university, thanked the Ku Klux Klan for a donation with the sign-off "Faithfully yours."

Years have elapsed since the *Rolling Stone* story. Much of what Erdely wanted to achieve with her reporting has, within the past two years, come to pass. The public has been galvanized by sexual assault reporting, riveted by stories of abuse and institutional indifference. I sometimes wonder: if *Rolling Stone* hadn't botched this piece in such a spectacular fashion, would the wave that came later have been so relatively impeccable? With the coverage of the accusations against Bill Cosby, starting with *New York*'s groundbreaking 2015 cover, and with the Harvey Weinstein story and everything that followed, reporters avoided presenting any single woman or experience as broadly representative. They demanded a lot of their subjects, and in doing so, strengthened their subjects' positions. They showed their readers what they, as reporters, knew and did not know.

Things have started to change at UVA, too. Students have stopped yelling *"Not gay!"* during the school song. (Now they yell *"Fuck Tech!,"* a reference to UVA's Virginia Tech rivalry.) No one says "GDI." Young people readily call themselves feminists. There's a discussion about renaming Alderman Library, and there's a Charlottesville chapter of the Democratic Socialists of America. Sexual assault prevention is now a major part of new student orientation—even though this sort of programming is, at any school, effective mostly in that it raises awareness of the issue. The percentage of UVA students who report confidence in their school's ability to handle a sexual assault complaint has doubled, although the total percentage remains under fifty. And during the year that followed the Weinstein story, the year that ended with Brett Kavanaugh's confirmation to the Supreme Court, female students at UVA continued to write to me, telling me, often, that they'd been assaulted and essentially written off.

I recently talked to a young woman who I'll call by her middle name, Frances—a preternaturally bright-eyed and indomitable character, the sort of person you'd expect to see riding a bicycle with tulips in the basket down a sunny street. Frances had started school at UVA in the fall of 2017, and a month into her first semester, she told me, she was sexually assaulted in her dorm room. The next morning, she asked a friend to take photos of the bruises on her neck, where her assailant had choked her. She reported the assault that day, and her assailant was suspended indefinitely within a week. "I felt so unilaterally supported by the student body," she told me—as well as by the police department, which charged her assailant with sexual battery and strangulation and, later, perjury. (On the positivity of her police interactions, she acknowledged, matter-of-factly, "I'm also a white girl.") In the months that followed her assault, she tried to keep busy with the bureaucracy of the reporting process; she got a therapist, whom she talked to about her recurring dreams about her assailant. In one of these dreams, she'd be alone in a room with him, unable to unlock her phone to call for help.

Frances and I spent a long time talking about the way UVA sells itself. She grew up in the Pacific Northwest, and visited UVA for the first time in the fall of her junior year of high school. "I was in love immediately, from that first moment, stepping onto the Lawn at night," she said. "It was perfect." After that visit, she put photos of the Rotunda and Charlottesville on her computer and phone screens. "I wanted all of it, the carols on the Lawn by candlelight, this bastion of the 'illimitable freedom of the human mind,'" she said, quoting Jefferson. She was thirteen when the *Rolling Stone* story came out, and she didn't read it. She still hasn't. She knew it was discredited. And maybe, she thought, UVA could still be all the things that it said it was.

After months of investigation, UVA found Frances's assailant not guilty. He was free to return to campus. (She wrote to me in the fall of her second year—he had, in fact, returned.) The school issued a 127-page report that effectively concludes that she is un-reliable. "They painted me as some drunken party girl who was out to flirt, and things got a little out of control, and I was embarrassed and couldn't handle the consequences," she told me. I read the entire report, and by the end felt physically debilitated. In a writ-ten statement, her assailant agreed that there was a sexual encoun-ter, and that Frances had physically struggled against him in her attempt to end the encounter. He asserted that he had stopped at an appropriate time. The report noted that—understandably enough—there were significant incongruities between Frances's behavior toward her assailant before the incident and her state-ments after the incident occurred. Following from this, and from the school's obligation to presume non-responsibility, the encoun-ter was essentially deemed acceptable: the unspoken conclusion was that Frances was either lying, or deceiving herself, or rightfully to blame. It filled me with anesthetizing despair to remember that her experience was itself the product of enormous change. Frances had been taken seriously by her friends and by the police depart-ment. UVA had suspended her assailant and conducted a thorough and procedurally correct inquiry. But still, she had been assaulted after a party her first semester. Still, the school had decided it wouldn't be fair to hold her assailant responsible. The things that defined her selfhood—her verve, her confidence, her eagerness—had been devastated just as they were reaching a peak. Everyone was technically doing what they were supposed to, and yet it felt like a glass structure was being constructed around some unfath-omable rot.

The recent shift in the broader social understanding of sexual assault has been so dramatic and so overdue that it has obscured the fact that our systems still mostly fail on this particular topic—that, as demonstrated by the Kafkaesque Title IX bureaucracy, these systems are unequal to a crime that our culture actively manufactures. No crime is confounding and punitive the way rape is. No other violent offense comes with a built-in alibi that

can instantly exonerate the criminal and place responsibility on
the victim. There is no glorified interpersonal behavior that can
be used to explain robbery or murder the way that sex can be
used to explain rape. The best-case scenario for a rape victim in
terms of adjudication is the worst-case scenario in terms of experience: for people to believe you deserve justice, you have to be
destroyed. The fact that feminism is ascendant and accepted does
not change this. The world that we believe in, that we're attempting to make real and tangible, is still not the world that exists.

I've begun to think that there is no room for writing about
sexual assault that relies on any sense of anomaly. The truth about
rape is that it's not exceptional. It's not anomalous. And there is
no way to make that into a satisfying story.

While writing this, I found Jackie's long-dormant wedding registry on the internet. As I snooped through it, I pictured the house
where she lives under a new last name—its cheerful kitchen, with
red enamel apples on the paper-towel holder; the sign in the en-
tryway that says, "Gratitude Turns What We Have into Enough."
I felt an awful contempt flooding through me. Earlier that day, I'd
read her entry on Encyclopedia Dramatica, the troll Wikipedia:
"Does this mean lying whore Jackie . . . owes us a free gangbang
now?" it asked. "How about Sabrina Rubin Erdely? SHE deserves
a good chokefucking, no?" I had recoiled, partly because of the
language and partly out of a shocking sense of recognition: I resent
the two of them, too. There's a part of me that feels as if Jackie
and Erdely inadvertently sentenced me to a life of writing about
sexual violence—as if I learned to report on a subject so personal
that it imprinted on me, as if I will always feel some irrational
compulsion to try to undo or redeem two strangers' mistakes.

But I know how easily anger is displaced on this particular topic.
I know that what I really resent is sexual violence itself. I resent the
boys who never thought for a second that they were doing any-

thing wrong. I resent the men they've become, the power they've amassed through subordination, the self-interrogation they ostentatiously hold at bay. I hate the dirty river I'm standing in, not the journalist and the college student who capsized in it. I understand that we have all shared in the same project, in some way. Schambelan writes, in her *n+1* essay:

> This is the story I've come up with, about the story Jackie told: she did it out of rage. She had no idea she was enraged, but she was. Something had happened, and she wanted to tell other people, so that they would know what happened and how she felt. But when she tried to tell it—maybe to somebody else, maybe to herself—the story had no power. It didn't sound, in the telling, anything like what it felt like in the living. It sounded ordinary, mundane, eminently forgettable, like a million things that had happened to a million other women—but that wasn't what it felt like to her.

At the close of her piece, Schambelan guesses at what Jackie might have been trying to say. It "can't be said reasonably," she writes. "It must be said melodramatically. Something like: Look at this. Don't you fucking dare not look. . . . You're going to know what we've decided is worth sacrificing, what price we've decided we're willing to pay to maintain this league of men, and this time, you're going to remember."

When I think about Jackie now, I think about the year that I came within striking distance of this fevered derangement—never at UVA, only after I graduated, when I moved to Kyrgyzstan, an obscure, beautiful, illogical post-Soviet republic, to serve in the Peace Corps. A week after our arrival in March, the government was overthrown in a conflict that killed eighty-eight people and injured almost five hundred. Later that summer, there was a rash of genocidal violence against the country's Uzbek population: two thousand people were killed, and one hundred thousand people were displaced. I was evacuated twice to the now-closed American military base near the Kyrgyz capital, which staged air force missions to Afghanistan, and a third time to the border of Kazakhstan. Between these periods of upheaval, I lived in a mile-long village tucked deep in the snowy mountains, taught English to high school students, and completely lost my mind.

Kyrgyzstan, by some official measures, was far ahead of the United States in terms of gender equality. The interim president after the 2010 revolution was a woman. Female politicians were introducing waves of progressive legislation in parliament. The country's constitution, unlike ours, ensured equal rights. But in the texture of everyday living, the country was run on what seemed like astonishingly constrictive male terms. In public, I made sure my knees and shoulders were covered. Soon after I met my preteen host sister, she earnestly warned me to watch out for men who would grab me on the bus. There's an old Kyrgyz tradition of "bride kidnapping," in which men snatch up women in public and then hold them hostage until they agree to get married. Today this tradition is mostly staged, as a form of elopement, but it hasn't disappeared. Domestic violence was ubiquitous. Women volunteers were harassed constantly—Asian women in particular, because we bore some plausible resemblance to the locals. I got used to cab drivers taking long detours and engaging me in extraordinarily invasive conversations before they finally relented and took me home. When Andrew came to visit, a local man asked him—jokingly, but repeatedly—if he had a gun, and if he would be willing to fight to keep his wife.

A claustrophobia began to set in on the dusty streets, on long bus rides, under the wide, extraterrestrial sky. Tight security restrictions had been imposed on us because of the ambient conflict, but of course I broke them, because I was lonely, and I wanted to hang out and keep busy, and I felt I had the right to do what I wanted to do. As that was not strictly the case, I spent several months "grounded" to my village as punishment, where I started to feel even more skittish—looking over my shoulder when I took walks in the mountains, never sure if the men I saw were following me or if I was just going insane. One day, my host father, drunk and leaning in, I thought, for a cheek kiss, grabbed me and kissed me on the mouth. I sprinted away and called a friend, then called a Peace Corps administrator, asking if I could go stay in the capital city for a little while. He suggested that, given my reputation in the office, I was just looking for an excuse to go party with my friends. And in fact, I *was* hoping to go party with my friends, because I wanted to distract myself from the fact that my host father had kissed me. The entire incident confused me deeply. Worse things had happened to me in college, and a kiss is whatever, and I didn't understand why this one suddenly felt like a big deal. I had always found it easy, even automatic, to dismiss sexual harassment as I had experienced it. I had always believed that unwanted sexual aggression was a sign of humiliating weakness in the aggressors; I'd always thought myself to be self-evidently better than anyone who would try to coerce or overpower me. But here, I was supposed to be humble. I wasn't better than anyone. I was supposed to—I wanted to—adhere to other people's norms.

Later on, after I left Kyrgyzstan, a year early, it became clear to me that I had been depressed. I was twenty-one, and I was trying my hardest to be permeable, to be alive to other people's suffering, but I didn't know how to stop being permeable when it was pointless, when it was ultimately narcissistic, when it did no good. I felt, monstrously, that there was no boundary between my situation and the larger situation, between my tiny injustices and the injustices everyone faced. I was so naïve, and violence seemed to be everywhere: a bus thundering through my village at night hit a person and kept driving; a drunk man threw a child against a wall. It was the first time that I fully understood myself to be subsumed within a social system that was unjust, brutal, punitive—that women were suffering because men had dominion over them, that men were suffering because they were expected to perform this dominion, that power had been stacked so unevenly, so long ago, that there was very little I could do.

This resulted in a state of mind that felt delusional and paranoid and underwater, so much so that I'm still not sure what exactly happened, whether I was overestimating or underestimating the danger I was in in any given situation, whether I was imagining the boys at the market who grabbed me as I walked past them on a side road, or the extra twenty minutes I spent in the cab begging the driver to take me home—or if, in the fifteen seconds that elapsed between my host father kissing me and me calling my friend, I had somehow simply imagined, or, worse, somehow *instigated*, the whole encounter. I was furious when my administrator blew me off, and I buried my anger because I understood that I was being entitled: I could terminate my service anytime I wanted to; I had it so easy compared to every local woman I knew. But even the suggestion that I was making something out of nothing made me wonder if I was, in fact, making something out of nothing. I started *wanting* things to happen to me, as if to prove to myself that I wasn't crazy, wasn't hallucinating. Spiky with resentment, I glared at men who looked at me too closely, daring them to give me another event to write down in my little secret file of incidents, daring them to make visible the dawning sense I had of women living in a continual state of violation, daring them to help me realize that I wasn't making any of this up. I wish I had known—then, in Peace Corps, or in college—that the story didn't need to be clean, and it didn't need to be satisfying; that, in fact, it would never be clean or satisfying, and once I realized that, I would be able to see what was true.

The Cult of the Difficult Woman

Over the past decade, there's been a sea change that feels both epochal and underrecognized: it is now completely normal for women to understand their lives, and the lives of other women, on feminist terms. Where it was once standard to call any unmanageable woman crazy or abrasive, "crazy" and "abrasive" now scan as sexist dog whistles. Where media outlets used to scrutinize women's appearances, they still do—but in a *feminist way*. Slut-shaming went from a popular practice in the early 2000s to a what-not-to-do buzzword in the late 2000s to a hard cultural taboo by 2018. The ride from Britney Spears getting upskirted on tabloid covers to Stormy Daniels as likable political hero has been so bumpy, so dizzying, that it can be easy to miss the profundity of this shift.

The reframing of female difficulty as an asset rather than a liability is the result of decades and decades of feminist thought coming to bear—suddenly, floridly, and very persuasively—in the open ideological space of the internet. It's been solidified by a sort of narrative engineering conducted both retrospectively and in real time: the rewriting of celebrity lives as feminist texts. Feminist celebrity discourse operates the way most cultural criticism does in the social media era, along lines of "ideological pattern-recognition," as Hua Hsu put it in *The New Yorker*. Writers take a celebrity's life and her public narrative, shine the black light on it, and point to the sexism as it starts to glow.

Celebrities have been the primary teaching tools through which online feminism has identified and resisted the warping force of patriarchal judgment. Britney Spears, initially glossed as a vapid, oversexed ingénue-turned-psycho, now seems perfectly sympathetic: the public required her to be seductive, innocent, flawless, and bankable, and she crumbled under the impossibility of these competing demands. In life, Amy Winehouse and Whitney Houston were often depicted as strung-out monsters; in death, they are understood to have been geniuses all along. Monica Lewinsky wasn't a dumb slut, she was an ordinary twentysomething caught in an exploitative affair with the most powerful boss in America. Hillary Clinton wasn't a shrill charisma vacuum incapable of winning the trust of ordinary people, but rather an overqualified public servant whose ambitions were thwarted by her opponents' bigotry and rage.

Analyzing sexism through female celebrities is a catnip pedagogical method: it takes a beloved cultural pastime (calculating the exact worth of a woman) and lends it progressive political import. It's also a personal matter, because when we reclaim the stories that surround female celebrities, stories surrounding ordinary women are reclaimed, too. Within the past few years, feminist coverage—fair coverage, in other words—has increasingly become standard across the media. The Harvey Weinstein story, and everything that followed, was possible in no small part because women were finally able to count upon a baseline of feminist narrative interpretation. Women knew their stories of victimization would be understood—not by everyone, but by many people—on their terms. Annabella Sciorra could acknowledge that rape had led to her effective banishment from the industry; Asia Argento could acknowledge that she dated Weinstein after he raped her. (Weinstein has yet to face trial for these allegations, and continues to deny them.) Both women could trust that these facts would not, in this new climate, render them suspicious or pathetic. (The coverage of the awful coda to Argento's story—the allegation, denied by Argento, that she had later sexually assaulted a much younger co-star—was also relatively complex and measured, with outlets condemning her behavior and acknowledging that abuse begets abuse.)

In turn, when presented with stories about famous women as *subjects*, not objects, massive numbers of ordinary women recognized themselves in what they saw. Women were able to articulate facts that often previously went unspoken: that entering a relationship with someone doesn't preclude being victimized by them, but sometimes follows it, and that being sexually harassed or assaulted can ruin your career. Women could see, through Hillary Clinton, how much this country despises a woman who wants power; through Monica Lewinsky, sold out by both Clintons, how easily we become casualties of other people's ambition; through the coverage of Britney Spears's breakdown, how female suffering is turned into a joke. Any woman whose story has been altered and twisted by the force of male power—so, any woman—can be framed as a complicated hero, entombed by patriarchy and then raised by feminists from the dead.

But when the case for a woman's worth is built partly on the unfairness of what's leveled at her, things get slippery, especially as the internet expands the range and reach of hate and unfair scrutiny into infinity—a fact that holds even as feminist ideas become mainstream. Every woman faces backlash and criticism. Extraordinary women face a lot of it. And that criticism always exists in the context of sexism, just like everything else in a woman's life. These three facts have collapsed into one another, creating the idea that harsh criticism of a woman is itself always sexist, and furthermore, more subtly, that receiving sexist criticism is in itself an indication of a woman's worth.

When the tools of pop-feminist celebrity discourse are applied to political figures like Kellyanne Conway, Sarah Huckabee Sand-

ers, Hope Hicks, and Melania Trump—as they are, increasingly—
the limits of this type of analysis start to show. I have wondered if
we're entering a period in which the line between valuing a
woman *in the face of* mistreatment and valuing her *because* of that
mistreatment is blurring; if the legitimate need to defend women
from unfair criticism has morphed into an illegitimate need to
defend women from criticism categorically; if it's become possible
to praise a woman specifically because she is criticized—for that
featureless fact alone.

The underlying situation is simple. We are all defined by our historical terms and conditions, and these terms and conditions have
mostly been written by and for men. Any woman whose name has
survived history has done so against a backdrop of male power.
Until very recently, we were always introduced to women through
a male perspective. There is always a way to recast a woman's life
on women's terms.

You could do this—and people have done this—with the entire Bible, starting with Eve, whom we might see not as a craven
sinner but as a radical knowledge-seeker. Lot's wife, turned into a
pillar of salt for daring to look back at burning Sodom and Go-
morrah, could exemplify not disobedience but rather the dispro-
portionate punishment of women. Lot, after all, was the one who
offered up his two virgin daughters to be raped by a mob of
strangers, and later impregnated both of them while living in a
cave. My Sunday school teachers spoke kindly of Lot, as a man
who had to make difficult choices; in art, he's portrayed as an
Everyman, overcome by the temptations of young female flesh. In
contrast, all his wife did was crane her neck around, and she was
smited forever, unglamorously. And the temptresses, of course,
beg for a retelling: Delilah, portrayed as a lying prostitute who
delivered her lover to the Philistines, seems today like just another woman seeking pleasure and survival in a compromised

world. From the biblical perspective, these women are cautionary tales. From the feminist one, they demonstrate the limits of a moral standard that requires women to be subservient. Either way, their allure is baked right in. "Of course the bitch persona appeals to us. It is the illusion of liberation," Elizabeth Wurtzel writes in her 1998 book *Bitch*, a precursor to the wave of feminist cultural criticism that has now become standard. Delilah, writes Wurtzel, "was a sign of life. I lived in a world of exhausted, taxed single mothers at the mercy of men who overworked and underpaid them. . . . I had never in my life encountered a woman who'd brought a man down. Until Delilah."

Delilah is a useful example, as the power she seized was inextricable from the expectation that she would be powerless. Samson was a colossus: as a teenager, he ripped a lion apart limb from limb. He killed thirty Philistines and gave their clothing to his groomsmen. He killed a thousand men using just a donkey's jawbone. And so Delilah seemed harmless to Samson, even as she badgered him for the truth about where his strength came from, and playfully tied him up at night with rope. Samson told her the truth—that his strength was in his hair, which had never been cut—and then fell asleep in her lap. Delilah, following instructions from the Philistines, grabbed her knife.

It's after this that Samson ascends to his true greatness. The Philistines capture him, gouge out his eyes, and chain him to a millstone, making him grind corn like a mule. Eventually, they drag him to a ritual sacrifice, and the weakened Samson prays to God, who gives him a last burst of divinity. He breaks the pillars at the temple, killing thousands of his captors and taking his own life. In this, he triumphs over evil, defying the cruelty of the Philistines and their dirty seductress, Delilah, whom Milton describes as "thorn intestine" in the poem *Samson Agonistes*. "Foul effeminacy held me yoked / Her bond-slave," Milton's Samson cries. The admission of hatred is an acknowledgment of her power. Wurtzel writes: "Delilah, to me, was clearly the star."

By nature, difficult women cause trouble, and that trouble can almost always be reinterpreted as good. Women claiming the power and agency that historically belonged to men is both the story of female evil and the story of female liberation. To work for the latter, you have to be willing to invoke the former: liberation is often mistaken for evil as it occurs. In 1905, Christabel Pankhurst kicked off the militant phase of the English suffrage movement when she spat at a police officer at a political meeting, knowing that this would lead to her arrest. From then on, the Women's Social and Political Union got themselves dragged out of all-male rooms, imprisoned, force-fed. They smashed windows and set buildings on fire. The suffragettes were written about as if they were wild animals, which swiftly highlighted the injustice of their position. In 1906, the *Daily Mirror* wrote in sympathy: "By what means, but by screaming, knocking, and rioting, did men themselves ever gain what they were pleased to call their rights?"

Condemnation historically accompanies most female actions that fall outside the lines of strict obedience. (Even the Virgin Mary, the most thoroughly venerated woman in history, faced it: according to the book of Matthew, Joseph found out about the pregnancy and asked for a divorce.) But praise comes to disobedient women, too. In 1429, seventeen-year-old Joan of Arc, high on spiritual visions, persuaded the dauphin Charles to place her at the head of the French army; she went into battle and helped clinch the throne in the Hundred Years' War. In 1430, she was imprisoned, and in 1431, she was tried for heresy and cross-dressing, and burned at the stake. But Joan was also simultaneously celebrated. During her imprisonment, the theorist and poet Christine de Pizan—who authored *The Book of the City of Ladies*, a utopian fantasy about an imaginary city in which women were respected—wrote that Joan was an "honor for the feminine." The man who executed her reported that he "greatly feared to be damned."

In 1451, twenty years after her death, Joan of Arc was retried posthumously, and deemed a virtuous martyr. The two stories—

her disobedience, her virtue—continued to intertwine. "The people who came after her in the five centuries [following] her death tried to make everything of her," writes Stephen Richey in his 2003 book *Joan of Arc: The Warrior Saint*. "Demonic fanatic, spiritual mystic, naïve and tragically ill-used tool of the powerful, creator and icon of modern popular nationalism, adored heroine, saint." Joan was loved and hated for the same actions, same traits. When she was canonized, in 1920, she joined a society of women—St. Lucy, St. Cecilia, St. Agatha—who were martyred because of their purity, the same way we now canonize pop-culture saints who were martyred over vice.

Rewriting a woman's story inevitably means engaging with the male rules that previously defined it. To argue against an ideology, you have to acknowledge and articulate it. In the process, you might inadvertently ventriloquize your opposition. This is a problem that kneecaps me constantly, a problem that might define journalism in the Trump era: when you write against something, you lend it strength and space and time.

In 2016, the writer Sady Doyle published a book called *Train-wreck: The Women We Love to Hate, Mock, and Fear . . . and Why*. It analyzed the lives and public narratives of famously troubled women: Britney Spears, Amy Winehouse, Lindsay Lohan, Whitney Houston, Paris Hilton, as well as figures further back in history—Sylvia Plath, Charlotte Brontë, Mary Wollstonecraft, even Harriet Jacobs. The book was a "well-rounded, thoughtful analysis," according to *Kirkus*, and a "fiercely brilliant, must-read exegesis," according to *Elle*. Its subtitle indicated an underlying uncertainty, one that elucidates a central ambivalence in feminist discourse. Who is the "we" that loves to hate, mock, and fear these women? Is it Doyle's audience? Or are feminist writers and readers duty bound to take personal ownership of the full extent of the hate, fear, and mockery that exists in other people's brains?

Doyle describes her book as an "attempt to reclaim the train-wreck, not only as the voice for every part of womanhood we'd prefer to keep quiet, but also as a girl who routinely colors outside the lines of her sexist society." The "we" in that sentence almost necessarily excludes both Doyle and her reader, and it becomes, throughout the book, an impossible amalgamation of the misogy-nist and the feminist—both of whom are interested, for opposite reasons, in plumbing the depths of female degradation and pain. In a chapter about Amy Winehouse, Whitney Houston, and Mar-ilyn Monroe, Doyle writes, "By dying, a trainwreck finally gives us the one statement we wanted to hear from her: that women like her really can't make it, and shouldn't be encouraged to try." At the end of a chapter about sex—which takes on "good-girl-gone-queer Lindsay Lohan, divorced single mother Britney Spears, Caitlyn Jenner with her sultry poses, Kim Kardashian having the gall to show up on the cover of *Vogue* with her black husband," who are all "tied to the tracks and gleefully run over"—Doyle writes, "We keep women's bodies controlled, and women them-selves in fear, with the public immolation of any sexual person who is or seems feminine." Do *we* really? Admittedly, it's always tricky to generalize in the collective first person, but this use case is indicative: in our attempts to acknowledge the persistence of structural inequality, *we* sometimes end up unable to see the pres-ent popular culture for what it is.

Trainwreck's project is, explicitly, to identify mistreatment of famous women in the past and thus prevent it in the future; it hopes to obviate the harm done to ordinary women in a culture that loves to watch female celebrities melt down. Doyle wreaths this worthy cause in arch, fatalistic hyperbole, exemplifying a tone that was, for years, a mainstay of online feminist discourse. In a chapter about *Fatal Attraction*, she writes, "A woman who wants you to love her is dangerously close to becoming a woman who demands the world's attention." The trainwreck is "crazy be-cause we're *all* crazy—because, in a sexist culture, being female is an illness for which there is no cure." Society makes Miley Cyrus into "a stripper, the devil, and the walking embodiment of predatory lust." When we get on the internet, the "#1 trending topic is still a debate about whether Rihanna is a Bad Role Model for Women," and "the verdict for Rihanna is never favorable." Valerie Solanas is remembered as a "bogeyman" of the "dirty, angry, fucked-up, thrown-away women of the world," while violent Norman Mailer is remembered as a genius. (I would guess that plenty of women in my millennial demographic semi-ironically venerate Solanas, and know Mailer mainly as the misogynist who stabbed his wife.) Doyle is motivated, she writes, by "a life spent watching the most beautiful, lucky, wealthy, successful women in the world reduced to deformed idiot hags in the media, and battered back into silence and obscurity through the sheer force of public disdain."

There is an argument to be made that this is what you have to do to counteract a force as old as patriarchy—that, in order to eradicate it, you have to fully reckon with its power, to verbalize and confront its worst insults and effects. But the result often verges on deliberate cynicism. "The leap from Paris Hilton to Mary Wollstonecraft may seem like a long one," Doyle writes. "But in practice, it's hardly even a bunny hop." She's referring to the fact that Wollstonecraft's sex life overshadowed, for some time, her canonical work *A Vindication of the Rights of Woman*, and that William Godwin published Wollstonecraft's salacious letters after her death. It's possible to draw a bright line between this and Rick Salomon selling a sex tape without Hilton's permission. But what changed between 1797 and 2004 shouldn't be underestimated or undercomplicated—nor should what changed between 2004 and 2016. I'd venture that our reality is not actually one in which the most beautiful, lucky, successful women in the world are being turned into "deformed idiot hags." Women are the drivers and rulers of the celebrity industry; they are rich; they have rights, if not as many as they ought to. The fact that women receive huge amounts of unfair criticism does not negate these facts but *informs* them, and in very complicated ways. Female celebrities are now venerated for their difficulty—their flaws, their complications, their humanity—with the idea that this will allow us, the ordinary women, to be flawed, and human, and possibly venerated, too.

I've been thinking about this argument since 2016—and specifically, since the week when, within a couple of days of each other, Kim Kardashian was robbed at gunpoint and Elena Ferrante was doxed. An online feminist outcry interpreted these two incidents as a single parable. *Look at what happens to ambitious women,* people wrote. *Look how women are punished for daring to live the way they want.* This was true, I thought, but in a different way than everyone seemed to be thinking. The problem seemed deeper—rooted in the fact that women have to slog through so many obstacles to become successful that their success is forever refracted through those obstacles. The problem seemed related to the way that the lives of famous women are constantly interpreted as crucial referenda on what we have to overcome to be women at all.

There's a limit, I think, to the utility of reading celebrity lives like tea leaves. The lives of famous women are determined by exponential leaps in visibility, money, and power, whereas the lives of ordinary women are mostly governed by mundane things: class, education, housing markets, labor practices. Female celebrities *do* indicate the rules of self-promotion—what's palatable and marketable to a general public in terms of sexuality and looks and affect and race. In today's world, this can seem like an essential question. But famous women do not always exist at the bleeding edge of what's possible. Attention is in many respects constrictive. Female celebrities are dealing with approval and backlash at such high, constant levels that it can be significantly more complicated for them to win the thing we're all ostensibly after—social permission for women to live the lives they want.

In 2017, Anne Helen Petersen published *Too Fat, Too Slutty, Too Loud: The Rise and Reign of the Unruly Woman*, a book that took the double-edged sword of female difficulty as its thesis. Unruly women have taken on an "outsized importance in the American imagination," Petersen writes. To be unruly is both profitable and risky; an unruly woman has to toe an ever-moving line of acceptability, but if she can do so, she can accrue enormous cultural cachet.

Petersen's book focuses on this sort of lauded unruliness— "unruliness that's made its way into the mainstream." She writes about, among others, Melissa McCarthy, Jennifer Weiner, Serena Williams, Kim Kardashian—who bested society's attempts to categorize them as (respectively) too fat, too loud, too strong, and too pregnant. "Does their stardom contribute to an actual sea change of 'acceptable' behaviors and bodies and ways of being for women today?" she asks. ". . . That answer is less dependent on the women themselves and more on the way we, as cultural consumers, decide to talk and think about them." These women, in all their unruliness, "*matter*—and the best way to show their gravity and power and influence is to refuse to shut up about why they do." Each chapter is dedicated to a woman who seems to possess some contested quality in excess, but who has nonetheless risen to the top of her field. These women are difficult and successful. Unruliness, Petersen writes, is "endlessly electric," fascinating, cool.

As a category, unruliness is also frustratingly large and amorphous. So many things are deemed unruly in women that a woman can seem unruly for simply existing without shame in her body— just for following her desires, no matter whether those desires are liberatory or compromising, or, more likely, a combination of the two. A woman is unruly if anyone has incorrectly decided that she's too much of something, and if she, in turn, has chosen to believe that she's just fine. She's unruly even if she is *hypothetically* criticized: for example, Caitlyn Jenner's entire celebrity narrative exists in reference to a massive wave of mainstream backlash that never actually came. Trans women have some of the hardest and most dangerous lives in America by any metric, but Caitlyn was immediately, remarkably exceptional. She was insulated to an unprecedented degree by her wealth and whiteness and fame (and perhaps by her credentials as a former Olympian). She came out in a corset on the cover of *Vanity Fair;* she got her own TV show; her political opinions—including her support for a president who would soon roll back protections for the trans community—made headlines. That this was possible while states were simultaneously passing "bathroom bills," while the murder rate for black trans women remained five times higher than the murder rate for the general population, is often presented as evidence for Caitlyn Jenner's bravery. It should at least as often be framed as proof of the distance between celebrity narratives and ordinary life.

In another chapter, Petersen writes about Caitlyn's stepdaughter Kim Kardashian. Kim had wanted, as she said on her show, a "cute" pregnancy, one in which only her belly would broaden. Instead, she gained weight everywhere. She continued to wear tight clothing and heels, and in doing so, "she became the unlikely means by which the cracks in the ideology of 'good' maternity became visible." Kim wore "outfits with see-through mesh strips, short dresses that showed off her legs, low-plunging necklines that revealed her substantial cleavage, high-waisted pencil skirts that broadened, rather than hid, her girth. She kept wearing heels, and full makeup . . . performing femininity and sexuality the same way she had her entire celebrity career." In response, she was compared to a whale, a sofa; close-ups of her swollen ankles in Lucite heels were all over the news. Kim, while pregnant, faced cruel, sexist criticism. But what is either implicit or cast aside in the chapter is the fact that what illuminates Kim as unruly in this situation is less her actual size than her unflagging commitment to eroticizing and monetizing the body. Her adherence to the practice of self-objectification is the instinct that makes her, as Petersen puts it, an "accidental activist" but an "activist nonetheless."

The bar is uniquely low with Kim Kardashian, who is frequently written about—much less in Petersen's book than elsewhere—as some sort of deliciously twisted empowerment icon. Kim has benefited from the feminist tendency to frame female courage as maximally subversive, when, just as often, it's *minimally* so. It is not "brave," strictly speaking, for a woman to do the things that will make her rich and famous. For some women, it is difficult and indeed dangerous to live as themselves in the world, but for other women, like Kim and her sisters, it's not just easy but extraordinarily profitable. It's true that the world has told Kim Kardashian that she's too pregnant, as well as "too fat, too superficial, too fake, too curvy, too sexual," and that this policing, as Petersen notes, reflects a larger misogynist anxiety about Kim's success and power. But Kim is successful and powerful not in spite of but *because of* these things. It actively behooves her to be superficial, fake, curvy, sexual. She is proof of a concept that is not very complicated or radical: today, it's possible for a beautiful, wealthy woman with an uncanny talent for self-surveillance to make her own dreams of increased wealth and beauty come true.

Petersen articulates this critical angle most clearly in the Madonna chapter, which focuses on the superstar in her fiftysomething biceps-and-sinew-and-corset iteration. In embracing and performing extreme fitness and sexuality, Madonna "may have outwardly refused the shame of age, but the effort she applied to fighting getting older stunk of it," Peterson writes. Onstage, she jumped rope while singing; she attended the Met Ball in a breastless bodysuit and assless pants. She was asserting her right to be sexual past the age deemed socially appropriate, but this taboo-breaking operated on an extremely specific basis: Madonna wasn't suggesting "that *all women* in their fifties and sixties should be relevant. Rather, she believes that women *who look like her* can be

relevant." The effective message was that women who exercise
three hours each day and maintain a professionally directed diet
can just barely wedge open the Venn diagram between "aging"
and "sexy." This type of rule-breaking operates, by definition, on
the level of the extraordinary individual. It's not built to translate
to ordinary life.

It's true, of course, that women who become famous for pushing social boundaries do the work of demonstrating how outdated
these boundaries are. But what happens once it becomes common
knowledge that these boundaries are outdated? We've come into
a new era, in which feminism isn't always the antidote to conventional wisdom; feminism is suddenly conventional wisdom in
many spheres. Women are not always—I'd argue that they're now
rarely—most interesting when breaking uninteresting restrictions. Melissa McCarthy's genius is more odd and specific than
the tedious, predictable criticism she's gotten for being fat. Abbi
Jacobson and Ilana Glazer of *Broad City* are more complicated
than the taboo on female grossness that they flouted on their
show. Celebrities, again, do not always indicate the frontier of
what people find appealing or even tolerable. Often, celebrity
standards lag far behind what women make possible in their individual lives every day. *Broad City* and *Girls*—Lena Dunham is the
subject of Petersen's "too naked" chapter—were groundbreaking
on television because they represented bodies and situations that,
for many people, were already ordinary and good.

There is a blanket, untested assumption, in feminist celebrity
analysis, that the freedom we grant famous women will trickle
down to us. Beneath this assumption is another one—that the
ultimate goal of this conversation is empowerment. But the
difficult-woman discourse often seems to be leading somewhere
else. Feminists have, to a significant degree, dismantled and rejected the traditional male definition of exemplary womanhood:
the idea that women must be sweet, demure, controllable, and
free of normal human flaws. But if men placed women on pedes-

tals and delighted in watching them fall down, feminism has so far mostly succeeded in reversing the order of operations—taking toppled-over women and re-idolizing them. Famous women are still constantly tested against the idea that they should be maximally appealing, even if that appeal now involves "difficult" qualities. Feminists are still looking for idols—just ones who are idolized on our own complicated terms.

Elsewhere, outside the kingdom of the difficult woman, a different type of female celebrity reigns. In *Too Fat, Too Slutty, Too Loud*, Petersen notes that unruly women "compete against a far more palatable—and, in many cases, more successful—form of femininity: the lifestyle supermom." She goes on:

> Exemplified by Reese Witherspoon, Jessica Alba, Blake Lively, Gwyneth Paltrow, and Ivanka Trump, these women rarely trend on Twitter, but they've built tremendously successful brands by embracing the "new domesticity," defined by consumption, maternity, and a sort of twenty-first-century gentility. They have slim, disciplined bodies and adorable pregnancies; they never wear the wrong thing or speak negatively or make themselves abrasive in any way. Importantly, these celebrities are also all white—or, in the case of Jessica Alba, careful to elide any connotations of ethnicity—and straight.

This type of woman—the woman who would never be difficult, kakistocratic political takeovers excepted—includes a wide variety of micro-celebrities: lifestyle bloggers, beauty and wellness types, generic influencers with long Instagram captions and predictable tastes. These women are so incredibly successful that a sort of countervailing feminist distaste for them has arisen—a displeasure at the *lack* of unruliness, at the disappointment of watching women adhere to the most predictable guidelines of what a woman should be.

In other words, just like the difficult women, the lifestyle types fall short of an ideal. They, too, are admired and hated simultaneously. Feminist culture has, in many cases, drawn a line to exclude or disparage the Mormon mommy bloggers, the sponsored-content factories, the "basics," the Gwyneths and Blakes. Sometimes—often—these women are openly hated: sprawling online forums like Get Off My Internets host large communities of women who love tearing into every last detail of an Instagram celebrity's life. There's an indicative line in *Trainwreck*, where Doyle writes, "Women hate trainwrecks to the extent that we hate ourselves. We love them to the extent that we want our own failings and flaws to be loved. The question, then, is choosing between the two." But why would these ever be our only options? The freedom I want is located in a world where we wouldn't *need* to love women, or even monitor our feelings about women as meaningful—in which we wouldn't need to parse the contours of female worth and liberation by paying meticulous personal attention to any of this at all.

In 2015, Alana Massey wrote a popular essay for *BuzzFeed* titled "Being Winona in a World Made for Gwyneths." It began with an anecdote from her twenty-ninth birthday, when a guy she was seeing made the unnerving disclosure that his ideal celebrity sex partner would be Gwyneth Paltrow. "And in that moment," Massey writes, "every thought or daydream I ever had about our potential future filled with broad-smiled children, adopted cats, and phenomenal sex evaporated. Because there is no future with a Gwyneth man when you're a Winona woman, particularly a Winona in a world made for Gwyneths." The essay that followed expanded the space between, as Massey put it, "two distinct categories of white women who are conventionally attractive but whose public images exemplify dramatically different lifestyles and worldviews." Winona Ryder was "relatable and aspirational," her life "more authentic . . . at once exciting and a little bit sad." Gwyneth, on the other hand, "has always represented a collection of tasteful but safe consumer reflexes more than she's reflected much of a real personality." Her life was "so sufficiently figured out as to be both enviable and mundane."

For women, authenticity lies in difficulty: this feminist assumption has become dominant logic while still passing as rare. The Winonas of the world, Massey argues, are the ones with stories worth telling, even if the world is built to suit another type of girl. (The world, of course, is also built to suit Winonas: though Massey acknowledges the racial limitations of her argument, the fact that a wildly popular essay could be built on analyzing the spectrum of female identity represented between Gwyneth Paltrow and Winona Ryder indicates both the stranglehold of whiteness on celebrity discourse and the way celebrity irregularity is graded on an astonishing curve.) Later on, Massey wrote about the period of success that followed the publication of this essay, in which she bought a house, went platinum blond, and upgraded her wardrobe. She looked at herself in a mirror, seeing "the expertly blown out blonde hair and a designer handbag and a complexion made dewy by the expensive acids and oils that I now anoint myself with. . . . I had become a total. fucking. Gwyneth." The hyper-precise calibration of exemplary womanhood either mattered more than ever or didn't matter at all.

Massey included the Winona/Gwyneth piece in her 2017 book, *All the Lives I Want: Essays About My Best Friends Who Happen to Be Famous Strangers*, which took on a familiar set of female icons: Courtney Love, Anna Nicole Smith, Amber Rose, Sylvia Plath, Britney Spears. The operating concept seemed to be that the world under patriarchy had badly aestheticized the suffering of women—and that, perhaps, women could now aestheticize that suffering in a good way, an incandescent and oracular way, one that was deep and meaningful and affirming and real. As the title suggests, we could *want* their trouble, their difficulty. In this book, celebrity lives are configured as intimate symbols. Sylvia Plath is "an early literary manifestation of a young woman who takes endless selfies and posts them with vicious captions calling herself fat and ugly." Britney Spears's body is the Rosetta stone through which Massey decodes her own desire to be thin and sexually irresistible. Courtney Love, a "venomous witch," is "the woman I aspire to be rather than the clumsy girl I have so often been." Like a priestess, Massey spoke a language that conjured glory through persecution and deification through pain. Every bit of hardship these difficult women experienced was an indication of their worth and humanity. They were set apart—fully alive, fully realized—in a way the bland women could never be.

As I read Massey's book, I kept thinking: womanhood has been denied depth and meaning for so long that every inch of it is now almost impossibly freighted. Where female difficulty once seemed perverse, the *refusal* of difficulty now seems perverse. The entire interpretive framework is becoming untenable. We can analyze difficult women from the traditional point of view and find them controversial, and we can analyze bland women from the feminist point of view and find them controversial, too. We have a situation in which women reject conventional femininity in the interest of liberation, and then find themselves alternately despising and craving it—the pattern at work in Massey's spiritual journey away from Gwyneth and then back to her, as well as in the message-board communities where random lifestyle bloggers are picked apart. Feminists have worked so hard, with such good intentions, to justify female difficulty that the concept has ballooned to something all-encompassing: a blanket defense, an automatic celebration, a tarp of self-delusion that can cover up any sin.

By 2018, as the boundary between celebrity and politics dissolved into nothing, the difficult-woman discourse, perfected on celebrities, had grown powerful enough to move into the mainstream political realm. The women in the Trump administration manifest many of the qualities that are celebrated in feminist icons: they are selfish, shameless, unapologetic, ambitious, artificial, et cetera. Their treatment as celebrities illuminates something odd about the current moment, something that is greatly exacerbated by the dynamics of the internet. On the one hand, sexism is still so ubiquitous that it touches all corners of a woman's life; on the other, it seems incorrect to criticize women about anything— their demeanor, even their behavior—that might intersect with sexism. What this means, for the women of the Trump administration, is that they can hardly be criticized without sexism becoming the story. Fortuitously for them, the difficult-woman discourse intercepts the conversation every time.

Every female figure in Trump's orbit is difficult in a way that could serve as the basis for a bullshit celebratory hagiography. There's Kellyanne Conway, mocked for visibly aging, for how she dresses, slut-shamed for sitting carelessly on the sofa—a tough-as-nails fighter, emerging triumphant from every snafu. There's Melania, written off because she was a model, because she was uninterested in pretending to be a happy Easter-egg-rolling First Lady, who rejected conventional expectations of White House domesticity and redefined an outdated office on her own terms. There's Hope Hicks, also written off because she was a model, viewed as weak because she was young and quiet and loyal, who nonetheless became one of the few people the president really trusted. There's Ivanka, *also* written off because she was a model, criticized as unserious because she designed shoes and wore bows to political meetings, who transcended the liberal public's hatred of her and worked quietly behind the scenes. And there's Sarah Huckabee Sanders, mocked for her frumpiness and prickly attitude, who reminded us that you don't need to be bone-thin or cheerful to be a public-facing woman at the top of your field. The pattern—woman is criticized for something related to her being a woman; her continued existence is interpreted as politically meaningful—is so ridiculously loose that almost anything can fit inside it. There, look at the Trump women, proving that female power doesn't always come the way we want it to. Look at them carrying on in the face of so much public disapproval, refusing to apologize for who they are, for the unlikely seat of power they've carved out for themselves, for the expectations they've refused.

This narrative is in fact alive to some degree. It's just not often written by feminists, although some pieces have come fairly close. Olivia Nuzzi's March 2017 cover story for *New York* was titled "Kellyanne Conway Is a Star," and it detailed how Conway had become the subject of endless "armchair psychoanalysis, outrage, and exuberant ridicule. But rather than buckling, she absorbed all of it, coming out the other side so aware of how the world perceives her that she could probably write this article herself." She projected "blue-collar authenticity," had a fighter's instinct; she had a "loose relationship to the truth" and a "very evident love of the game." This had propelled her, despite the constant criticism about her unmanageable looks and demeanor, to the position of being the "functional First Lady of the United States." Nuzzi also wrote about Hope Hicks twice: the first piece, for GQ in 2016, was called "The Mystifying Triumph of Hope Hicks, Donald Trump's Right-Hand Woman," and detailed how a "person who'd never worked in politics had nonetheless become the most improbably important operative in this election." The second piece came out in *New York* after Hicks resigned in early 2018. Nuzzi painted her both as a woman utterly in charge of her own destiny and a sweet, innocent, vulnerable handmaiden to an institution that was falling apart.

The media conversation around the women of the Trump administration has been conflicted to the point of meaninglessness. They have benefited from the pop-feminist reflex of honoring women for achieving visibility and power, no matter how they did so. (The situation was perfectly encapsulated by *Reductress*'s 2015 blog post "New Movie Has Women in It.") What began as a liberal tendency now brings conservative figures into its orbit. In 2018,

Gina Haspel, the CIA official who oversaw torture at a black site in Thailand and then destroyed the evidence, was nominated to be director of the agency—the first woman to hold this office. Sarah Huckabee Sanders tweeted, "Any Democrat who claims to support women's empowerment and our national security but opposes her nomination is a total hypocrite." Many other conservatives echoed this view, with varying degrees of sincerity. There's a joke that's circulated for the past few years: leftists say *abolish prisons*, liberals say *hire more women guards*. Now plenty of conservatives, having clocked feminism's palatability, say *hire more women guards*, too.

The Trump administration is so baldly anti-woman that the women within it have been regularly scanned and criticized for their complicity, as well as for their empty references to feminism. (It's arguable that we could understand the institution of celebrity itself as similarly suspicious: despite the prevailing liberalism of Hollywood, the values of celebrity—visibility, performance, aspiration, extreme physical beauty—promote an approach to womanhood that relies on individual exceptionalism in an inherently conservative way.) But the Trump women have also been defended and rewritten along difficult-women lines. Melania merely wearing a black dress and a veil to the Vatican, looking vaguely widowy, was enough to prompt an onslaught of yes-bitch jokes about dressing for the job you want. The *Times* ran a column on Melania's "quiet radicalism," in which the writer assessed Melania as "defiant in her silence." When Melania boarded a plane to Houston in the middle of Hurricane Harvey wearing black stiletto heels, she was immediately slammed for this tone-deaf choice, and then defended on the terms of feminism: it was shallow and anti-woman to comment on her choice of footwear—she has the right to wear whatever sort of shoes she wants.

By 2018, the Trump administration was weaponizing this predictable press cycle. In the midst of the outrage about family separation at the southern border, Melania boarded a plane to visit the caged children in Texas wearing a Zara jacket emblazoned with the instantly infamous slogan "I Really Don't Care, Do U?" It was a transparent act of trolling: a sociopathic message, delivered in the hopes of drawing criticism of Melania, which could then be identified as *sexist* criticism, so that the discussion about sexism could distract from the far more important matters at hand.

And, because of the feminist cultural reflex to protect women from criticism that invokes their bodies or choices or personal presentation in any way, the Trump administration was also able to rely on liberal women to defend them. In 2017, a jarring, loaded image of Kellyanne Conway began making the rounds on the internet: she appeared to be barefoot, with her legs spread apart, kneeling on a couch in the Oval Office in a room full of men. This was a gathering of administrators from historically black colleges—black men in suits, conducting themselves with buttoned-up propriety, while Conway acted as if the Oval Office were the family TV room. There was an uproar about this general unseemliness, which was immediately followed by full-throated defenses of Conway, including a tweet by Chelsea Clinton. *Vogue* then wrote that Chelsea's gesture of support was "a model for how feminists *should* respond to powerful women being demeaned and diminished on the basis of their gender," and that this was a "great way to beat Conway and other 'post-feminist' political operatives at their own game." Conway "wins," *Vogue* wrote, when people point out that she looks tired, or haggard, or "when she's belittled for purportedly using her femininity as a tool." Then the writer made an about-face and looked right at the point. Conway "is using her femininity against us. It's not out of the realm of possibility—and is in fact quite likely—that Conway has considered that no matter what she says or does . . . she will be criticized in bluntly sexist terms because she is a woman." I'd add that she also likely knows that, on the terms of contemporary feminism, she will be *defended* in equally blunt terms, too.

Later on, Jennifer Palmieri, the director of communications for Hillary Clinton's presidential campaign, lamented in the *Times* that Steve Bannon was seen as an evil genius while Conway, equally manipulative, was just seen as crazy. When *Saturday Night Live* portrayed Conway like Glenn Close in *Fatal Attraction* in a sketch, that, too, was sexist, as were the memes that compared Conway to Gollum and Skeletor. But if you stripped away the sexism, you would still be left with Kellyanne Conway. Moreover, if you make the self-presentation of a White House spokesperson off-limits on principle, then you lose the ability to articulate the way she does her job. Misogyny insists that a woman's appearance is of paramount value; these dogged, hyper-focused critiques of misogyny can have an identical effect. Generic sexism is not meaningfully disempowering to Kellyanne Conway in her current position as an indestructible mouthpiece for the most transparently destructive president in American history. In fact, through the discourse established by feminism, she can siphon some amount of cultural power from this sexism. *SNL* called her a needy psycho? Nevertheless, Kellyanne persists.

Of all the Trump administration women, none have been defended more staunchly and reflexively than Hope Hicks and Sarah Huckabee Sanders. After Hicks resigned in early 2018, Laura McGann wrote a piece at *Vox* arguing that "the media undermined Hicks with sexist language right up until her last day." News outlets kept citing the fact that she was a model, McGann noted, and calling her a neophyte—whereas, if Hicks were a man, she'd be a wunderkind, and the media wouldn't dwell on her teenage part-time job. Journalists wrote too much about her "feminine" personality. Outlets have "questioned her experience, doubted [her] contributions to the campaign and inside the White House, and implied her looks are relevant . . . to anything. It adds up to another insidious narrative about a woman in power that is familiar to successful women everywhere." In order to scrutinize Hicks the way she deserved to be scrutinized, McGann wrote, we needed to forget about her "tweenage modeling career."

The idea—impeccable in the abstract—was that we could and should critique Hicks without invoking patriarchy. But women are shaped by patriarchy: my own professional instincts are different because I grew up in Texas, in the evangelical church, on a cheerleading squad, in the Greek system. My approach to power has been altered by the early power structures I knew. Hicks worked as a model while growing up in bedroom-community Connecticut; she attended Southern Methodist University, a private school outside Dallas with an incredibly wealthy and conservative population; she became a loyal, daughterly aide to an open misogynist. She seems to have been shaped at a deep, true, essential level by conservative gender politics, and she has consistently acted on this, as is her right. Talking about Hicks without acknowledging the role of patriarchy in her biography may be *possible*, but to say that it's politically necessary seems exactly off the point. In *Vox*, McGann cited *Times* coverage of Hicks as implicitly sexist; after her resignation, a *Times* piece cited me as implicitly sexist, in turn. I was one of the members of the media dismissing Hicks "as a mere factotum," the *Times* wrote, quoting a tweet of mine: "Goodbye to Hope Hicks, an object lesson in the quickest way a woman can advance under misogyny: silence, beauty, and unconditional deference to men."

It is entirely possible that I'm wrong in assuming that these attributes made Hicks valuable in Trump's White House. Maybe she wasn't as deferential as reporters claimed. (She was certainly silent, never speaking on the record to the media; she's certainly beautiful.) But it doesn't seem coincidental that a president who has married three models, was averse to his first wife's professional ambitions, and is upsettingly proud of his daughter's good looks picked a young, beautiful, conventionally socialized woman to be his favored aide. Of course, Hicks was hardworking, and had legitimate political instincts and abilities. But with Trump, a woman's looks and comportment are inseparable from her abilities. To him, Hicks's beauty and silence would have translated as rare skills. Her experience as a model is, I think, *incredibly* relevant: the modeling industry is one of the very few in which women are able to engage misogyny to get ahead, to outearn men. A model has to figure out a way to appeal to an unseen, changing audience; she has to understand how to silently invite people to project their desires and needs onto her; under pressure, she has to radiate perfect composure and control. Modeling skills are distinct and particular, and they would prepare a person well for a job working under Trump. Nonetheless, perhaps this is another one of those situations where identifying misogyny means ventriloquizing it; maybe I'm extending sexism's half-life now, too.

This sort of discursive ouroboros was most obvious, perhaps, after the White House Correspondents' Dinner in 2018, when the comedian Michelle Wolf poked fun—as was her task for the evening—at Sarah Huckabee Sanders. "I love you as Aunt Lydia in *The Handmaid's Tale*," Wolf said. She joked that, when Sanders walked up to the lectern, you never knew what you were going to get—"a press briefing, a bunch of lies, or divided into softball teams." Finally, she complimented Sanders for being resourceful. "Like, she burns facts, and she uses the ash to create a perfect smoky eye. Maybe she's born with it, maybe it's lies. It's probably lies." The blowback from these jokes swallowed a news cycle. MSNBC's Mika Brzezinski tweeted, "Watching a wife and mother be humiliated on national television for her looks is deplorable. I have experienced insults about my appearance from the president. All women have a duty to unite when these attacks happen and the WHCA owes Sarah an apology." Maggie Haberman, the *Times*'s star Trump reporter, tweeted, "That @PressSec sat and absorbed intense criticism of her physical appearance, her job performance, and so forth, instead of walking out, on national television, was impressive." In response to Haberman, Wolf replied,

"All these jokes were about her despicable behavior. Sounds like you have some thoughts about her looks though?" Feminists, and people eager to prove their feminist bona fides, echoed Wolf's point en masse: the jokes were *not* about Sanders's looks!

But they were. Wolf didn't insult Sanders's appearance outright, but the jokes were constructed in such a way that the first thing you thought about was Sanders's physical awkwardness. She does conjure something of the stereotypical softball coach, inelegant and broad-shouldered, the sort of person who doesn't belong in shift dresses and pearls. She *does* look older than she is, which is part of the reason the Aunt Lydia reference hit. And the joke within that perfect-smoky-eye joke is that Sanders's eye makeup is in fact messy, uneven, and usually pretty bad. All of this remained off-limits, however, due to the unquestioned assumption that a woman's looks are so precious, due to sexism, that joking about them would render Wolf's set inadmissible by default.

A month later, another news cycle was swallowed when Samantha Bee called Ivanka a cunt. She did this on her show, in a segment about border separation, noting that, as news outlets reported stories about migrant children who were being locked up and abused in prisonlike detention centers, Ivanka had posted a photo of herself doting on her youngest son, Teddy. "You know, Ivanka," Bee said, "that's a beautiful photo of you and your child, but let me just say, one mother to another: Do something about your dad's immigration practices, you feckless cunt! He listens to you!" A tidal wave of outrage descended from the right and the center—not about the migrant families, but about the use of the word "cunt." Conservatives were once again weaponizing a borrowed argument. The White House called for TBS to cancel her show, and then Bee apologized, and I felt as if a feminist praxis was turning to acid and eating through the floor. It's as if what's signified—sexism itself—has remained so intractable that we've mostly given up on rooting out its actual workings. Instead, to the great benefit of people like Ivanka, we've been adjudicating inequality through cultural criticism. We have taught people who don't even care about feminism how to do this—how to analyze women and analyze the way people react to women, how to endlessly read and interpret the signs.

Hovering over all of this is the loss of Hillary Clinton to Trump in the 2016 election. Throughout her campaign, Clinton had been cast—and had attempted to cast herself—as a difficult woman, a beloved figure of the mainstream feminist zeitgeist. She fit the model. For decades, her public narrative had been determined by sexist criticism: she was viewed as too ambitious, too undomestic, too ugly, too calculating, too cold. She had drawn unreasonable hatred for pursuing her ambitions, and she had weathered this hatred to become the first woman in American history to receive a major party's presidential nomination. As the election approached, she was held to a terrible, compounded double standard, both as a serious candidate going up against an openly corrupt salesman, and as a woman facing off against a man. Clinton attempted to make the most of this. She turned misogynist slights into marketing tactics, selling "Nasty Woman" merchandise after Trump used the term to disparage her during a debate. This merchandise was popular, as was the reclaimed insult: on Twitter, rather embarrassingly, feminists called themselves "nasty women" all day long. But if we really loved nasty women so much, wouldn't Clinton have won the election? Or at least, if this sort of pop feminism was really so ascendant, wouldn't 53 percent of white women have voted for *her* instead of for Trump?

Clinton was in fact celebrated for outlasting—until November, at least—her sexist critics. Her strength and persistence in response to misogyny were easily the things I liked most about her. I felt great admiration for the Clinton who had once refused to change her name, who couldn't stand the idea of staying home and baking cookies. I believed in the politician who sat patiently through eleven hours of interrogation on Benghazi and was still called "emotional" on CNN for choking up when she talked about the Americans who had died. I was moved, watching Clinton white-knuckle herself into stoicism, in 2016, as Trump stalked her around the debate stage. No woman in recent history has been miscast and disrespected quite like Clinton. Years after the election, at Trump rallies across the country, angry crowds of men and women were still chanting, "Lock her up!"

But the gauntlet of sexism that Clinton was forced to fight through ultimately illuminated little about her other than the fact that she was a woman. It did her—and us, eventually—the crippling disservice of rendering her generic. Misogyny provided a terrible external structure through which Clinton was able to demonstrate commitment and tenacity and occasional grace; misogyny also demanded that she pander and compromise in the interest of survival, and that she sand down her personality until it could hardly be shown in public at all. The real nature of Clinton's campaign and candidacy was obscured first and finally by sexism, but also by the reflexive defense against sexism. She was attacked so bluntly, so unfairly, and in turn she was often upheld and shielded by equally blunt arguments—defenses that were about nasty women, never really about *her*.

Clinton's loss, which I will mourn forever, might reiterate the importance of making space for the difficult woman. It might also point toward the way that valuing a woman for her difficulty can, in ways that are unexpectedly destructive, obscure her actual, particular self. Feminist discourse has yet to fully catch up to the truth that sexism is so much more mundane than the celebrities who have been high-profile test cases for it. Sexism rears its head no matter who a woman is, no matter what her desires and ethics might be. And a woman doesn't have to be a feminist icon to resist it—she can just be self-interested, which is not always the same thing.

I Thee Dread

My boyfriend maintains a running Google spreadsheet to keep track of the weddings we've been invited to together. There are columns for the date of the event, the location, our relationship to the couple, and—the ostensible reason for this record-keeping—whether or not we've sent a present yet, and which of us sent the gift. The spreadsheet was first a function of his personality: where I am careless about most things outside my writing, Andrew, an architect, is meticulous even about irrelevant details, a monster of capability who rearranges the dishwasher with a fervor that borders on organizational BDSM. But at some point, the Google spreadsheet became a necessity. Over the past nine years, we've been invited to forty-six weddings. I myself do not want to get married, and it's possible that all these weddings are why.

Andrew is thirty-three, and I'm thirty, and to some degree we are having a demographically specific experience. Our high school friends are mostly upper-middle class and on the conservative side, the type to get married like clockwork and have big, traditional weddings, and we both went to the University of Virginia, where people tend to be convention-friendly, too. We also haven't actually attended all of these weddings. We used to split up some weekends to cover two simultaneously—packing our formalwear, driving to the airport, and waving goodbye in the terminal before boarding separate flights. We've skipped maybe a dozen weddings altogether, sometimes to save money that we would spend going to other weddings, since for about five years one or both of us was on a grad school budget, and we always seemed to live a plane ride away from the event.

But we love our friends, and we almost always love the people they marry, and like most wedding cynics—an expansive population that includes most married people, who will happily bitch about nuptial excess at weddings outside their own—Andrew and I love every wedding once we're physically present: tipsy and tearing up and soaked in secondhand happiness, grooving to Montell Jordan alongside the groom's mom and dad. So we've done it, over and over and over, booking hotel rooms and rental cars, writing checks and perusing Williams-Sonoma registries, picking up tux shirts from the cleaners, waking up at sunrise to call airport cabs. At this point the weddings blend together, but the spreadsheet conjures a series of flashes. In Charleston, a peacock wandering through a lush garden at twilight, the damp seeping through the hem of my thrift-store dress. In Houston, a ballroom leaping to its feet at the first beat of Big Tymers. In Manhattan, stepping out onto a wide balcony at night overlooking Central Park, everyone in crisp black-and-white, the city twinkling. In rural Virginia, the bride walking down the aisle in rain boots as the swollen gray sky held its breath. In rural Maryland, the groom riding a white horse to the ceremony as Indian music drifted through a golden field. In Austin, the couple bending to receive Armenian crowns underneath a frame of roses. In New Orleans, the bomb-pop lights of the cop car clearing the street for the parasols and trumpets of the second line parade.

It's easy for me to understand why a person would want to get married. But, as these weddings consistently reminded me, the understanding doesn't often go both ways. Whenever someone would ask me when Andrew and I might get married, I'd demur, saying that I didn't know, maybe never, I was lazy, I didn't wear jewelry, I loved weddings but didn't want one of my own. I'd usually try to change the subject, but it never worked. People would immediately start probing, talking to me like I was hiding something, suddenly certain that I was one of those girls who'd spend years proclaiming that she was too down-to-earth for anything but elopement until the second she thought she could get someone to propose. Often people would launch into a series of impassioned arguments, as if I'd just presented them with a problem that needed fixing, as if I were wearing a sandwich board with "Change My Mind" written on it—as if it were a citizen's duty to encourage betrothal the way we encourage people to vote.

"Never?" they'd say, skeptically. "You know, there's something really amazing about a ritual, especially at a time when we have so few rituals left in society. There's really no other time when you can get everyone you love together in the same room. *My* wedding was super low-key—I just wanted everyone to have fun, you know? I just wanted to have a really great party. You really get married for other people. But also, in this really deep way, you do it for you." At the next wedding, the discussion would continue. "Is marriage still not on the table?" people would ask, checking in. "You know you can get married without having a wedding, right?" One man told me, at a wedding, six years after I had attended his wedding, that I was missing out on something amazing. "There's something deeper about our relationship now," he said. "Trust me—when we got married, something just *changed*."

Andrew is asked about this less often than I am, as it is presumed that marriage is more emotionally exciting for women: within straight couples, weddings are frequently described as the most special day of *her* life, if not necessarily his. (And of course the questioning is similarly gender-slanted, and far more intrusive, for people who don't want to have kids.) But still, Andrew gets asked about it often enough. "Doesn't it bother you?" I asked him recently, after he recounted a couple of phone calls with old friends, one male and one female, both of whom seemed obliquely concerned about our lack of legally binding commitment. "No," he told me, switching lanes on the Taconic Parkway.

"Why not?" I asked.

"I . . . don't really care what people think," he said.

"Yeah!" I said. "I normally don't, either!"

"Sure," he said, audibly bored with this already.

"I usually *really* don't care what people think," I said, getting steamed.

Andrew nodded, his eyes on the road.

"It's just this *one thing*," I said. "It's like the *one thing* people say to me that I take personally. And I guess it's a circular situation—like, people shouldn't take *us* not wanting to get married personally, but they *do* take it personally; otherwise we wouldn't have to fucking *talk* about it so much. And it's like the more I have to talk about it, the more it creates this problem I didn't have in the *first* place—like I've constructed this *spiderweb* of *answers* about why I don't want to get *married* that's probably concealing my *actual* thoughts about, like, family structure and love. And then I resent the question even *more*, because *it's* stupid and predictable, and so it makes *me* stupid and predictable, and I have all these, like, *meta-narratives* in my head, when the fact of the matter is that the whole thing is just trans*parently* ridiculous, starting from the idea that a man just *proposes* to a woman and she's supposed to be just *lying in wait* for the moment *he* decides he's ready to *commit* to a situation where *he* statistically benefits and she statistically becomes *less happy* than she would be if she was *single*, and then *she's* the one who has to wear this tacky *ring* to signify *male ownership*, and she's supposed to be *excited* about it, this new *life* where *doubt* becomes this thing you're supposed to experience *in private* and *certainty* becomes the *default affect* for the *entire rest of your life* . . ."

I trailed off because I knew that Andrew had long ago stopped listening to me and started thinking about which nineties wres-

tling match he was going to watch that evening, and that he, unlike me, had long ago made peace with the desires and decisions
that I could not stop explaining, because I, on the topic of weddings, like so many women before me, had gone a little bit insane.

Here, according to the current advice of the wedding industry, is
what a newly engaged person is expected to do in preparation for
the event. (Within a straight couple, it is universally assumed—if
not actually true, as a rule—that the person who will invest the
most energy in this process is the bride-to-be.) Assuming a twelve-
month engagement, the affianced is supposed to immediately
begin planning an engagement party, looking for a wedding plan-
ner (average cost $3,500), choosing a venue (average cost $13,000),
and fixing on a date. With eight months to go she's expected to
have created a wedding website (average cost $100—a bargain)
and selected her vendors (florals: $2,000; catering: $12,000;
music: $2,000). She should have purchased presents to "propose"
to her bridesmaids (packages including custom sippy cups and
notepads run up to $80, but a "Will You Join My Bride Tribe?"
note card is a mere $3.99), assembled a wedding registry (here,
thankfully, she can expect to recoup around $4,800), chosen a
photographer ($6,000), and shopped for a dress ($1,600, on average, though at the iconic bridal mecca Kleinfeld, the average customer spends $4,500).

With six months to go, the bride should have arranged for the
engagement photos ($500), designed invitations and programs
and place cards ($750), and figured out where they'll go on their
honeymoon ($4,000). At four months out, she should have gotten
the wedding rings ($2,000), purchased gifts for her bridesmaids
($100 per bridesmaid), found gifts for the groomsmen ($100 per
groomsman), secured wedding favors ($275), dealt with her wed-
ding showers, and ordered a wedding cake ($450). As the wed-
ding draws near, she needs to apply for a marriage license ($40),

do her final gown fittings, test out her wedding shoes, go away for her bachelorette party, prepare the seating chart, send a music list to her band or DJ, and do a final consultation with her photographer. In the days before the wedding, she passes through the final gauntlet of grooming processes. The night before, there's the rehearsal dinner. On her wedding day, a year of planning and approximately $30,000 of spending are unleashed over the span of about twelve hours. The next morning, she gets up for the brunch send-off, then goes on her honeymoon, sends her thank-you notes, orders the photo album, and, most likely, starts getting the paperwork together to change her name.

All of this is conducted in the spirit of fun but the name of tradition. There's a vague idea that, when a woman walks down the aisle wearing several thousand dollars' worth of white satin, when she pledges her fealty and kisses her new husband in front of 175 people, when her guests trickle back to the tent draped in twinkle lights and find their seats at tables festooned with peonies and then get up in the middle of their frisée salads to thrash around to a Bruno Mars cover—that this joins the bride and groom to an endless line of lovebirds, a golden chain of couples stretching back for centuries, millions of dreamers who threw lavish open-bar celebrations with calligraphy place cards to celebrate spending together forever with their best friend.

But for centuries, weddings were entirely homemade productions, brief and simple ceremonies conducted in private. The vast majority of women in history have gotten married in front of a handful of people, with no reception, in colored dresses that they had worn before and would wear again. In ancient Greece, wealthy brides wore violet or red. In Renaissance Europe, wedding dresses were often blue. In nineteenth-century France and England, lower-class and middle-class women got married in black silk. The white wedding dress didn't become popular until 1840, when twenty-year-old Queen Victoria married Prince Albert, her cousin, in a formal white gown trimmed with orange blossoms.

The event was not photographed—fourteen years later, after the appropriate technology had developed, Victoria and Albert would pose for a reenactment wedding portrait—but British newspapers provided lengthy descriptions of Victoria's wedding crinolines, her satin slippers, her sapphire brooch, her golden carriage, and her three-hundred-pound wedding cake. The symbolic link between "bride" and "royalty" was forged with Victoria, and would eventually intensify into the idea of a wedding as "a sort of Everywoman's coronation," as Holly Brubach wrote in *The New Yorker* in 1989.

Very soon after Queen Victoria's wedding, her nuptial decisions were being enshrined as long-standing tradition. In 1849, *Godey's Lady's Book* wrote, "Custom has decided, from the earliest age, that white is the most fitting hue [for brides], whatever may be the material." The Victorian elite, copying their queen, solidified a wedding template—formal invitations, a processional entrance, flowers and music—with the help of new businesses dedicated exclusively to selling wedding accessories and décor. The rapidly developing consumer marketplace of the late nineteenth century turned weddings into a staging ground for upperclass lifestyle: for a day, you could purchase this lifestyle, even if you weren't actually upper-class. As middle-class women attempted to create an impression of elite social standing through their weddings, white dresses became more important. In *All Dressed in White: The Irresistible Rise of the American Wedding*, Carol Wallace writes that "a white dress in pristine condition implied its wearer's employment of an expert laundress, seamstress, and ladies' maid."

By the turn of the twentieth century, middle-class families were spending so much money on weddings that there was a cultural backlash. Critics warned against love's commercialization, and advice writers cautioned families against endangering their finances for a party. In turn, elite women raised the bar in response to middle-class social performances. In *Brides, Inc.: Amer-*

ican Weddings and the Business of Tradition, Vicki Howard describes
a custom among wealthy families of displaying presents, allowing
guests to "peruse . . . long cloth-covered tables laden with silver,
china, jewels, and even furniture. . . . Newspaper announcements
recounted society gift viewings, noting the designer or manufac-
turer of gifts." A Tennessee bride invited more than fifteen hundred people to her 1908 wedding, and received "seventy silver
gifts, fifty-seven glass and crystal items, thirty-one pieces of china,
nine sets of linens, and sixty miscellaneous items."

The growing wedding industry figured out that the best way to
get people to accept the new, performative norms of nuptial excess was to tell women—as *Godey's Lady's Book* had done in 1849
with the white wedding dress—that all of this excess was extremely *traditional*. "Jewelers, department stores, fashion design-
ers, bridal consultants, and many others became experts on
inventing tradition," Howard writes, "creating their own versions
of the past to legitimize new rituals and help overcome cultural
resistance to the lavish affair." In 1924, Marshall Field's invented
the wedding registry. Retailers began issuing etiquette instructions, insisting that purchasing fine china and engraved invitations
was simply the way that things had always been done.

In 1929, the financial crash put a damper on wedding spending. But then, retailers picked up the pitch that "love knows no
depression." Throughout the thirties, newspapers ramped up
their wedding coverage, describing gowns and reception menus,
giving their readership vicarious thrills. Wallace writes that, by
the thirties, brides had become "momentary celebrities." When
the socialite Nancy Beaton married Sir Hugh Smiley in 1933 at
Westminster, the dreamy photographs taken by her brother Cecil
were all over the papers—shots of Nancy looking slouchy and al-
luring, her eight bridesmaids linked by one long floral garland,
two boys in white satin holding up her veil. "There was so much
poverty that we all craved glamour," an eighty-seven-year-old former dressmaker told the *Mirror* in 2017, producing her own

Beaton-inspired wedding portrait. "It was our chance to feel like a star for the day." In 1938, a De Beers representative wrote to the ad agency N. W. Ayer & Son, asking if "the use of propaganda in various forms" could juice the engagement-ring market. In 1947, the N. W. Ayer copywriter Frances Gerety coined the slogan "A Diamond Is Forever," and ever since then, diamond engagement rings have been all but mandatory—an $11 billion industry in America as of 2012.

In the forties, getting married "went from a transition to a kind of apotheosis," Wallace writes. A wedding no longer marked a woman's shift from single to married, but rather, it indicated her ascension from ordinary woman to bride and wife. As this glorification was demarcated mainly through purchases, a publishing industry sprang up to tell women what they should buy. In 1934, the first American bridal magazine was founded, under the title *So You're Going to Be Married.* (It was later renamed *Brides* and purchased by Condé Nast.) In 1948, the first weddings-only advice book, *The Bride's Book of Etiquette*, gave women guidance that would persist through decades: "It's your privilege to look as lovely as you know how," and "You are privileged to make your wedding anything you want it to be," and "You are privileged to have all eyes center on you."

Against the backdrop of World War II, weddings took on a new, fierce importance. In 1942, nearly two million Americans got married—an 83 percent increase from a decade before, with two thirds of those brides marrying men who had newly enlisted in the military. The wedding industry capitalized on wartime ceremonies as a symbol of all that was precious about America. "A bride could be forgiven for believing that it was her patriotic duty to insist on a formal wedding, white satin and all," Wallace writes. The war also gave jewelry companies a lasting boon. Attempts to market engagement rings for men had previously flopped, as such rings were incompatible with the still-prevalent idea that engagement is a thing that men do to women. But in a war context, the male *wedding* band started to seem logical: with a wedding band, men could cross the ocean wearing a reminder of wife, country, and home. A tradition of bride and groom exchanging rings at the ceremony was rapidly invented. By the fifties, it was as if the double-ring ceremony had existed since the beginning of time.

After the war was over—and along with it, wartime fabric rationing—American wedding dresses grew more elaborate. Synthetic fabrics had become widely available, and full skirts of tulle and organza bloomed. Brides, already young, got even younger. (The average age of first marriage for women was twenty-two at the turn of the twentieth century, but by 1950 it had dropped to 20.3.) By the late fifties, three quarters of women between twenty and twenty-four were married. As the two-decade slump of depression and wartime gave way to peace, prosperity, and a brand-new mass consumer economy, weddings symbolized the beginning of a couple's catalog-perfect future—the house in the suburbs, the brand-new washing machine, the living room TV.

In the sixties, with social upheaval on the horizon, weddings continued to provide a vision of domestic tradition and stability. Brides adopted a Jackie Kennedy look, wearing pillbox hats, empire waists, and three-quarter sleeves. In the seventies, the wedding industry adapted to accommodate the counterculture, catering to a new wave of young couples who wished to avoid the previous generation's aesthetic. It was in this decade—with the so-called narcissism epidemic and the rise of what Tom Wolfe called the "Me Generation"—that the idea of the wedding as a form of deeply individual expression took hold. Men wore colored tuxes. Bianca Jagger got married in an Yves Saint Laurent Le Smoking jacket. "Extremely quirky weddings got publicity," writes Wallace, "like the couples who married on skis or underwater or stark naked in Times Square."

Then, in the eighties, the pendulum swung back. "For many of us who stood on the beach in the nineteen-seventies and looked on while the maid of honor sang 'Both Sides Now' and the barefoot couple plighted its troth with excerpts from Kahlil Gibran's *The Prophet*," Holly Brubach wrote in *The New Yorker*, "the news that in the eighties weddings seemed to be taking a turn for the more traditional came as a relief. Who could have foreseen that the results would often be, in their way, no less preposterous?" She noted the odd "pastiche of elements from Dior's New Look and Victorian fashion" that had taken over bridal attire in the years following Diana Spencer's televised royal wedding bonanza. Like Diana's dress, the eighties wedding look ran counter to fashion, with full skirts, mutton sleeves, bustles and bows.

In the nineties, with the rise of Vera Wang and the ascendancy of Calvin Klein minimalism, wedding dresses realigned with trends. Brides wore white slip dresses with spaghetti straps, à la Carolyn Bessette-Kennedy—a Calvin Klein publicist before her marriage, and a silky blond exemplar of East Coast good taste. From the West Coast, a Playboy Mansion licentiousness entered the bridal aesthetic. Cindy Crawford got married on the beach in a minidress that resembled lingerie. Consumerist raunch—*Girls Gone Wild, MTV Spring Break*—came crashing into the industry. Brides-to-be insisted on bachelorette parties involving hot-cop strippers and penis straws.

In the aughts, weddings took on the high-res bloat of reality television. *Who Wants to Marry a Multi-Millionaire?* aired, disastrously, in February 2000. Betrothal was the end goal of the *Bachelor* franchise, the raw material for the assembly line of *Say Yes to the Dress*. The aerial-scale wedding celebration—the type so preposterous that it required subsidization by the TV network that would broadcast it—entered the realm with Trista Rehn and Ryan Sutter's 2003 *Bachelorette* wedding, which cost $3.77 million and attracted 17 million viewers on ABC. (Rehn and Sutter were paid $1 million for the TV rights.) And then, in the 2010s, came the elaborate monoculture of Pinterest, the image-sharing social network that produced a new, ubiquitous, "traditional" wedding aesthetic, teaching couples to manufacture a sense of authenticity through rented barns, wildflowers in mason jars, old convertibles or rusty pickup trucks.

The industry churns on today, riding high and manic in the wake of two recent bride coronations: Kate Middleton, rigorously thin in her Alexander McQueen princess gown ($434,000), and Meghan Markle, doe-eyed in boatneck Givenchy ($265,000). Despite the economic precarity that has threatened the American population since the 2008 recession, weddings have only been getting more expensive. They remain an industry-dictated "theme park of upward mobility," as Naomi Wolf put it: a world defined by the illusion that everyone within it is upper-middle class.

This illusion is formalized further by the social media era, in which clothes and backdrops are routinely sought out and paid for in large part to broadcast the impression of cachet. Weddings have long existed in this sort of performative ecosystem: "A great set of wedding photographs can be called upon to justify all the expense that preceded them, and the anticipation of acquiring a good set of photographs can also encourage that expense in the first place," Rebecca Mead writes in *One Perfect Day: The Selling of the American Wedding*. Today, Instagram encourages people to treat life itself like a wedding—like a production engineered to be witnessed and admired by an audience. It has become common for people, especially women, to interact with themselves as if they were famous all the time. Under these circumstances, the vision of the bride as celebrity princess has hardened into something like a rule. Expectations of bridal beauty have collided with the wellness industry and produced a massive dark star of obligation. *Brides* recommends that its affianced readers take healing naps in salt chambers and cleanse themselves with crystals. *Martha Stewart Weddings* prices out a fireworks show at your reception ($5,000 for three to seven minutes). *The Knot* recommends underarm Botox ($1,500 per session). A friend of mine was recently quoted $27,000 for a single day of wedding photography. There are social media consultants for weddings; there are "bridal boot camp" fitness programs all over the nation; there is a growing industry for highly staged, professionally photographed engagements. One day these will probably seem traditional, too.

Despite my personality, or what you might guess if you've ever talked to me after I've had a single drink of alcohol, I have been in straight and monogamous relationships for more than twelve out of the past thirteen years. But my apathy toward weddings—the apparent culmination of these relationships—is lifelong. Girls are trained in childhood to take an interest in bridal matters, through Barbies (which I didn't care about) and make-believe (I mostly fantasized through reading) and feature-length Disney musicals, in which a series of beautiful princesses enchant a series of inter-changeable men. I loved these movies *except* for the love interests. I fantasized about being Belle, swinging around ladders in the li-brary; Ariel, swimming around the deep ocean with a fork; Jas-mine, alone in the starlight with her phenomenal tiger; Cinderella, getting a makeover from the mice and the birds. Toward the end of these movies, when things got real with the princes, I would get bored and eject my VHS tapes. While I was writing this, I pulled up the weddings from *Cinderella* and *The Little Mermaid* on You-Tube, and felt like I was watching deleted scenes.

It's not that I was averse to the bridal building blocks. I was girly as a kid, and I loved attention. I had pink sheets, pink cur-tains, pink walls in my room. I pored over descriptions of fancy dresses in books, feeling deeply pained in *Gone with the Wind* when Scarlett couldn't wear her favorite one, "the green plaid taf-feta, frothing with flounces and each flounce edged in green vel-vet ribbon," because, relatably, there was "unmistakably a grease spot on the basque." Sometimes, at family gatherings, I would demand an audience and sing "Colors of the Wind," in honor of the Disney princess that I felt most connected to—Pocahontas, with her neon sunrises and raccoon friend and bare feet. I was

only four years old when I started writing impassioned notes to
my mother to persuade her to take me to Glamour Shots, the
iconically tacky mall photo studio where you could take a portrait
of yourself in sequins. When she acquiesced, I wrote a thank-you
note *to God*. ("Thank you for the chance to go to Glammer Shots,"
I scrawled, "and for making me sneaky.") For the photo, I proudly
wore a white dress with puffy sleeves and flowers in my hair.

In middle school, I went on my first "date," dropped off at the
mall for a romantic matinee showing of the Adam Sandler vehicle
Big Daddy. Around then I started to desperately want guys to like
me; at the same time, I was repulsed by the predictability of that
desire. In high school, I carried on a series of intense male friendships and odd secretive dalliances, and mostly, within a graduat-
ing class of ninety people who had all gone to school together for
a decade, I didn't date. In college, I fell in love very quickly with a
guy who all but moved into my apartment in the fall of my second
year, when I was seventeen. Around then, I recounted one of our
conversations in my LiveJournal:

> He was telling me what scares him—that he's just fulfilling the
> part of, you know, like the left-wing existentialist college boy-
> friend after which I settle down with the Marriage Type. . . .
> What I told him, and what I really think, is that what are we all
> ever doing except playing a part that fulfills a role at its appro-
> priate time?

This is the only time the word "marriage" occurs in the entire archive, which covers my whole adolescence. Watching myself
obliviously shift a personal tension into an abstract social inquiry,
I can glimpse, for a second, a shadow of all the things I have neglected to admit to myself in the elaborate project of justifying
what I want.

Anyway, I broke up with that boyfriend my fourth year of college, suddenly confused as to why I had ever voluntarily done

someone else's laundry. When I moved home after graduation, I got bored and messaged Andrew, whom I had met the year before at a Halloween party. He'd been dressed as the wrestler Rowdy Roddy Piper. (I was dressed, politically incorrectly, as Pocahontas, and my date was draped in feather boas—the Colors of the Wind.) At the time, he was dating a pint-size brunette in my sorority, who later broke up with him before he moved to Houston for grad school.

Andrew was new to Texas, and I thought I was leaving for Peace Corps any minute. Freed by the mutual acknowledgment that this would be temporary, we glued ourselves to each other, and then six months passed in this way. One morning we woke up on a deflated air mattress in my friend Walt's apartment, hungover, with light filtering through the dust like magic, and when I looked at him I felt that if I couldn't do this forever I would die. A few days later, we went to DC for, of all things, a black-tie fraternity reunion. I got wasted and went outside to savor the taste of several delicious menthols, and then came back inside reeking of smoke, which Andrew hated. "I'd quit for you," I told him, "but . . ." My departure for Central Asia was, by then, just two weeks away. Andrew, who is a sweet boy, started crying. We went back to our hotel room and admitted that we loved each other. I woke up surrounded by cans of Budweiser, which I had drunkenly used as cold compresses for my tear-swollen face.

We decided to try to stay together, even though I was leaving. I boarded a plane to Kyrgyzstan, where, several months into my volunteer service, I reached my single peak of wedding ideation to date. My friend Elizabeth had sent me a care package full of wonderful, frivolous things—an issue of *Martha Stewart Weddings* among them. Everything in the magazine was pristine, useless, beautiful, predictable. I loved it, and I reread it all the time. One night, after climbing halfway up a mountain to try to get cell service on my tiny Nokia, after failing to reach Andrew and sinking into a wormhole of dread that I was ruining something irreplaceable, I fell asleep reading my wedding magazine and got married to him in a dream. It was an intense, vivid, realistic vision, soundtracked by 2011. There was a vast, open green plain, with flowers drifting in the air, the guitar loop from José González's cover of "Heartbeats" playing, a sense of shattering freedom and security, like an ascension, or possibly like a death; then, a dark room that glittered like a disco, and Robyn's "Hang with Me" thudding through the air. I woke up shocked, and then curled into a ball, my eyes smarting. For weeks afterward I nursed that fantasy, even though I was never able to imagine anything but light and music and weather. I could never see myself, could never imagine bridesmaids, a dress, a cake.

I left Peace Corps early. On the plane back from Kyrgyzstan, I was a raw nerve, fragile in a way that I had never been before—flattened out by the awful juxtaposition between my obscene power as an American and my obscene powerlessness as a woman, and by an undiagnosed case of tuberculosis, and by my own humiliating inability to live comfortably in a situation where I couldn't achieve or explain my way out of every bind. I went straight from the airport to Andrew's apartment in Houston and never left. He was, at the time, oppressively busy, coming home from his grad school studio to catch five hours of sleep a night. I occupied myself with my two Peace Corps hobbies: doing yoga and cooking elaborate meals. Alone in the kitchen, rolling out pastry crusts and checking vinyasa schedules, I started to feel uncomfortable flashbacks to college, as if I had once again, at a freakishly young age, found myself playing the role of wife.

At the time, I didn't technically need a job right away. Andrew had gotten a full scholarship to Rice, and so his parents paid his— now our—$500 rent, giving him the money they had saved to subsidize grad school tuition. This year of free rent was transformative, as free rent tends to be. But I was terrified of what it meant to depend on someone else's money. I was afraid of making myself useful through sex and dinner. I spent hours every day on

Craigslist looking for work and, in the process, discovered lifestyle blogs, wedding blogs—websites that overwhelmed me with despair. I stopped cobbling together grant-writing gigs and started "helping" rich kids with their college application essays, which effectively meant writing them. Propping up the class system paid terrifically, and with this ill-gotten cash, I bought myself a sense of permission. I wrote some short stories and got into Michigan's MFA program. In 2012, we moved to Ann Arbor. We were invited to eighteen weddings over the course of the next year.

By that point Andrew and I were a team, fully. We had a dog, we split the housework and our credit card statement, and we had never spent a holiday apart. When I curled up to him in the mornings I felt like a baby sea lion climbing on a sunlit rock. One weekend in 2013 we flew back to Texas for a wedding in Marfa, where the whole thing was a vision of heaven: a mournful Led Zeppelin riff thrumming through a church, the heat of the desert, the supernatural happiness of the young couple, the sunset gradient fading away as they danced. That night I sat under the stars in a black dress, drinking tequila, wondering if my heart was as incorrect as it seemed to me in that moment—thudding with the certainty that I didn't want any of this at all.

The pressure of this thought intensified until my ears seemed to be ringing. I told Andrew what I was thinking, and his face crumpled. He had been thinking the exact opposite, he told me. This was the first wedding where he'd really understood what all of this was for.

Half a decade has gone by since then. Andrew has long ago forgiven me for making him cry in Marfa; he has also, possibly due to a lack of desirable alternatives, lost interest in making anything official. Our lives are full of pleasure but almost completely stripped of mass ritual: we don't do anything for Valentine's Day, or celebrate an "anniversary," or give each other

Christmas presents, or put up a tree. For my part, I have stopped feeling guilty about not wanting to marry such a marriageable person. I now understand that it is an extremely ordinary and unremarkable thing to feel overwhelmed by weddings, or even averse to them. As a society we do not lack for evidence that weddings are often superficial, performative, excessive, and annoying. There is a strong strain of wedding hatred in our culture underneath all the fanaticism. The hatred and fanaticism are, of course, intertwined.

This tension crops up in many wedding movies, which tend to depict weddings as a site of simultaneous love and resentment. (Or, in the case of the soothing and relatable *Melancholia*, a site of impending comet apocalypse.) Often, in wedding movies, it is the romantic partner who is loved and the family who generates the resentment, as in *Father of the Bride* or *My Big Fat Greek Wedding*. But more recently, these movies have been about how women love and resent the wedding itself. The 2011 Paul Feig blockbuster *Bridesmaids* played this tension for slapstick comedy and sweetness. The 2012 Leslye Headland movie *Bachelorette* did it again, on a dark, acidic palette.

Before that, there was *27 Dresses*, released in 2008, starring Katherine Heigl, and 2009's *Bride Wars*, starring Kate Hudson and Anne Hathaway. These deeply upsetting rom-coms were supposed to be *about* women who love weddings and *for* women who love weddings. But both movies seemed to really hate weddings, and to hate those women, too. *27 Dresses* was about Jane, an uptight, sentimental, perpetually exhausted bridesmaid-handmaiden who became obsessed with weddings after she fixed a rip in a bride's dress when she was a kid. "I knew I had helped someone on the most important day of her life," Jane says breathily, in the opening sequence, "and I just couldn't wait for my special day." Throughout the movie, she compulsively denies herself self-worth and happiness, hoarding both things for her imaginary future wedding, planning other people's rehearsal dinners and accruing huge piles of resentment in her soul.

Bride Wars is worse. Hathaway's Emma and Hudson's Liv are best friends who have also been obsessed with weddings since childhood. They get engaged simultaneously and accidentally plan their weddings at the Plaza for the same day. An all-out battle erupts as a result of this preposterously fixable situation. Emma, a public-school teacher who pays the $25,000 venue fee from the wedding nest egg that she's been building since she was a teenager, sends Liv chocolates every day so that she'll get fat. Liv, a lawyer with a treadmill in her office, sneaks into a spray-tan salon to turn Emma bright orange. Both women are essentially friendless, and they treat their husbands-to-be like crash-test dummies. Just before she walks down the aisle, Emma snaps at the coworker whom she's forced to be maid of honor:

> Deb, I've been dealing with versions of you my whole life, and I'm gonna tell you something that I should've told myself a long time ago. Sometimes it's about me, okay? Not all the time, but every once in a while it's my time. Like today. If you're not okay with that, feel free to go. But if you stay, you have to do your job, and that means smiling and talking about my bridal beauty, and most importantly, not making it about you . . . Okay? Can you do that?

Like Jane, Emma has been broken by the cultural psychosis that tells women to cram a lifetime's supply of open self-interest into a single, incredibly expensive day.

In 2018, Michelle Markowitz and Caroline Moss published the humor book *Hey Ladies!*, a series of hellish fictional emails sent among a group of female friends in New York City who are constantly sentencing one another to elaborate social obligations— a problem that worsens once members of the group start getting

engaged. A sample email, from when the bride-to-be's mother
chimes in on the bridal shower:

> Since we all know Jen has always loved flowers, I'm thinking
> we do a garden luncheon bridal shower at our country club in
> Virginia at the turn of the season. I know Virginia is a trek
> from New York City and Brooklyn, but I already checked Am-
> trak train tickets for the last weekend in April, and it looks like
> it will only be ~$450 per person round trip (a deal!).
>
> Ali, since you're the Maid of Honor I'll let you handle dress
> code, but please, ladies, be prepared to wear a pastel or muted
> shade that goes well with your skin tone. If you're not sure,
> google! Or go to a high-end luxury clothing store and make a
> consultation appointment with a stylist. As for shoes, just be-
> cause this will be outside doesn't mean you should sacrifice
> looking good for being comfortable. I am going to have a pho-
> tographer on site, so keep that in mind! As for hair and makeup,
> please call Meegan at Hair Today in VA for consecutive day-of
> appointments so we can have consistency in looks.

It's satire, of course, and perfectly exaggerated. But real emails
like this frequently go viral on Twitter. And, although until 2014
I never made more than $35,000 annually, I have spent, at a bare
minimum, at least $35,000 on weddings to date.

So: the expense, the trouble, the intensity. And then there are
the predictable feminist things, too. Historically, marriage has
mostly been bad for women and fantastic for men. Confucius defined a wife as "someone who submits to another." Assyrian law
declared, "A man may flog his wife, pluck her hair, strike her and
mutilate her ears. There is no guilt." In early modern Europe,
writes Stephanie Coontz, in *Marriage, a History*, a husband "could
force sex upon [his wife], beat her, and imprison her in the family
home, while it was she who endowed him with all her worldly
goods. The minute he placed that ring upon her finger he con-

trolled any land she brought to the marriage and he owned outright all her movable property as well as any income she later earned." The legal doctrine of coverture, which held that, as Sir William Blackstone put it in 1753, "the very being, or legal existence of the woman is suspended during the marriage or at least is incorporated or consolidated into that of her husband," was implemented in the Middle Ages and was not fully dismantled in America until the late twentieth century. Until 1974, women were frequently required to bring their husbands with them while applying for a credit card. Until the eighties, legal codes in many states specified that husbands could not be held responsible for raping their wives.

Part of my aversion to getting married is my sense of incompatibility with the word "wife," which—outside the *Borat* context, which is perfect, and will be perfect forever—feels inseparable from this dismal history to me. At the same time, I understand that people have been objecting to inequality in marriage for centuries, from both the inside and the outside of the institution, and that, in recent years, what it means to be a wife, a married partner, has changed. In the summer of 2015, in *Obergefell v. Hodges*, the Supreme Court guaranteed same-sex couples the right to marry each other—a decision that validated the relatively recent conception of marriage as a mutual affirmation of love and commitment, and also reconfigured it as an institution that could be entered into on gender-equal terms. "No union is more profound than marriage, for it embodies the highest ideals of love, fidelity, devotion, sacrifice, and family," reads the final paragraph of the decision. "In forming a marital union, two people become something greater than once they were. . . . It would misunderstand these men and women to say they disrespect the idea of marriage. Their plea is that they do respect it, respect it so deeply that they seek to find its fulfillment for themselves. Their hope is not to be condemned to live in loneliness, excluded from one of civilization's oldest institutions. They ask for equal dignity in the eyes of the law." On the Friday that the decision was handed down, I'd planned on staying in, but then the news electrified me with such happiness that I went out, and ended up at the club on mushrooms. I remember standing still, people dancing all around me, my heart like Funfetti cake, reading the decision's final paragraph on my phone screen over and over as I cried.

The constitutional right to gay marriage brings the institution into its viable future. To many people at the tail end of my generation, and to much of the generation that follows, it may already seem incomprehensible that gay couples once did not have the right to marry—as incomprehensible as it feels to me when I imagine not being able to apply for a credit card on my own. This is an era in which marriage is generally understood not as the beginning of a partnership but as the avowal of that partnership. It's an era in which women graduate from college in greater numbers than men, and often outearn men in their twenties; an era in which women are no longer expected to get married to have sex or to build a stable adulthood, and are consequently delaying marriage, sometimes forgoing it altogether. Today, only around 20 percent of Americans are married by age twenty-nine, compared to nearly 60 percent in 1960. Marriage is becoming more equal on every front. "In part, that's because when we delay marriage, it's not just women who become independent," Rebecca Traister writes in *All the Single Ladies*. "It's also men, who, like women, learn to clothe and feed themselves, to clean their homes and iron their shirts and pack their own suitcases."

Many of the weddings I've been to have reflected this shift. The fetishization of virginal purity has been largely removed from the picture: even in Texas, among religious conservatives, it is often implicitly acknowledged that the engaged couple has prepared for a life together in ways that include having sex. Thankfully, I can't remember the last time I saw a bouquet toss. Often, both parents walk the bride down the aisle. One ceremony featured the bride and groom's daughters as flower girls. One of my

Peace Corps friends proposed to her male partner on a beach in Senegal. While writing this, I went to a wedding in Cincinnati where, post-kiss, the officiant proudly announced the couple as "Dr. Katherine Lennard and Mr. Jonathon Jones." A few weeks later, I attended another wedding, this one in Brooklyn, where the couple entered the ceremony together, and the bride, the writer Joanna Rothkopf, delivered her vows in two sentences, one of which was a *Sopranos* joke. ("I love you more than Bobby Bacala loves Karen, and luckily I can't cook so you'll never have to eat my last ziti.") A few weeks after *that*, I drove upstate for another wedding, where my friend Bobby was preceded down the aisle by the four women in his wedding party, and he and his husband, Josh, walked to the altar holding hands.

On the whole, though, the "traditional" wedding—meaning the traditional straight wedding—remains one of the most significant re-invocations of gender inequality that we have. There is still a drastic mismatch between the cultural script around marriage, in which a man grudgingly acquiesces to a woman salivating for a diamond, and the reality of marriage, in which men's lives often get better and women's lives often get worse. Married men report better mental health and live longer than single men; in contrast, married women report *worse* mental health, and die earlier, than single women. (These statistics do not suggest that the act of getting married is some sort of gendered hex: rather, they reflect the way that, when a man and a woman combine their unpaid domestic obligations under the aegis of tradition, the woman usually ends up doing most of the work—a fact that is greatly exacerbated by the advent of kids.) There's an idea that women get to Scrooge-dive in heaps of money after divorce proceedings, but in fact, women who worked while married see their incomes go down by 20 percent on average after a divorce, whereas men's incomes go up by more than that.

Gender inequality is so entrenched in straight marriage that it persists in the face of cultural change as well as personal intentions. A 2014 study of Harvard Business School alumni—a group of people primed for high ambitions and flexibility—showed that more than half of men from their thirties to their sixties expected that their careers would take priority over their spouses' careers: three quarters of these men had their expectations fulfilled. In contrast, less than a quarter of their female peers expected their spouses' careers to take precedence over theirs, but this nonetheless happened 40 percent of the time. Biology plays a role here, obviously—we have not yet cracked the situation in which people whose bodies are consistent with female biology have to have the children, if children are to be had—but social convention and public policy produce a thicket of unforced problems. The study of Harvard Business School graduates showed that the younger female respondents, in their twenties and early thirties, were on track for a similar mismatch between outcome and desire.

There is a harbinger of this inequality in marriage, and a symbol, in the way that straight women are still often expected to formally adopt the identities of their husbands. In *Jane Eyre*, which Charlotte Brontë published in 1847, the narrator feels a sense of dislocation when, on the eve of her wedding, she sees "Mrs. Rochester" on her luggage tags. "I could not persuade myself to affix them, or have them affixed. Mrs. Rochester! she did not exist," Jane thinks. ". . . It was enough that in yonder closet, opposite my dressing-table, garments said to be hers had already displaced my black stuff Lowood frock and straw bonnet: for not to me appertained that suit of wedding raiment. . . . I shut my closet to conceal the strange, wraith-like apparel it contained." In Daphne du Maurier's *Rebecca*, published in 1938, Rebecca feels the same sense of self-estrangement at the prospect of marriage. "Mrs. de Winter. I would be Mrs. de Winter. I considered my name, and the signature on cheques, to tradesmen, and in letters asking people to dinner." She repeats the name, dissociating. "Mrs. de Winter. I would be Mrs. de Winter." After a few minutes, she realizes that she has been eating a sour tangerine, and that she has "a sharp, bitter taste in my mouth, and I had only just noticed it." Mrs. Rochester and Mrs. de Winter both end up near-fatally embroiled in their husbands' previous problems, which themselves stem from marriage; it's notable that Brontë and du Maurier restore a sort of balance in these novels by burning both husbands' estates to the ground.

The first woman in America to keep her birth name after marriage was the feminist Lucy Stone, who wed Henry Blackwell in 1855. The two of them published their vows, which doubled as a protest against marriage laws that "refuse[d] to recognize the wife as an independent, rational being, while they confer upon the husband an injurious and unnatural superiority, investing him with legal powers which no honorable man would exercise, and which no man should possess." (Stone was later barred from voting in a school board election under her maiden name.) Nearly seven decades later, a group of feminists formed the Lucy Stone League, agitating for the right of married women to check into a hotel, or open a bank account, or get a passport, in their own names. This fight for name equality dragged on until fairly recently: the oldest women in that Harvard Business School study would have been required, in some states, to take their husbands' last names if they wanted to vote. It took until the 1975 Tennessee State Supreme Court case *Dunn v. Palermo* for the final law to this effect to be struck down. "Married women," wrote Justice Joe Henry, "have labored under a form of societal compulsion and economic coercion which has not been conducive to the assertion of some rights and privileges of citizenship." A requirement that a woman take her husband's name "would stifle and chill virtually all progress in the rapidly expanding field of human liberties. We live in a new day. We cannot create and continue conditions and then defend their existence by reliance on the custom thus created."

Women began keeping their names in the seventies, when it became broadly possible to do so. In 1986, *The New York Times* began using the honorific "Ms." to refer to women whose marital status was unknown, as well as to married women who wished to use their birth names. The trend of name independence peaked in the nineties, at a rather paltry 23 percent of married women, and today less than 20 percent keep their names. The decision "is one of convenience," Katie Roiphe wrote at *Slate* in 2004. "The politics are almost incidental. Our fundamental independence is not so imperiled that we *need* to keep our names. . . . At this point—apologies to Lucy Stone, and her pioneering work in name keeping—our attitude is: Whatever works."

Roiphe's laissez-faire postfeminist view remains common. Women believe that their names are personal, not political—in large part because the decision-making around them remains so culturally restricted and curtailed. A woman keeping her name is making a choice that is expected to be limited and futile. She will not pass the name down to her children, or bestow it upon her husband. At most—or so people tend to think—her last name will be crammed into the middle of her children's names, or packed around a hyphen, and then later dropped for space reasons. (And in fact, a Louisiana law still requires the child of a married couple to bear the husband's last name in order for a birth certificate to be issued.) We find it inappropriate for women to treat their names the way that men, by default, feel entitled to. On this front, as on so many others, a woman is allowed to assert her independence as long as it doesn't affect anyone else.

Of course, there are no clear-cut ways to navigate family names even with a presumption of gender equality: hyphenated names dissolve after a single generation, and generally speaking, one name has got to go. But there's a flexibility with which queer couples approach the issue of naming children—as well as wedding-related conventions in general, particularly proposals—that is conspicuously absent from the heterosexual scene. In marriage, too, gay couples divide household work more equally than straight couples do, and when they adopt "traditional" gender roles, they "tend to reject the notion that their labor arrangements are imitative or derivative of those of heterosexual couples," as Abbie Goldberg writes in a 2013 study. Instead, "they interpret their arrangements as pragmatic and chosen." Gay couples are also more likely to find their division of labor to be fair than straight couples—a statistic that holds, crucially, even when the work is not divided evenly. (In other words, their hopes and their outcomes are more closely aligned.) The institution works differently without the power imbalance that historically defined it. Like any social construct, marriage is most flexible when it is new.

How is it possible that so much of contemporary life feels so arbitrary and so inescapable? Thinking about weddings has not been very useful to me: developing an understanding of the material conditions that produced the wedding ritual, its basis in inequality and its role in perpetuating that inequality, hasn't really meant a thing. It doesn't remove me from a culture that is organized through marriage and weddings; it certainly doesn't make it any less sensible to do what all the affianced of the past, present, and future have done and are doing, which is taking these opportunities for ritual pleasure and sweetness whenever they can.

And still I wonder how much harder it would be to get straight women to accept the reality of marriage if they were not first presented with the fantasy of a wedding. I wonder if women today would so readily accept the unequal diminishment of their independence without their sense of self-importance being overinflated first. It feels like a trick, a trick that has worked and is still working, that the bride remains the image of womanhood at its most broadly celebrated—and that planning a wedding is the only period in a woman's life where she is universally and unconditionally encouraged to conduct everything on her terms.

The conventional vision of a woman's life, in which the wedding plays a starring role, seems to be offering an unspoken trade-off. Here, our culture says, is an event that will center you absolutely—that will crystallize your image when you were young and gorgeous, admired and beloved, with the whole world rolling out in front of you like an endless meadow, like a plush red carpet, sparklers lighting up your irises and petals drifting through your lavish, elegant hair. In exchange, from that point forward, in the eyes of the state and everyone around you, your needs will slowly cease to exist. This is of course not the case for everyone, but for plenty of women, becoming a bride still means being flattered into submission: being prepared, through a rush of attention and a series of gender-resegregated rituals—the bridal shower, the bachelorette party, and, later, the baby shower—for a future in which your identity will be systematically framed as secondary to the identity of your husband and kids.

The paradox at the heart of the wedding comes from the two versions of a woman that it conjures. There's the glorified bride, looming large and resplendent and almost monstrously powerful, and there's her nullified twin and opposite, the woman who vanishes underneath the name change and the veil. These two selves are opposites, bound together by male power. The advice book chirping "You are privileged to have all eyes center on you" and Anne Hathaway snapping "Sometimes it's about me, okay?" at her maid of honor are inextricable from the laws that required women to take their husband's name if they wanted to vote in elections and the fact that the post-marriage benefit package of health, wealth, and happiness is still mostly distributed to men. Underneath the confectionary spectacle of the wedding is a case study in how inequality bestows outsize affirmation on women as compensation for making us disappear.

It is easy, so easy, to find all of this beautiful. I recently pulled up an archive of *Martha Stewart Weddings* to see if I could find the issue that I pored over in Kyrgyzstan almost a decade ago. I spotted the cover immediately: the peach backdrop, the redhead with a huge smile and bright lipstick—like a Disney princess, with butterflies alighting on the tulle skirt of her strapless white dress. "Make It Yours," the cover commands. I bought it, and read through it one more time, remembering the tea-length skirts, the bouquets of anemones and ranunculus, the apricot champagne sparklers, these things I had mentally surrounded myself with when all I wanted was for something good to last.

The woman on the cover reminded me of Anne of Green Gables, L. M. Montgomery's thoughtful, talkative, carrot-headed heroine. I couldn't remember when in the series she got married, or how, or what it looked like—even though I had, of course, nurtured a crush on her boy-next-door sweetheart Gilbert Blythe. I looked up *Anne's House of Dreams*, the fifth book in the series, and found the wedding scene. It's a September day, full of sunshine, and the chapter opens with Anne in her old room at Green Gables, thinking about cherry trees and wifehood. Then she descends the stairs in her wedding dress, "slender and shining-eyed," her arms full of roses. In this pivotal moment, she does not think or speak. The narration passes to Gilbert. "She was his at last," he thinks, "this evasive, long-sought Anne, won after years of patient waiting. It was to him she was coming in the sweet surrender of the bride."

It's such a natural scene. It's lovely. It's so perversely familiar. It occurs to me that I crave independence, that I demand and expect it, but never enough, since I was a teenager, to actually be alone. It's possible that, just as marriage conceals its true nature through the elaborate ritual of the wedding, I have been staging this entire production to hide from myself some reality about my life. If I object to the wife's diminishment for the same reason that I object to the bride's glorification, maybe this reason is much simpler and more obvious than I've imagined: I don't want to be diminished, and I *do* want to be glorified—not in one shining moment, but whenever I want.

This seems true, but I still feel that I can't trust it. Here, the more I try to uncover whatever I'm looking for, the more I feel that I'm too far gone. I can feel the low, uneasy hum of self-delusion whenever I think about all of this—a tone that gets louder the more I try to write and cancel it out. I can feel the tug of my deep and recurring suspicion that anything I might think about myself must be, somehow, necessarily wrong.

In the end, the safest conclusions may not actually be conclusions. We are asked to understand our lives under such impossibly convoluted conditions. I have always accommodated everything I wish I were opposed to. Here, as in so many other things, the "thee" that I dread may have been the "I" all along.

Acknowledgments

Though all of these essays were written for this book, several of them influenced my work at *The New Yorker*, and vice versa. A few of them build on things I wrote at *Jezebel* and *The Hairpin*. I am thankful to have started writing inside the *Awl* family: thank you to Logan Sachon and Mike Dang, the first editors to publish me; to Jane Marie, my dreamy first *Hairpin* editor; to Choire Sicha and Alex Balk, who used to confuse me when they would bitch about the internet—lol.

I'm thankful to the Repentagon for the lasting education, and for the friends, too—Lauren, Rachel, Annabel, Lara, thanks for seeing it all. Robert, I'm as glad for you now as I was when we saw the construction angels.

At my beloved University of Virginia: thank you to the Jefferson Scholars Foundation for the lifetime of student debt freedom, to Michael Joseph Smith, to Caroline Rody, to Walt Hunter, to Rachel Gendreau. Kevin, Jamie, Ryan, Tory, Baxa, Juli, and Buster Baxter: thank you for the permanent spiritual home.

It was during my short time in the Peace Corps that I started considering the unlikely possibility of writing for a living. Lola, Yan, Kyle, thank you for letting me cry when my laptop was stolen, and Akash, thank you forever for lending me yours so that I could start writing again. David, you're the best *kuya*. Dinara Sultanova, you're the most wonderful woman I've ever met.

I owe so much to the funding and space provided by the University of Michigan Helen Zell Writers' Program. Thank you to Nicholas Delbanco for encouraging me immediately, and to Brit Bennett, Maya West, Chris McCormick, and Mairead Small Staid for your easygoing brilliance. Rebecca Scherm, Barbara Linhardt, Katie Lennard: see you at the barre, etc.

My friendships in New York have kept a little part of the world warm and steady: thank you to Help Group, to 2018, and to the opera cunts. I'm grateful to Amy Rose Spiegel, a guardian angel; to Derek Davies, for so much musical ecstasy; to Frannie Stabile, the patron saint of butt optimization. Puja Patel, I'm sorry that I never filed that one time at SXSW. Luce de Palchi, I'll never forget being at a loss for words, on deadline, the night after the election, and you told me that I didn't need to do anything other than be honest—that what I thought would be enough.

At Gawker Media: Tom Scocca, thank you for your excruciating edits. To my beloved freaks at *Jezebel*, please come over for a bottle of rosé each.

To Rebecca Mead, Rebecca Solnit, and Rebecca Traister— Andrew would always ask me *which* Rebecca I was going on about this time—I admire all of you and your work so much, and I felt crushed by happiness when you looked out for me early on. Thank you to Jeff Bennett, who gave me invaluable notes on this manuscript, and to the genius Marlon James for introducing us. To Gideon Lewis-Kraus, thank you for X-raying this book and my personhood. Thanks to the remarkable Mackenzie Williams, who provided research assistance on several essays, most notably "We Come from Old Virginia" and "I Thee Dread." My dear wife Haley Mlotek, thank you for handing me the subtitle of this book on the day it was due. And to Emma Carmichael: thank you for giving me a career, and a close-up look at how to bring the best out of people, and above all a friendship that I really can't imagine my life without.

I am so grateful to the MacDowell Colony for giving me a month in paradise. To my incredible agent, Amy Williams, thank you for every last thing you do. Thank you to Jenny Meyer, and to Anna Kelly at Fourth Estate. I still find it laughable that I am employed at *The New Yorker*—my brilliant colleagues, you fill me with awe. Emily Greenhouse, thanks for adopting me in London. Jeanie Riess, thank you for fact-checking this book. Bruce Diones, thank you for keeping it all running. Nick Thompson, thank you for hiring me. Thank you to Dorothy Wickenden and Pam McCarthy. To David Haglund, my editor, you are the very best—thank you for making me better. Thank you to David Remnick for not firing me (yet) when I tweet about my bong.

Carrie Frye, you are the most generous reader, the most supernatural editor, the loveliest person—thank you for guiding me with such meticulous grace and insight through the entire process of turning this proposal into a manuscript. I couldn't have written this book without you. I'm grateful to everyone at Random House for taking such good care of me—especially to Andy Ward, Susan Kamil, Molly Turpin, and Dhara Parikh. To my editor, Ben Greenberg, thank you for making this book a reality—for championing it, sharpening it, and always making me feel that I was in great hands.

Finally: to Lynn Stekas and John Daley, thank you for being family to me since 2010, for the values you passed down to your children, and for your example of mutual love and respect. Clare and Matt and CJ and Quinn, I'm so glad you guys are in my life. To my brother, Martin, I'm sorry I made you pretend to be my dog before we got Gretzky. To my actual dog, Luna, thank you for being the best fluffy pal—with you, I could never be lonely. To Aida Adia, my beautiful grandmother, I know that I'm a reader because of you. To my mom and dad, I'm in your debt forever:

your sacrifices made me tough and capable and alive to the world's strangeness, and taught me about unconditional love. And to Andrew Daley, my partner-in-everything: thank you for growing up with me, for building me a desk and a life, and for being so attractive. In truth, I've felt married to you for a long time.

Background Reading

The I in the Internet

Carr, Nicholas. *The Shallows: What the Internet Is Doing to Our Brains*. W.W. Norton, 2010.

Forster, E. M. "The Machine Stops." *Oxford and Cambridge Review*, November 1909.

Gilroy-Ware, Marcus. *Filling the Void: Emotion, Capitalism, and Social Media*. Repeater, 2017.

Goffman, Erving. *The Presentation of Self in Everyday Life*. Anchor Books, 1959.

Hermann, John. "The Content Wars." *Awl*, 2015.

Lanier, Jaron. *You Are Not a Gadget: A Manifesto*. Penguin, 2011.

Milner, Ryan, and Whitney Phillips. *The Ambivalent Internet: Mischief, Oddity, and Antagonism Online*. Polity, 2017.

Nagle, Angela. *Kill All Normies: Online Culture Wars from Tumblr and 4chan to the Alt-Right and Trump*. Zero Books, 2017.

Odell, Jenny. *How to Do Nothing*. Melville House, 2019.

Phillips, Whitney. *This Is Why We Can't Have Nice Things: Mapping the Relationship Between Online Trolling and Mainstream Culture*. MIT Press, 2016.

Read, Max. "Does Even Mark Zuckerberg Know What Facebook Is?" *New York*, October 2, 2017.

Ronson, Jon. *So You've Been Publicly Shamed*. Picador, 2016.

Schulman, Sarah. *Conflict Is Not Abuse: Overstating Harm, Community Responsibility, and the Duty of Repair*. Arsenal Pulp Press, 2017.

Silverman, Jacob. *Terms of Service: Social Media and the Price of Constant Connection*. Harper Perennial, 2016.

Wu, Tim. *The Attention Merchants*. Atlantic, 2017.

Always Be Optimizing

Brodesser-Akner, Taffy. "Losing It in the Anti-Dieting Age." *New York Times Magazine*, August 2, 2017.

Buchanan, Matt. "How to Power Lunch When You Have No Power." *Awl*, January 22, 2015.

Foucault, Michel. *Discipline and Punish*. Pantheon, 1977.

Haraway, Donna. "A Cyborg Manifesto: Science, Technology, and Socialist-Feminism in the Late Twentieth Century." In *Simians, Cyborgs and Women: The Reinvention of Nature*. Routledge, 1991.

Kinsella, Sophie. *My Not So Perfect Life*. Dial Press, 2017.

Lacey, Catherine. *The Answers*. Farrar, Straus & Giroux, 2017.

Shelley, Mary. *Frankenstein*. 1818; Dover, 1994.

Sudjic, Olivia. *Sympathy*. Houghton Mifflin Harcourt, 2017.

Weigel, Moira. "Pajama Rich." *Real Life*, August 22, 2016.

Weiss, Emily. "The Little Wedding Black Book." *Into the Gloss*, 2016.

Widdows, Heather. *Perfect Me*. Princeton University Press, 2018.

Wolf, Naomi. *The Beauty Myth*. Chatto & Windus, 1990.

Pure Heroines

Alcott, Louisa May. *Little Men*. Roberts Brothers, 1871.

———. *Little Women*. Roberts Brothers, 1869.

Austen, Jane. *Pride and Prejudice*. T. Egerton, 1813.

Beauvoir, Simone de. *The Second Sex*. Penguin, 1949.

Blume, Judy. *Starring Sally J. Freedman as Herself*. Bradbury, 1978.

———. *Tiger Eyes*. Bradbury, 1981.

Chopin, Kate. *The Awakening*. Herbert S. Stone & Co., 1899.

Collins, Suzanne. *The Hunger Games*. Scholastic, 2008.

Didion, Joan. *Play It as It Lays*. Farrar, Straus & Giroux, 1970.

Edwards, Julie Andrews. *Mandy*. HarperCollins, 1971.

Eliot, George. *Middlemarch*. William Blackwood and Sons, 1871.

Eugenides, Jeffrey. *The Marriage Plot*. Picador, 2011.

———. *The Virgin Suicides*. Farrar, Straus & Giroux, 1993.

Ferrante, Elena. *My Brilliant Friend*. Europa, 2012.

———. *The Days of Abandonment*. Europa, 2005.

Fitzhugh, Louise. *Harriet the Spy*. Harper & Row, 1964.

Flaubert, Gustave. *Madame Bovary*. Michel Lévy Frères, 1856.

Flynn, Gillian. *Gone Girl*. Crown, 2012.

Gergen, Mary. "Life Stories: Pieces of a Dream." In *Toward a New Psychology of Gender*. Routledge, 1997.

Grossman, Lev. *The Magicians*. Viking, 2009.

Hardy, Thomas. *Tess of the D'Urbervilles*. James R. Osgood, 1891.

James, E. L. *Fifty Shades of Grey*. Vintage, 2011.

James, Henry. *Portrait of a Lady*. Houghton, Mifflin and Company, 1881.

Konigsburg, E. L. *From the Mixed-Up Files of Ms. Basil E. Frankweiler*. Atheneum, 1967.

Kraus, Chris. *I Love Dick*. Semiotext(e), 1997.

Larsson, Stieg. *The Girl with the Dragon Tattoo*. Norstedts Förlag, 2005.

Lovelace, Maud Hart. *Betsy-Tacy and Tib*. Thomas Y. Crowell, 1941.

Lowry, Lois. *Anastasia Krupnik*. Houghton Mifflin, 1979.

Meyer, Stephenie. *Twilight*. Little, Brown, 2005.

Milan Women's Bookstore Collective. *Sexual Difference: A Theory of Social-Symbolic Practice*. Indiana University Press, 1990.

Miller, Nancy. *The Heroine's Text: Readings in the French and English Novel*. Columbia University Press, 1980.

Mitchell, Margaret. *Gone with the Wind*. Macmillan, 1936.

Montgomery, L. M. *Emily of New Moon*. Frederick A. Stokes, 1923.

———. *Anne of Green Gables*. L .C. Page & Co., 1908.

Naylor, Phyllis Reynolds. *The Agony of Alice*. Atheneum, 1985.

Offill, Jenny. *Dept. of Speculation*. Vintage Contemporaries, 2014.

Pascal, Francine. *Double Love*. Macmillan, 1983.

Plath, Sylvia. *The Bell Jar.* Heinemann, 1963.

Roth, Veronica. *Divergent.* HarperCollins, 2011.

Rowling, J. K. *Harry Potter and the Prisoner of Azkaban.* Scholastic, 2001.

Smith, Betty. *A Tree Grows in Brooklyn.* Harper & Bros., 1943.

Solnit, Rebecca. *The Mother of All Questions.* Haymarket, 2017.

Taylor, Sydney. *All of a Kind Family.* Follett, 1951.

Thackeray, William. *Vanity Fair.* Bradbury & Evans, 1848.

Tolstoy, Leo. *Anna Karenina.* The Russian Herald, 1878.

Warner, Gertrude Chandler. *The Boxcar Children.* Albert Whitman & Co., 1942.

Ecstasy

The Alister Hardy Archive. www.uwtsd.ac.uk/library/alister-hardy-religious-experience-research-centre.

Beverly, Julia. *Sweet Jones: Pimp C's Trill Life Story.* Shreveport Ave., 2015.

Carson, Anne. *Decreation: Poetry, Essays, Opera.* Vintage, 2006.

Eisner, Bruce. *Ecstasy: The MDMA Story.* Ronin Publishing, 1993.

Faniel, Maco L. *Hip Hop in Houston: The Origin and the Legacy.* History Press, 2016.

Hall, Michael. "The Slow Life and Fast Death of DJ Screw." *Texas Monthly,* April 2001.

Hitt, Jack. "This Is Your Brain on God." *Wired,* November 1, 1999.

Holland, Julie. *Ecstasy: The Complete Guide: A Comprehensive Look at the Risks and Benefits of MDMA.* Park Street Press, 2001.

Huxley, Aldous. *The Perennial Philosophy.* Harper & Bros., 1945.

James, William. *The Varieties of Religious Experience.* Longmans, Green & Co., 1902.

Julian of Norwich. *Revelations of Divine Love.* 1670; Dover, 2006.

Kierkegaard, Søren. *Fear and Trembling.* C. A. Reitzel, 1843.

Lewis, C. S. *Perelandra.* The Bodley Head, 1943.

———. *The Screwtape Letters.* Geoffrey Bles, 1942.

Malinar, Angelika, and Helene Basu. *The Oxford Handbook of Religion and Emotion.* Oxford University Press, 2007.

Porete, Marguerite. *The Mirror of Simple Souls.* c. 1300; Paulist Press, 1993.

Weil, Simone. *Gravity and Grace*. Librairie Plon, 1947.

Wright, Laurence. *God Save Texas*. Knopf, 2018.

The Story of a Generation in Seven Scams

Amoruso, Sophia. *#GIRLBOSS*. Portfolio, 2015.

Bowles, Nellie. "Unfiltered Fervor: The Rush to Get Off the Water Grid." *New York Times*, 2017.

Braucher, Jean, and Barak Orbach. "Scamming: The Misunderstood Confidence Man." *Yale Journal of Law and Humanities* 27, no. 2 (2015).

Bruder, Jessica. "Driven to Despair." *New York*, May 21, 2018.

Cairns, James Irvine. *The Myth of the Age of Entitlement: Millennials, Austerity, and Hope*. University of Toronto Press, 2017.

Carreyrou, John. *Bad Blood*. Knopf, 2018.

Chocano, Carina. "From Wells Fargo to Fyre Festival, the Scam Economy Is Entering Its Baroque Phase." *New York Times Magazine*, May 16, 2017.

Craig, Scott. "Mast Brothers: What Lies Beneath the Beards." *Dallas Food*, 2015.

Harris, Malcolm. *Kids These Days: Human Capital and the Making of Millennials*. Little, Brown, 2017.

Konnikova, Maria. *The Confidence Game*. Penguin, 2017.

Lewis, Michael. *Liar's Poker*. W.W. Norton, 1989.

———. *The Big Short*. W.W. Norton, 2010.

McClelland, Mac. "I Was a Warehouse Wage Slave." *Mother Jones*, March–April 2012.

Pressler, Jessica. "Maybe She Had So Much Money She Just Lost Track of It." *New York*, May 28, 2018.

Stone, Brad. *The Upstarts: How Uber, Airbnb, and the Killer Companies of the New Silicon Valley Are Changing the World*. Little, Brown, 2017.

We Come from Old Virginia

Anthony, David and Dorcas R. Brown. "Midwinter dog sacrifices and warrior initiations in the late Bronze Age at the site of Krasnosamarskoe, Russia." Hartwick College, 2012.

Coronel, Sheila, Steve Coll, and Derek Kravitz. "*Rolling Stone*'s Investigation: 'A Failure That Was Avoidable.'" *Columbia Journalism Review*, April 5, 2015.

Dorr, Lisa Lindquist. *White Women, Rape, and the Power of Race in Virginia, 1900–1960*. University of North Carolina Press, 2004.

Doyle, Jennifer. *Campus Sex, Campus Security*. Semiotext(e), 2015.

Eisenberg, Emma. "'I Am a Girl Now,' Sage Smith Wrote. Then She Went Missing." *Splinter*, July 24, 2017.

Reed, Annette Gordon. *Thomas Jefferson and Sally Hemings: An American Controversy*. University of Virginia Press, 1997.

Santos, Carlos, and Rex Bowman. *Rot, Riot, and Rebellion: Mr. Jefferson's Struggle to Save the University That Changed America*. University of Virginia Press, 2013.

Schambelan, Elizabeth. "League of Men." *n+1*, Spring 2017.

Seccuro, Liz. *Crash Into Me: A Survivor's Search for Justice*. Bloomsbury, 2011.

Shane, Charlotte. "Obstruction of Justice." *Harper's*, August 2018.

Syrett, Nicholas L. *The Company He Keeps: A History of White College Fraternities*. University of North Carolina Press, 2009.

"Take Back the Archive." University of Virginia Library's Scholars' Lab.

The Cult of the Difficult Woman

Doyle, Sady. *Trainwreck: The Women We Love to Hate, Mock, and Fear . . . and Why*. Melville House, 2016.

Gay, Roxane. *Bad Feminist*. Harper Perennial, 2014.

Massey, Alana. *All the Lives I Want: Essays About My Best Friends Who Happen to Be Famous Strangers*. Grand Central, 2017.

———. "The Year I became a (Total Fucking) Gwyneth." *Medium*. 2016.

Petersen, Anne Helen. *Too Fat, Too Slutty, Too Loud: The Rise and Reign of the Unruly Woman*. Plume, 2017.

Wurtzel, Elizabeth. *Bitch: In Praise of Difficult Women*. Doubleday, 1998.

I Thee Dread

Brontë, Charlotte. *Jane Eyre*. Smith, Elder & Co., 1847.

Brubach, Holly. "In Fashion for Better or Worse." *New Yorker*, July 10, 1989.

Coontz, Stephanie. *Marriage, a History: How Love Conquered Marriage*. Penguin, 2006.

Du Maurier, Daphne. *Rebecca*. 1938; William Morrow, 2006.

Dunn v. Palermo. Tennessee State Supreme Court, 1976.

Goldberg, Abbie E. "'Doing' and 'Undoing' Gender: The Meaning and Division of Housework in Same-Sex Couples." *Journal of Family Theory*. June 2013.

Howard, Vicki. *Brides, Inc.: American Weddings and the Business of Tradition*. University of Pennsylvania Press, 2008.

Mead, Rebecca. *One Perfect Day: The Selling of the American Wedding*. Penguin, 2008.

Montgomery, L. M. *Anne's House of Dreams*. McClelland, Goodchild and Stewart, 1917.

Moss, Caroline, and Michelle Markowitz. *Hey Ladies!: The Story of 8 Best Friends, 1 Year, and Way, Way Too Many Emails*. Harry N. Abrams, 2018.

Obergefell v. Hodges. U.S. Supreme Court, 2015.

Wallace, Carol. *All Dressed in White: The Irresistible Rise of the American Wedding*. Penguin, 2004.

Wolf, Naomi. "Brideland." In *To Be Real: Telling the Truth and Changing the Face of Feminism*, edited by Rebecca Walker. Anchor Books, 1995.

Yalom, Marilyn. *A History of the Wife*. Harper Perennial, 2002.

About the Author

JIA TOLENTINO is a staff writer at *The New Yorker*. Raised in Texas, she studied at the University of Virginia before serving in Kyrgyzstan in the Peace Corps and receiving her MFA in fiction from the University of Michigan. She was a contributing editor at *The Hairpin* and the deputy editor at *Jezebel*, and her work has appeared in *The New York Times Magazine*, *Grantland*, *Pitchfork*, and other publications. She lives in Brooklyn.

jia.blog
Twitter: @jiatolentino
Instagram: @jiatortellini

About the Type

This book was set in Berling. Designed in 1951 by Karl-Erik Forsberg (1914–95) for the type foundry Berlingska Stilgjuteri AB in Lund, Sweden, it was released the same year in foundry type by H. Berthold AG. A classic old-face design, its generous proportions and inclined serifs make it highly legible.